Visual Basic .NET
Weekend Crash Course™

Visual Basic .NET
Weekend Crash Course™

Richard Mansfield

Hungry Minds™

Best-Selling Books • Digital Downloads • e-Books • Answer Networks • e-Newsletters • Branded Web Sites • e-Learning

Cleveland, OH • Indianapolis, IN • New York, NY

Visual Basic .NET Weekend Crash Course™
Published by
Hungry Minds, Inc.
909 Third Avenue
New York, NY 10022
www.hungryminds.com

LOC: 2001089329
ISBN: 0-7645-4824-7
Printed in the United States of America
10 9 8 7 6 5 4 3 2 1
1B/TQ/RR/QR/IN
Distributed in the United States by Hungry Minds, Inc.
Distributed by CDG Books Canada Inc. for Canada; by Transworld Publishers Limited in the United Kingdom; by IDG Norge Books for Norway; by IDG Sweden Books for Sweden; by IDG Books Australia Publishing Corporation Pty. Ltd. for Australia and New Zealand; by TransQuest Publishers Pte Ltd. for Singapore, Malaysia, Thailand, Indonesia, and Hong Kong; by Gotop Information Inc. for Taiwan; by ICG Muse, Inc. for Japan; by Intersoft for South Africa; by Eyrolles for France; by International Thomson Publishing for Germany, Austria, and Switzerland; by Distribuidora Cuspide for Argentina; by LR International for Brazil; by Galileo Libros for Chile; by Ediciones ZETA S.C.R. Ltda. for Peru; by WS Computer Publishing Corporation, Inc., for the Philippines; by Contemporanea de Ediciones for Venezuela; by Express Computer Distributors for the Caribbean and West Indies; by Micronesia Media Distributor, Inc. for Micronesia; by Chips Computadoras S.A. de C.V. for Mexico; by Editorial Norma de Panama S.A. for Panama; by American Bookshops for Finland.

For general information on Hungry Minds' products and services please contact our Customer Care department within the U.S. at 800-762-2974, outside the U.S. at 317-572-3993 or fax 317-572-4002.

For sales inquiries and reseller information, including discounts, premium and bulk quantity sales, and foreign-language translations, please contact our Customer Care department at 800-434-3422, fax 317-572-4002 or write to Hungry Minds, Inc., Attn: Customer Care Department, 10475 Crosspoint Boulevard, Indianapolis, IN 46256.

For information on licensing foreign or domestic rights, please contact our Sub-Rights Customer Care department at 212-884-5000.

For information on using Hungry Minds' products and services in the classroom or for ordering examination copies, please contact our Educational Sales department at 800-434-2086 or fax 317-572-4005.

For press review copies, author interviews, or other publicity information, please contact our Public Relations department at 317-572-3168 or fax 317-572-4168.

For authorization to photocopy items for corporate, personal, or educational use, please contact Copyright Clearance Center, 222 Rosewood Drive, Danvers, MA 01923, or fax 978-750-4470.

Hungry Minds‌ is a trademark of Hungry Minds, Inc.

About the Author

Richard Mansfield (High Point, NC) is an author and programmer whose recent titles include *Visual Basic .NET ASP.NET Programming* and *Visual Basic .NET Database Programming For Dummies*. While editor of *COMPUTE!* magazine from 1981 through 1987, he wrote hundreds of magazine articles and two columns. From 1987 to 1991, Richard was editorial director and partner in Signal Research. He began writing books full-time in 1991 and has written 27 computer books.

to David Lee Roach

Credits

Acquisitions Editor
Sharon Cox

Project Editors
Sharon Nash
Mildred Sanchez

Technical Editor
Brian D. Patterson

Copy Editor
Kathryn Duggan

Editorial Assistant
Cordelia Heaney

Editorial Manager
Colleen Totz

Senior Vice President, Technical Publishing
Richard Swadley

Vice President and Publisher
Joseph B. Wikert

Project Coordinator
Maridee Ennis

Graphics and Production Specialists
Sean Decker, Joyce Haughey,
Gabriele McCann, Kristin McMullan,
Laurie Petrone, Jill Piscitelli, Betty Schulte

Quality Control Technicians
Laura Albert, Vickie Broyles, David Faust,
Carl Pierce, Dwight Ramsey

Permissions Editor
Laura Moss

Media Development Specialist
Greg Stephens

Proofreading and Indexing
TECHBOOKS Production Services

Preface

If this is your first time working with Visual Basic .NET, you're in for a treat. In my opinion, Visual Basic — whatever version — provides by far the most fun you'll ever have programming. And I've been working with computer languages for more than 20 years.

Or, if you're here for a quick refresher course, you'll be reminded of why you chose to come back to VB: It's not only great fun to work with, it's also the fastest route on this planet from programming concept to finished application.

Who Should Read This Book

This Crash Course is designed to provide you with a set of short lessons that you can grasp quickly — in one weekend. The book is for three categories of readers:

- First, there are an estimated 4 to 8 million Visual Basic users, and many of them want to migrate from traditional VB to Internet-ready VB .NET. This book provides a bridge to help you leverage your existing knowledge of classic Visual Basic techniques and find out how to accomplish what you want to do in VB .NET.

- Second, this book is for people who want to learn the Visual Basic .NET language fast. You may need to learn it to get a job, to be eligible for a promotion, to pass a course, and so on. You don't have the luxury of taking your time to gain this knowledge. You need to learn it quickly. You may be entirely new to programming, or you may have experience programming in another language and just need to apply your knowledge to a new language.

- A third audience for this book consists of people who have some knowledge of Visual Basic but haven't used it in a while. You need a quick refresher course.

Whatever your circumstances, you'll find that this book gives you the guidance you need to start working with Visual Basic .NET to produce excellent Windows and Internet applications.

What Results Can You Expect?

Is it possible to learn Visual Basic .NET in one weekend? Yes, it is. For one thing, VB is a straightforward, easy-to-understand language. Its vocabulary is quite like English, so you'll often see easily understood lines of programming code like this:

```
If Temperature = 98.6 Then Patient = "Healthy"
```

rather than the crypto reverse Polish notations of some other languages, where the code can look like this (as you can see, it truly deserves the name *code*):

```
main(int, char **argv)
{
    int  i = 4408;
    int  n = atoi(argv[2]);
}
```

What's more, this book has been designed so that you'll learn everything you need to know to create fully professional, tested, effective Visual Basic .NET programs. But you'll learn only what you need to know. This is not a reference book, so the VB vocabulary has been carefully surveyed to determine which commands you need to know for nearly all programming. VB .NET's vocabulary consists of several hundred commands, but fewer than 50 are essential. The rest are highly specialized or rarely, if ever, used. So, in this book, you'll learn all of the useful concepts and commands — but I will not fog things up with the obscure or merely technical commands.

Finally, Visual Basic includes dozens of Wizards, add-ins, prewritten components, and other built-in assistants that can greatly simplify common programming tasks. Throughout this book, you'll be relying on these helpful features to get your programs up and running fast. If VB .NET has a tool that makes connecting your program to a database and displaying the data in a table (grid) format a snap (and it does), why do things the hard way with pages of hand programming? Visual Basic was the first, and is still the best, RAD language. RAD means *rapid application development*. And that's not an empty promise, as you'll see in many of the sessions in this book.

Layout and Features

No one should try to simply propel themselves through this material without a break. This book is arranged so that each session lasts about a half-hour, and they're grouped into sets of two or three hours each. After each session, and at the end of each part, you'll find some questions to check your knowledge and give you a little practice exercising your newfound skills. Take a break, grab a snack, refill that beverage glass or cup, and plunge into the next one!

Along the way, you'll find some features of the book that help you keep track of how far along you are and that point out interesting bits of information you shouldn't miss. First, as you're going through each session, check for this in the margin:

**20 Min.
To Go**

This icon and others like it let you know how much progress you've made through each session. There are also several icons that highlight special kinds of info for you:

This is a flag to clue you in to an important piece of information you should file away in your head for later.

 This gives you helpful advice on the best ways to do things, or a neat little technique that can make your programming easier.

 This cautions you about a possible danger.

Conventions Used in This Book

Aside from the icons you've just seen, there are only two conventions in this book:

- To indicate a menu choice, we use the ⇨ symbol, as in:

  Choose File ⇨ Save All to save your work.
- To indicate programming code, we use a special font, like this:

  Notice the line at the end: Me.Text = "Deleted". When the user clicks the OK button, you want this message to appear. The Me.Text command displays your message in the form's title bar.

Where to Go from Here

Now you're ready to begin. Stake out a weekend, stockpile some snacks, heat or cool your beverage of choice, and get ready to enjoy accomplishing startling results with what I think is the greatest computer language ever invented. Visual Basic is also, by far, the world's most popular programming language, so a lot of people must agree with me.

Session 1 gets you started by exploring in detail just what it is about Visual Basic .NET that makes it so powerful, effective, and — let's be honest — just plain fun to work with (don't tell your boss).

Acknowledgments

First, I'd like to thank my acquisitions editor, Sharon Cox, for her thoughtful advice. My project editors, Mildred Sanchez and Sharon Nash, deserve credit for their discernment, and the high quality of their editing. The technical editor, Brian Patterson, carefully reviewed the entire manuscript and made important suggestions. The production coordinator, Maridee Ennis, ensured that this book sailed smoothly through production, and Kathryn Duggan, the copy editor, combed through every line of my prose, making some improvements. To all these, and the other good people at Hungry Minds who contributed to this book, my thanks for the enhancements they made.

Contents at a Glance

Contents

Visual Basic .NET
Weekend Crash Course™

☑ **Friday**

☐ Saturday

☐ Sunday

PART

I

Friday
Evening

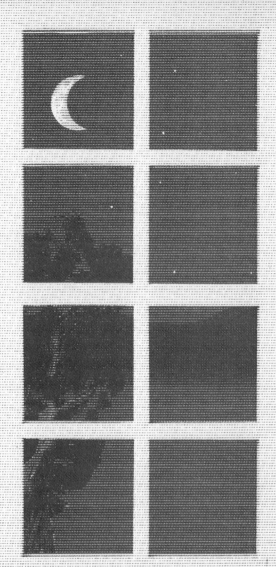

Introducing Visual Basic .NET

Session Checklist

✔ Designing an application using Visual Basic's built-in components

✔ Drawing the user interface

✔ Understanding Visual Basic's English-like programming language

✔ How VB .NET differs from previous versions

**30 Min.
To Go**

There are dozens of computer languages — each one has its fans. My favorite language is Visual Basic (VB), and I'm not alone — it's the most popular programming language in the world. Nobody knows exactly, but estimates of the number of VB programmers range from 4–8 million people. All other computer languages combined can claim only a fraction of this many users.

In many ways, VB has more power than other languages, for several reasons. It has continued to be polished for ten years now, improved for a decade by some of the most talented computer programmers currently employed. It's usually the fastest (and most enjoyable) way to get from idea to running application.

One reason Visual Basic is so popular and so effective is that it doesn't ask you to reinvent the wheel. Some elements of any significant programming job are unique, so it's necessary to work those out yourself. But many elements of a job are likely not unique.

VB is filled with prewritten components: Wizards that step you through many programming jobs (and write the programming for you), templates that you merely customize, and add-ins of all kinds that make your programming life easier.

Visual Basic provides such a full set of built-in intelligent tools that creating programs for the Windows or Internet environment can be astonishingly easy. You can just double-click the icons for TextBoxes or PictureBoxes — or dozens of other components — and they're instantly added to your program. These components are fully functional, and you can modify their behavior and appearance in many ways by simply adjusting their properties with a click of the mouse.

With VB, you can write efficient, polished programs that are every bit as professional as commercial applications. Yet, creating a program with Visual Basic has always been much easier than with C or other computer languages.

I say *has always been* because the times are changing. VB .NET represents a fundamental shift in the Visual Basic language, but we'll cover that topic at the end of this session.

"Designing" instead of Writing

If you are new to programming, the first phase of writing a program in Visual Basic will seem more like designing a picture than writing out cryptic, half-mathematical instructions for a machine to follow. If you have struggled with more primitive languages, it will seem paradoxical that programming for sophisticated environments like Windows or the Internet should prove to be so simple.

Visual Basic contains so many built-in features that creating the user interface for a program is more like picking out lawn furniture from a catalog than building the chairs and tables yourself.

But Visual Basic's tools and custom controls are more than simply nice-looking; they also know how to do things. Perhaps the quickest way to grasp what makes Visual Basic so special is to think of it as a collection of prebuilt robot parts. You just choose the parts you want and add them to the surface (the windows) of your program with a double-click of your mouse.

Visual Basic provides all the visual components necessary for computer interaction: listboxes that automatically alphabetize and arrange items in columns, scrollbars, resizable windows, pushbuttons, and more.

These tools come with built-in capabilities

A TextBox automatically wraps words around to the next line and responds to arrow, Backspace, Delete, Enter, Caps Lock, and Shift keys. It would take days to hand-program a TextBox from scratch.

In addition, you can customize each tool by selecting qualities from the Properties window. For example, some of the choices for a TextBox's properties are BackColor, BorderStyle, Enabled, Font, ForeColor, Lines, MaxLength, Name, ReadOnly, ScrollBars, Size, TabStop, Text, and Visible. (*Note to users of previous versions of VB:* Lines, ReadOnly, and Size are new properties in VB .NET.)

Want to change the background color of a TextBox? Just click BackColor, click the down arrow button, then click the Custom tab and select from a palette of colors, as shown in Figure 1-1.

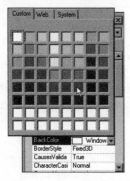

Figure 1-1 *Changing an object's color is as easy as clicking your mouse button a couple of times.*

You can edit objects globally

20 Min. To Go

Want to change the color of five labels? Drag the mouse around them to select them as a group. This is the same way you would group visual objects in a graphics program. You can also group them by holding down the Shift key and clicking each label you want to change. VB is so intelligent that its Properties window (where the qualities of objects, such as their size or color, are adjusted) will now display only those properties that the selected objects have in common.

After selecting all of the labels whose color you want to change, just click the Properties window BackColor item, the down-arrow button, then the Custom tab. The Color Palette will appear. Click the color you want and, voilà, all the selected labels change from white to magenta, or puce, or whatever you want.

Want to align a group of controls (by left, center, right, top, middle, or bottom) so they line up on screen and look good? Just drag your mouse around them to group them (or click each one as you're holding down the Ctrl key), then choose the menu item: Format ➪ Align. Want them to be the same size? Choose Format ➪ Make Same Size. The Format menu also includes a variety of other shortcuts.

Want to copy a group of selected objects within a given form or from one form to another, or cut and paste them? It's just as easy as copying and pasting text in a word processor. Delete, cut, copy, or paste them using the same Windows conventions that you would with words in a document: Click a component (or if you want to manipulate a group of objects, drag the mouse around them to select them). Once the component or components are selected, you're then free to copy, delete, or cut them. Remember, if you don't want to drag the mouse around them — perhaps they're not contiguous — simply hold down the Ctrl key and click the mouse. This adds an object to a selected group.

Then, you can manipulate the selected components just as you manipulate selected text in a word processor:

- The Del key deletes the object or group.
- Shift+Del cuts (deletes, but copies to the clipboard for any later pasting you might want to do) the object or group. This is the way you move objects from one window to another.

- Ctrl+Ins or Ctrl+C copies the selected object or objects to the clipboard, from which they can be pasted as often as you want. The properties of the objects — qualities such as color, width, text fonts, and so forth — will also be copied.
- Shift+Ins or Ctrl+V pastes the object or objects.

Keep in mind, we're only covering a few of VB's shortcuts and helpful tools in this introductory session. You'll learn about many more before your crash course is over.

Drawing in the Design Phase

One very important Visual Basic breakthrough is a reversal of the normal approach to programming. Instead of spending weeks writing instructions that tell the computer how to make your program respond and how it should look, you simply start out by *drawing* the program. You create the *user interface* as it's called, the surface that the user sees and interacts with when your program runs.

You create the user interface by dragging the various items you want from the Toolbox onto a window (called a Windows Form or WebForm in VB .NET), select their qualities, and then see how your program looks to the user. The Windows Form in VB .NET is what we've always called a VB form: it looks like a window when the user runs the program. The WebForm is new in VB .NET and when run, it looks like a Web page, and the user views it in his or her browser.

The VB .NET user interface design stage takes very little time. You don't write a single instruction — just click or drag. You can resize, reposition, and delete components very easily. Double-click a control in the Toolbox and it will be placed on the Design window. Click any control in your Design window to select it and you'll see that control's Properties window.

 If you have previously closed the Properties window, press F4 to bring it back. And if you don't see a window discussed in this book (such as the Solution Explorer or Toolbox) — simply open the View menu and you'll see all the common VB .NET windows. Where are the less common windows? Just choose View ⇨ Other Windows.

Organizing a program and designing the interface between computer and user is both quick and intuitive. You are, in effect, describing how the program should behave — how it should interact with the user — but you are describing it visually. Recall that many of the tools you assemble on a window or Web page come from the factory already functional, equipped to react intelligently when the program runs.

This design-first approach encourages you to think your program through before you get down to the details of programming. In Visual Basic, you draw your goals onscreen first so that the final product is there for you to see. You never lose sight of your overall design and the way that components work together to make your application effective.

And when you've created the user-interface and seen all the things it can do — you then see what it cannot do. Whatever it cannot do by itself is what you, the programmer, must provide by writing code.

How about Programming?

Well, you say, that's all good, but what about the actual programming? Isn't programming unforgiving? Yes, in many ways, a computer is the least flexible thing you'll ever try to communicate with. Put a comma — a little comma — in the wrong place and the computer will completely misunderstand what you're asking it to do. Misspell a word, even only slightly, and the computer will not understand it at all. There's no getting around it — at this stage of their development, computers are extremely literal critters. Communicating with them means doing it their way, or not at all.

However, in spite of this literal-mindedness, VB helps you out in various ways when you're programming. First, some of VB's commands — the words in VB's language — are familiar English words like stop, end, text, and timer. Second, you can sometimes combine VB commands into statements that are quite similar to English sentences, for example: If X = 12 Then Stop.

Sure, punctuation must be exact (a semi-colon means one thing, and a comma means something entirely different to VB). But always remember that Visual Basic hates to let you fail. While you're learning to program, you can turn on various kinds of training wheels that are built into VB. If you make a punctuation error or misspell a command, VB can make suggestions as you type each line of your program. Features like Auto Syntax Check and Auto Quick Info are always available. Perhaps experienced programmers might turn them off, but while you're still getting used to the idea of telling a machine what you want it to do (also known as programming), these various kinds of helpers are invaluable.

That's the topic of the next session. In Session 2, you take a tour of the VB editor — or Integrated Development Environment (IDE), as it's sometimes more grandly called. As you'll see, when you program in VB, the editor is there to assist you every step of the way.

Computers may be highly literal, but they can make up for it by offering you tireless and watchful assistance. If you mistype a VB command, VB itself will immediately show you the error and suggest how to fix it. And if you're not exactly sure what a particular command does — or how to use it — examples and tutorials for each command are only a key press away, key F1 to be specific. Just click a command in your programming code to select it, and then press F1. With VB, you're rarely left hanging and twisting in the wind.

VB .NET Differs from Previous Versions

10 Min.
To Go

VB .NET represents a major shift in the commands, syntax, diction, and other elements of Visual Basic. The *punctuation*, and some percentage of the other elements remain the same, but much is different. The primary goal of Microsoft's entire .NET set of languages is to move programmers from the familiar Windows operating system to the Internet. That's why it's called *.NET*. Internet programming requires a variety of new skills and techniques.

A secondary — yet quite dramatic — shift is that the various .NET languages (specifically VB, C++, and C#) now share a common syntax and diction, to a degree. In practical terms, if you're familiar with traditional VB, you'll feel that VB .NET contains many C-like qualities. Here's a very brief, very limited comparison to give you a sample of the fundamental changes:

Traditional VB	VB .NET
File Open	Streaming File I/O. Greater flexibility; more programmer control; more programming to write and test.
A largely self-describing library (few qualifiers required from the programmer).	Namespace references often required. Frequent object qualification (the VB .NET PrintDocument1.DefaultPageSettings = PageSetupDialog1.PageSettings as opposed to the VB 6 Printer.Print).
Simple procedure structures	More complex procedure syntax.

Here's another example. You use the following command to move a control left in VB:

```
Text1.Left = 100
```

To do the same thing in the VB .NET style:

```
TextBox1.Location = New System.Drawing.Point(100,100)
```

Here's an example of a procedure in VB:

```
Sub CommandButton1_Click()
```

and in VB .NET:

```
Private Sub Button1_Click(ByVal sender As System.Object, ByVal e As
System.EventArgs) Handles Button1.Click
```

There are many, many such changes. If you've programmed in VB before, you'll note the changes throughout this book.

In order to smooth the transition from VB to VB .NET — for those who might have as much as ten years of experience with VB — you can still use many traditional VB commands when working within VB .NET. If you find yourself in a snit (or a bind), and want to use an old-style VB traditional command rather than the new VB .NET version, try putting this line of code at the very top of your code window:

```
Imports Microsoft.VisualBasic
```

In many cases, referencing this "compatibility library" of legacy VB functions will permit you to use the older syntax, diction and punctuation from VB 6.

Done!

REVIEW

You were introduced to the world of Visual Basic in this session. You heard about its integrated design environment and its Toolbox full of prewritten solutions to programming problems, and you learned that this language is packed with templates, add-ins, wizards, and other tools to make a programmer's life easier. Then you saw some ways to efficiently create and modify a user interface using VB's components and the Properties window. Next you saw how organizing a project graphically during the design phase helps you see the overall structure of your emerging program. You were warned that computers are very literal, but comforted with the knowledge that VB includes various tools to help you avoid making errors, or at least fix them quickly. Finally, you were introduced to some of the changes made to the language in VB .NET.

QUIZ YOURSELF

1. What is the purpose of the Properties window? (See "These tools come with built-in capabilities.")
2. How would you change the font property of three labels simultaneously? (See "You can edit objects globally.")
3. What does the Align feature on the Format menu do? (See "You can edit objects globally.")
4. When a Visual Basic program runs, what do Windows Forms look like to a user? (See "Drawing in the Design Phase.")
5. VB .NET simplifies traditional VB syntax. True or False? (See "VB .NET Differs from Previous Versions.")

SESSION

A Tour of the Editor

Session Checklist

✔ How to use the VB .NET Toolbox to add controls to your project

✔ How to add more controls to the Toolbox

✔ What a form is when you're designing a project, and what it becomes for the user

✔ How to adjust the qualities of controls and forms using the Properties window

✔ Naming your controls

✔ How the Solution Explorer offers an overview of your entire project

**30 Min.
To Go**

The Visual Basic editor has been modified and improved for over ten years. By now, the majority of programmers consider it to be the world's most comfortable, efficient, and powerful programming editor. You can customize it extensively to suit your personal preferences, and you'll find it loaded with tools that can prevent or solve all kinds of programming problems.

In fact, calling it an *editor* seems insufficient — its proper name is Integrated Design Environment (IDE) — and it deserves that more elaborate name.

The VB IDE is so admirable that all Microsoft's other computer languages now use it as well. Microsoft bundles its new C# language — along with HTML, XML, VB .NET, and even C++ — into a single mega-development package known as the Visual Studio .NET "family." This book focuses on VB .NET, with a little excursion here and there into HTML or XML.

When you create VB programs, you work in the IDE — so you'll find tips and examples of how to use it throughout this book. This session covers the four main visible features in the IDE: the Toolbox, form, Solution Explorer, and Properties window. These are the primary tools that you'll use in all of your VB projects.

The Toolbox

Click the VS .NET icon to start the editor, or choose Start ⇨ Programs ⇨ Microsoft Studio .NET. You'll likely see the Start dialog box, shown in Figure 2-1.

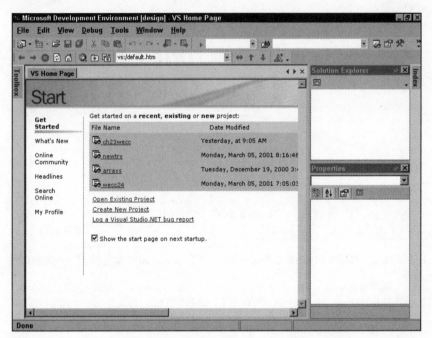

Figure 2-1   *This dialog box greets you when you first run VB.*

The VB .NET Start dialog box can also be displayed when you choose File ⇨ New|Project. It also appears, by default, each time you run the VB editor. You can prevent the dialog box from appearing by choosing Tools ⇨ Options, clicking the Environment folder, and then clicking the General option. Drop down the listbox titled At Startup to choose from several startup options.

Click the Create New Project link in the Start dialog box. You'll see a display of various kinds of projects (notably Windows and Web applications) that you can launch from the New Project dialog box, shown in Figure 2-2.

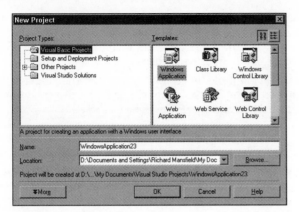

Figure 2-2   *Select the type of project you want to build in this dialog window.*

Double-click the Windows Application icon in the New Project dialog box. This is the simple, empty template you use to create traditional Windows applications or utilities.

You should now see the VB IDE layout shown in Figure 2-3.

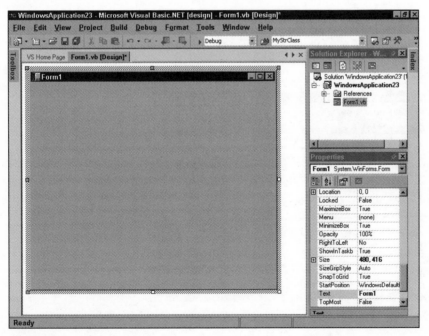

Figure 2-3   *Most programmers use this layout when working in VB, but you can drag the windows around, open new windows, and position or resize them to suit your needs.*

If you see a different layout than the one shown in Figure 2-3, fix it. (You will have a chance to do things your way soon enough, but for now, arrange your IDE as shown in Figure 2-3.) Make the Toolbox a tabbed item on the left. (If the Toolbox isn't visible, press F4; if the Toolbox isn't a tab, right-click the Toolbox's title bar and choose *auto-hide*.)

Put the Solution Explorer in the upper right of the VB .NET editor, and the Properties window just below the Solution Explorer. If the Solution Explorer or Properties window is not visible, click them on the View menu to make them visible.

A collection of controls

The Toolbox is where the controls (also called components) sit, waiting for you to double-click one to place it on the form. The controls you'll likely use often are clustered near the top: PictureBox, Label, TextBox, GroupBox (formerly Frame), Button (formerly CommandButton), CheckBox, RadioButton (formerly OptionButton), ComboBox, and ListBox.

The ScrollBars controls aren't of much use — the TextBox, where you're most likely to need scroll bars, includes its own ScrollBars property. The PictureBox is explained in Session 9. The DataGrid control is a quick way to connect an application to a database. And there are many, many other controls you can add to the Toolbox.

**20 Min.
To Go**

Adding more controls to the Toolbox

Right-click the Toolbox and choose Customize Toolbox from the context menu. You should see the dialog box shown in Figure 2-4.

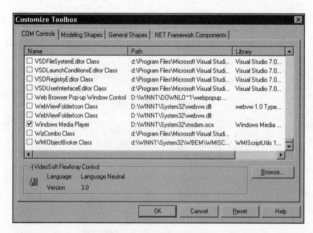

Figure 2-4   *Use this Customize Toolbox dialog box to add controls to your Toolbox.*

If you want to use any of the many additional controls listed in the Customize Toolbox dialog box in your VB project, go ahead and click the checkbox next to the control's name. When you close the dialog box, that control's icon will be added to the Toolbox.

As you can see in Figure 2-4, I chose the Microsoft Media Player control. Then I double-clicked its icon and, voila!, a fully functional Media Player is added to my VB project, as shown in Figure 2-5.

Figure 2-5   *Do you want to show movies in the VB application you're building? Just add Media Player to your Toolbox, and it's yours to use.*

To make Media Player work, locate a movie file type it can play (.MPG or .AVI) on your hard drive (or on the Internet) and then simply change the Media Player's Filename property either in the Properties window, or by assigning it in programming code (perhaps in response to the user's choice of file from the OpenFileDialog control, as described in Session 4).

Precisely which additional controls are available in the Components dialog box depends on which products you've installed on your system (some additional controls come with VB; others come with other applications). You can buy commercial controls as well. For information on these third-party controls, take a look at one of the VB magazines, or try http://searchvb.techtarget.com.

The Form and the Properties Window

The second and third of the four main IDE windows are the Form Designer and the Properties window. To illustrate how to use the Form Designer, you must also use the Properties window, which is why these two features are covered together in this section.

A form is Visual Basic's main method of organization. It holds the controls that make up the user interface. When your VB application runs, a form is a window that the user sees and can interact with. When you use Windows Forms, the user sees the classic Windows window; when you use WebForms, the user sees a Web page in her browser.

A VB application can have several forms, just as any other Windows application can have more than one window, or any Web site can have more than one page. Also, as you'll see in Session 4, forms act as logical containers to help you organize your programming.

Your first step when writing a VB program is to add some controls from the Toolbox to a form. You arrange the controls on the form as you wish — resizing and repositioning them by dragging them with the mouse. If you want to remove a control, just click it to select it and then press the Delete key. Only one control at a time on a form is *selected* — it's the one with eight small squares surrounding it, giving you a visual indication that you can drag those squares to resize the control.

Reposition the control by dragging the entire control — click anywhere within the control (to select it) and then hold your left mouse button down while moving the mouse.

You may want several controls lined up in a row, and want them to be all the same size, font, and color. For instance, a group of four CheckBoxes might offer the user four options. Rather than spending the time to adjust each of their Font, ForeColor (text color), and Size properties individually, just make all your changes to the first CheckBox. Then *clone* it, making as many copies (with the same properties) as you wish. To copy (clone) a control, click it to select it, and then press Ctrl+C. Now press Ctrl+V to paste a new clone onto the form. Note that all the properties will be the same, except the Name, TabIndex, Location and Text properties. However, the Location properties will be nearly identical — so your new clone will appear almost directly on top of the original control from which it was cloned. Drag the new clone to a different position on the form so you can see both the original and the clone.

Setting properties

This next example demonstrates how you can use the Properties window to adjust the qualities of a control.

Don't forget that each *form* also has a list of properties you can adjust. Just click the form itself, and its color and other qualities will be listed in the Properties window.

1. You want a larger form, so drag the lower-right corner of the form itself to make it bigger. (If you want your form really big, first drag the form's container window to enlarge it, and also close other windows so you have room onscreen to make the Design window — where the form resides — larger.)

   Now you've got some room to work with. Remember, the size that you make a form when creating your project is the size that the user will later see when viewing that form in your running application (assuming they use the same screen size that you use).

2. Double-click the CheckBox icon in the Toolbox. A CheckBox control appears in Form1.

3. I usually change the default font of Labels, CheckBoxes, TextBoxes, RadioButtons, and the like from the default MS Sans Serif 8 point (which is tiny) to Arial 11 point (which is more readable). To do this, click the ellipsis (...) next to the word Font in the Properties window. You'll now see the Font dialog box.

Before changing these properties, first make sure that the title bar of the Properties window says "CheckBox1," the name of your CheckBox — not "Form1." If it says "Form1," you've clicked the form and *its* properties are now listed in the Properties window rather than those of the CheckBox. To fix this, so that you see the properties of the CheckBox, click the CheckBox to select it. Whatever object is currently selected will be the one whose properties are listed — and therefore can be changed — in the Properties window.

4. Adjust the font so that Arial is selected and the size is set to 11. Click OK to close the Font dialog box. Now note that the CheckBox's font has grown larger.

5. Click the down-arrow button next to the ForeColor property in the Properties window. Click the Custom tab and click a dark blue for the text color.

6. Adjust any other properties that you want to customize. Now you've got your CheckBox looking just the way you want it.

Understanding the Name property

You'll have a chance to continue working on the form in a moment, but first note these two important features:

- Visual Basic automatically gives each new control a Name property. The first CheckBox you created by double-clicking its icon in the Toolbox was automatically named CheckBox1, and if you add a new one, or create a clone, the new one is given the name CheckBox2. (TextBoxes are named TextBox1, TextBox2, and so on.)

- VB automatically supplies a default Text (formerly *Caption*) property to each new control that has that property. However, some controls, like ScrollBars, don't have a Text property. The Text property given to new controls is, by default, the same as the control's default Name property. You always change the Text property because, in most cases, it informs the user of the purpose of the control. If a button shuts down your program, you would change its Text to Exit or some synonym like Quit, so the user knows what it does. Or if you wish, you can delete the Text property. Just drag your mouse pointer across it to select the text in the Properties window, and then press the Delete key.

Sometimes you need to refer to a particular control in your programming. For example, you can change many properties while a program is running, like this:

```
CheckBox1.Text = "New Text!"
```

The names of controls are the way that you, and VB, tell them apart. You can change the name of a control by merely clicking the Name property in the Properties window (however, the Name property is one of those than cannot be changed while a program is running).

The Name property is the second property listed, at the top of the Properties window. Some programmers like to rename each of their controls to something that identifies its purpose. They find that renaming makes it easier to read the source code if it becomes necessary to modify it later. For example, the purpose of this next line of programming is harder to understand

```
If CheckBox2.Checked = True Then Call ShowIt
```

than this version:

```
If chkShowThumbnail.Checked = True Then Call ShowIt
```

Other programmers feel that the default names that VB gives controls are just fine. In this book, I won't have you spending a lot of extra time individually renaming controls — except in some cases where I think it's necessary to help avoid confusion.

If you want to use the special identifier prefixes for the Names of your controls, Table 2-1 provides the recommended list. (There is no *official* list from Microsoft yet — the subject is under discussion at this time.)

Table 2-1   *Standardized Naming Conventions*

Prefix	Corresponding Object	Example
Acd	ActiveDoc	acdMainPage
Chk	CheckBox	chkBoldface
Cmb or Cbo	ComboBox	cboDropper
Cmd or Cm	ADO command (database)	cmMyCommand
Btn	Button	btnExit
Cmg	CommandGroup	cmgSelectOne
Cn	Connection (database)	cnMyConnex
Con	Container	cntFramed
Ctl or Ctr	Control	ctlSeeThis
Edt	EditBox	EdtWrite
Fld	Field (database)	FldTitles
Frm	Form	frmColors
Frs	FormSet	frsTypeIn
Grd	Grid	grdGoods
Grc	Column (in grid)	grcQuantity
Grh	Header (in grid)	grhYearsResults
Hpl	HyperLink	HplURL
Lbl	Label	lblContents
Lst	ListBox	lstNames
Pag	Page	PagTurn
Pgf	PageFrame	PgfRule
Prj	ProjectHook	prjSuzerine
Rb	RadioButton	rbBlueBackground
Rs	Recordset (database)	rsTotalSales
Sep	Separator	SepZone

Spn	Spinner	spnWatch
Txt	TextBox	txtAddress
Tmr	Timer	tmrAnimation
Tbr	ToolBar	tbrDropThis
Tbl	Table (database)	tblTitles

The Solution Explorer

The Solution Explorer window (see Figure 2-6) is the VB .NET equivalent of the Windows Explorer — it's your viewport into the overall organization of your project. All your forms are listed — and you can quickly switch among them by clicking their names in the Solution Explorer.

Also, any other large-scale elements of a VB project are displayed, organized by folders. For example, if you have five forms in a project (your application will have five windows) — you'll see each of these forms contained in the Forms folder in the Solution Explorer.

The elements that are displayed in the Solution Explorer can include modules, class modules, libraries, controls you've added to the Toolbox, user controls, user documents, property pages, and designers — things you'll learn about in future sessions.

Figure 2-6 *The Solution Explorer shows you the big picture — all of the major elements of your current VB project.*

In special situations, there might even be two different projects (or more) open in the VB IDE and therefore displayed in the Solution Explorer at the same time. (Choose File ➪ New|Project, and then click the Add to solution RadioButton in the New Project dialog box.) Interestingly, one category of VB project is designed to work within other VB projects. You can use VB to build your own custom controls in the VB IDE. A control that you build can be added to the Toolbox just like any other Toolbox control. It can then be added to any form in any standard VB application. To test a custom control that you're building, you need to have it in the VB IDE at the same time as an ordinary Windows Form or WebForm application. That's because you have to test it by adding it to a container Windows Form or WebForm. In this specialized case, the Solution Explorer will show these two completely separate projects.

Done!

REVIEW

In this session you were introduced to three primary Visual Basic features. The Toolbox is your container for controls — useful, prebuilt parts that you can assemble into an effective user interface. Then you looked at the primary unit of organization in VB — the form. During the design phase, you use it to create your program's appearance. When the program executes, the form becomes a traditional window or, in the case of a WebForm, a page in a Web browser. Finally, you looked at the Solution Explorer — the tool you use to see the overall organization of your project.

QUIZ YOURSELF

1. What is a WebForm? (See "The Form and the Properties Window.")
2. How do you put additional controls on the Toolbox? (See "Adding more controls to the Toolbox.")
3. What is the value of cloning controls? (See the Tip under "The Form and the Properties Window.")
4. Where do you change the name of a control? (See "Understanding the Name property.")
5. Name two items that might be found in the Solution Explorer window. (See "The Solution Explorer.")

Talk to Your User: Creating an Interface

✔ Understanding Rapid Application Development (RAD)

✔ Manipulating the properties of a TextBox

✔ Listing the features of your application

✔ Adding tooltips to assist the user

✔ Running and testing the application

✔ Saving the application

✔ Adjusting the TabIndex properties

**30 Min.
To Go**

Nowadays, the term *visual* is used in the names of dozens of languages and products — Visual C++, Visual Studio, and so on. But back in 1991, Visual Basic was the first language to offer what's now called RAD features (which are, in some cases, visual ways of working, hence the term *visual*).

RAD stands for Rapid Application Development, and it means a collection of tools that considerably lighten a programmer's burden. What's more, working with RAD is often just plain fun (don't tell the boss).

VB has had nearly a decade now to perfect its RAD tools. And those tools — along with VB's English-like vocabulary and syntax — are the primary reason that Visual Basic is the world's most popular programming language.

The RAD tools — drag-and-drop, add-ins, snap-ins, Wizards, templates, prebuilt functionality in components, designers, and other shortcuts — can seriously speed up your programming, and greatly assist with the later maintenance of that programming.

An important component of RAD is its visual approach to solving many common programming problems. Need a password-entry box? Don't program it. Don't even copy and
paste some programming code. Simply double-click a TextBox to put it onto your Windows
Form or WebForm. Drag the TextBox to the size and position you prefer. Then adjust the
PasswordChar property of the TextBox. You've got your password-entry box up and working
in a matter of seconds.

In this session and the next, you're going to build a word processor application. A side
benefit of creating your own application is that you construct it, so you fully understand it.
Also, you're writing the source code — the commands and lines of programming that make
it work — so you can customize it to your heart's content. Do you prefer a particular font or
font color? No problem. Would you rather have a larger entry window to type in? A little
dragging, and it's done. Your wish is VB's command.

In this session, you'll design the user interface — the components that a user works with.
In Session 4, you'll write your first programming code to support the user interface. (You'll
be surprised how little code can be required in VB, even to create a functioning, if simple,
word processor!)

Preparing a TextBox

Fire up VB .NET and click Create New Project when the Visual Studio IDE appears. Then type
MyApplication in the Name field in the New Project dialog box. Now double-click the
Windows Application icon in the New Project dialog box. (The Windows Application template
is merely an empty Form1 and is the starting point for creating an ordinary, traditional
Windows application.) Click OK to close the New Project dialog.

You want a fairly large window for this application, so close the Output window, Results
window, and any other window visible on the lower-left side of the IDE. Also, stretch Form1
so it is big enough to fill as much as possible of the IDE without covering the Solution
Explorer and Properties Windows, as shown in Figure 3-1.

The primary component used for text input or word processing in VB .NET is the TextBox
control. Double-click the TextBox icon on the Toolbox. Change the TextBox's MultiLine property to True (otherwise you cannot enlarge the TextBox). Now drag the TextBox so it takes
up most of the left side of the form, as shown in Figure 3-1.

Almost always, you have to adjust three properties of a TextBox when you first put it on
a form: its Text, Font, and MultiLine properties. First, delete the Text property. By default, a
TextBox includes a bit of sample text — the default name, TextBox1. You never want that
message to greet the user; instead, you want a blank, empty TextBox ready for the user to
type in text. So click the TextBox to select it, and then click the Text property in the
Properties window. Drag your mouse pointer across the default contents in the Property window: *TextBox1*. Then press the Delete key to delete it. Notice that it disappears in the visible
TextBox on the form as well. Usually, changes you make in the Properties window are immediately reflected in the object itself in the Design window as well. This is a nice feature.

Next, you'll want to change the font and enlarge the font size from the standard, and
tiny, 8-point MS Sans Serif. Click the Font property in the Properties window, and then click
the ellipsis button (...) to reveal the Font dialog box. Change the font to Times New Roman,
Windows's standard serif typeface. Change the size to 11 or whatever looks best at your
screen resolution, and then click OK to close the Font dialog box.

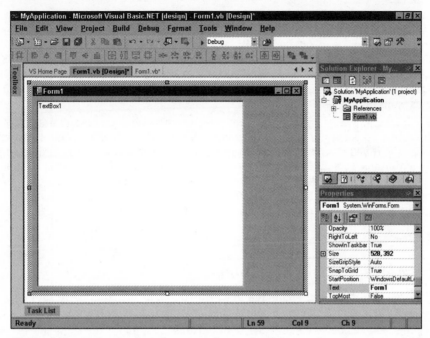

Figure 3-1 *Make the form large, so the user will have a lot of room in which to type.*

The third (and final) default TextBox property that nearly always needs changing is the MultiLine property. You've already fixed this one earlier in this session. When this property is set to False, a TextBox only displays a single line of text. If the user keeps typing after the first line is filled, the line scrolls horizontally. Put another way, there is no automatic word-wrap, and pressing the Enter key does not move you down a line. There is only that one single line, which can hold about 5000 words.

The standard VB .NET TextBox can hold around 10,000 words, so if you expect to need more storage (your diary, for instance, doubtless bursts with lengthy dramatic incidents), use the RichTextBox instead. It can hold a huge amount of text, because it's limited only by the amount of memory available in the computer. The RichTextBox isn't visible on the Toolbox until you click the small down-arrow icon at the bottom of the Toolbox, and scroll to see all the other controls on the Windows Forms tab in the Toolbox. Note that I use the ordinary TextBox in many examples in this book. The reason is that a RichTextBox has more features, properties and methods. I find that when illustrating programming principles and techniques, the simpler you can keep things, the better. While you are learning VB .NET programming, the plain old TextBox is less distracting.

Now that the TextBox is in good shape, you can add some buttons to handle the various features you want to offer your user.

**20 Min.
To Go**

In this example, you'll use an alternative approach to application design — using buttons to trigger features, instead of putting those features into menus. Buttons are more often used in smaller windows, with smaller ambitions than word processing. You've seen the smaller windows — usually dialog boxes — that often include three standard buttons: OK, Cancel, and Apply. Or the standard Internet buttons: Submit and Cancel. Larger applications like word processors usually avoid buttons and hide their many options within menus or display them as icons on toolbars.

Even though it's in a large window, you can consider this "word processor" example as a small-scale utility. So you'll use buttons instead of menus. That's my excuse and I'm sticking with it. Seriously, if you're writing an application for your own use, go ahead and do what feels most comfortable to you. I personally enjoy seeing an application's options all lined up as buttons whenever possible. Menus, and especially submenus, are to me a necessary evil. They're just harder to use, but I know that in applications of any complexity, menus are required because there are too many options and features to put them all on a set of visible buttons.

Deciding Which Features You Want

In Session 2, you used a cloning technique in which you defined the properties for a single component, and then used it to create copies that inherited those properties.

Let's say that you decide you want a series of buttons lined up on the right side of the form for this word-processor application. This sounds like a good candidate for the cloning technique.

1. Double-click the Button icon on the Toolbox to put a new button on the form.
2. Drag the button over to the right side of the form so it's not covering the TextBox.
3. Widen the button a bit.
4. Enlarge its font by double-clicking the Font property in the Properties window.
5. Change the font to Arial and the font's size to 11 points (or your preference).
6. Click OK to close the Font dialog box.

Naturally, you need a Close button to shut the application down. What other buttons would be useful? Surely you'll want New, Save, and Open buttons. A button for Import and one for Export would be nice (to paste and copy text to the clipboard). True, you can just use Ctrl+C or Ctrl+V for these features, but you've got room, so why not just add Import and Export buttons? While you're at it, why not create a Notepad button to bring up the Windows Notepad application? (It's often a useful alternative text-entry utility.) And, of course, you want Print. Finally, how about Options? At the least, you'll want to let users have the option of changing the font and font size.

OK. You've thought it over and you want to have a total of nine buttons: Close, New, Save, Open, Import, Export, Notepad, Print, and Options.

In this example, you can follow the naming conventions to give each button a meaningful, easily recognizable name. So change the name of the existing button from the default Button1 to btnClose. Click the button to select it, and then locate its Name property in the Properties Window and make the change. Finally, click the Text property and change it from Button1 to Close.

Now follow these steps to clone eight copies:

1. Click the button to select it.
2. Press Ctrl+C to copy it.
3. Press Ctrl+V to paste it.
4. A new clone button appears on top of the original button (it inherits its position, size and many other properties from the original button).
5. Drag the new button over to just underneath the existing buttons.
6. Change the new clone button's Name property to btnNew (or btnplus — use a name that reminds you of the button's purpose in your project).
7. Change the new clone's Text property to its function.

Repeat steps 1–7 until you've created buttons captioned for each feature in your application: Close, New, Save, Open, Import, Export, Notepad, Print, and Options.

It's nice to arrange a group of controls into a logical order. On most Windows application's menus, New, Open, and Save appear in that order. Close should be at the bottom of the form (at the end of the column of buttons). Also, it's useful to organize some of the buttons into logical groups. New, Open, and Save should be closer together than the other buttons — so they form a group of related features. Similarly, you might want to group the Import and Export buttons because they both employ the Windows clipboard. When you're done rearranging the buttons, they should look something like the organization in Figure 3-2.

One final step — horizontal alignment: Drag your mouse pointer around all of the buttons to select them. Choose Format ⇨ Align ⇨ Left to horizontally align the buttons.

To fine-tune the position of a control, click the control to select it, and then while holding down the CTRL key, repeatedly press (or hold down) the up, down, left, or right arrow key. You can also select multiple controls and move them all at the same time.

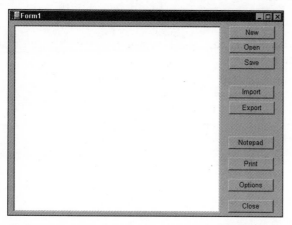

Figure 3-2   *Your new word processing application looks like it's ready to work.*

When you have the components positioned just the way you like them on your form, you might want to lock them down, because it's easy to accidentally click and move a button or some other component, messing up your careful, clean layout. To lock all the components in place, choose Format ⇨ Lock Controls (or right-click the form). You can tell that the controls have been locked because now when you click one of the buttons, it is no longer surrounded by drag handles (eight small boxes attached to the control, showing you where you can click to resize the control). And more importantly, you can no longer drag or resize it.

Adding Mini-Help Tooltips

10 Min. To Go

Users appreciate tooltips, those little boxes that pop out when you pause your mouse pointer on a button, toolbar icon, or other component. It's a handy feature that can remind you, with a succinct description, of the purpose of each component.

Adding tooltips to your buttons is a snap. With the Windows Forms tab selected in the Toolbox, scroll down until you locate the ToolTip icon. Double-click that icon to add the ToolTip capability to this form. Click each button, and then in the Properties window, type a description into its ToolTip property.

Some controls, such as the Timer, are not actually added to the form itself, but are displayed to the programmer in a special window, called the *tray*, located just below the Design window. These controls are never visible to the user when the program runs, so they are not displayed on the form itself.

Testing Your Application

Any time you want to see how your VB application works, you can run it. What you see is precisely what users will see when they run the application — it looks and acts just as it will later after you officially compile and distribute it.

How do you run it? Press F5. Suddenly you see the window you've been working on as a real Windows application. Click the buttons — they move down and up just like real Windows buttons (because they are real Windows buttons).

Test the tooltips you just added by pausing the mouse pointer over one of the buttons. You see a tooltip pop out, as shown in Figure 3-3.

Notice that the Output window automatically appears when you put VB in run mode. It displays the progress of the compilation (the building of your program) and also lists any errors it finds in your programming. (You'll find out how to use this window in Session 20.)

When you're finished running the application and playing with the tooltips, shut the application down by clicking the X icon in the upper-right corner of Form1 — or select Debug ⇨ Stop Debugging.

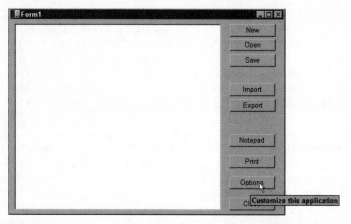

Figure 3-3   *Your application is now running, so the tooltips you added to these buttons will pop out when you pause the mouse pointer over them.*

Saving Your Work

You've gone to the effort to make a nice, thoughtful user interface. Now you should save your project to your hard drive so that if you lose power between now and Session 4 (if lightning strikes or some other disaster occurs), you won't have to repeat Session 3. When you're ready for Session 4, you can just reload the project back into VB. (In Session 4, you'll fill in the programming that makes all your Buttons actually do what their captions say they can do.)

To save your project, choose File ⇨ Save All. Now your work is secure. If you want to know where on your hard drive your file was stored, it's in the Visual Studio Projects folder found in this path in Windows Explorer: Documents and Settings\YourName\My Documents\Visual Studio Projects. (Web projects, on the other hand, can be found in the Inetpub folder.)

Courtesies for the Keyboard-bound: Adjusting the TabIndex Property

You should add two final niceties to your application before considering the user interface finished. Some people like to use the Tab key to move between the components. Each time they press Tab, the focus moves to the next component, as defined by the TabIndex property of each component. Pressing the spacebar triggers the component that currently has the focus. For example, when one of your buttons has the focus, pressing the spacebar will depress that button, just as if the button had been clicked with the mouse. Some people prefer to leave their hands on the keyboard when using a word processor, so you always want to take into account the TabIndex.

By default, each newly added component gets the next higher TabIndex. However, recall that you rearranged the buttons after creating them. So the TabIndexes are scrambled. In this application, you want to simply move down the buttons in order when the user repeatedly presses the Tab key. So leave the TextBox's TabIndex property alone — it's 0 (the first, lowest index number), and that's what you want. It means that when this application first runs, the TextBox will have the focus, and the user can start typing right away without having to click the TextBox or tab to it. A user can only type into a TextBox when it has the focus.

However, the buttons' TabIndexes are messed up. So click each button in turn, starting with New at the top of the column of buttons, and adjust their TabIndex properties from 1 to 9. VB is smart enough to prevent any of these index numbers from being duplicated — so by the time you get to the last button, Close, it will automatically have been changed to TabIndex 9. A shortcut trick if you want to change the Tab order of a number of controls is to start with the last control (the one you want to give the highest TabIndex number). Then work your way down the list, giving each one a TabIndex of 0. VB .NET will automatically number them correctly for you.

If you have a control that you do not want to be part of the tab group, set its TabStop property to False. That way, no amount of tabbing will ever set the focus to that control.

A second courtesy for keyboard-bound users is to add a shortcut keypress feature to each of your captions. Menu items and button text usually have one letter underlined — for example, File. This permits people to keep their hands on the keyboard, yet still activate a menu or button by pressing a key combination (Alt+F to trigger File, Alt+E for Edit, and so forth).

You add these underlined shortcuts to each button's Text property by adding an ampersand (&) immediately preceding the letter you want to underline. So change the Text properties of each button to: &New, &Open, &Save, &Import, &Export, No&tepad, P&rint, O&ptions, and &Close. (Notice that you have to use some interior letters so that each button has a unique shortcut letter — New uses up the *N*, so you put your ampersand before the *t* in Notepad.)

Now, to be on the safe side, save your work again — choose File ⇨ Save All.

Press F5 to run the application and try tabbing to make sure that the TabIndex series works as expected, and then try pressing Alt+C to see if the Close button gets the focus. Hopefully, all is well.

REVIEW

Done!

This session was intended to give you an idea of the powerhouse you're tapping into when you use Visual Basic. You can create a text-entry utility of surprising capabilities with very little real effort on your part. You saw how to get some of the benefits of RAD. Then you adjusted the properties of the TextBox and a set of buttons. You also saw how to run and save your new project, as well as how to provide the user with three nice features — tooltips, shortcut keys, and intelligent Tab-key cycling through the components on the form.

QUIZ YOURSELF

1. Name three features in Visual Basic that are considered RAD. (See the introduction to this session.)

2. What three properties do you nearly always have to change when adding a TextBox to a project? (See "Preparing a TextBox.")

3. What's the advantage of "cloning" a component? (See "Deciding Which Features You Want.")

4. What does a shortcut key do for the user? (See "Courtesies for the Keyboard-bound: Adjusting the TabIndex Property.")

5. What symbol do you add to a component's Text property to create a shortcut key? (See "Courtesies for the Keyboard-bound: Adjusting the TabIndex Property.")

Writing Your First Code

Session Checklist

✔ Knowing how to use the code window

✔ Understanding the four basic programming steps

✔ Learning how to assign text to a TextBox

✔ Interacting with the user through Dialog components

**30 Min.
To Go**

OK. We've been hanging around the shallow end now for three sessions. It's time to move to the deep water. Sure, Visual Basic makes life easy by doing a lot of the grunt work for you, but a programmer *programs*, by definition. You have to know a computer language and how to use it to make the computer do precisely what you want it to do.

It's fine to type in a caption like Close on a Button control, as you did in Session 3 by changing the Buttons' Text property, but now you have to write the code that actually shuts down a program when the user clicks that button.

In Visual Basic, you write much of your code in procedures called *event handlers* (formerly known as *events*). Each component has a whole set of events available for your use, if you wish to use them (although quite often you only use one event for each control in a typical program).

Events are things that can *happen to* a component — there are Click events, MouseOver events, LostFocus events, KeyPress events, and many others.

When programming for an Internet page, there is normally only *one* event — the Click event. That's because browsers are rather primitive when compared to full operating systems like Windows. The evolution of browsers has been seriously limited because Netscape and Microsoft have not been able to agree on standards, such as DHTML, which would permit more sophisticated user-browser interaction.

What do you want your application to do if the user clicks the Close button? You want the application to end. There is an End command in VB that does precisely that — shuts down the application. To program the behavior of the Close button, you put the End command into that button's Click event. It's that simple. Well, it's not usually *that* simple, but programming in VB .NET is a lot easier than programming in most other languages.

Using the Code Window

Let's see how it works. If you have shut down VB, restart it (when the Visual Studio IDE appears, choose Open Existing Projector click the filename of the project you created in Session 3 — the little word processing application).

By default, all Windows projects you start in VB .NET are named *WindowsApplication* (plus a number). If you prefer to launch the VS .NET IDE from within Windows Explorer, locate your project's folder and find the file with your project's name and a *.SLN* extension (for *solution*). Double-clicking that file will launch VB .NET with your project already loaded.

At this point, you will see the Design window (which shows how your form and its controls look). If you don't see your form, locate Form1.VB in the Solution Explorer — the Explorer-like window in the upper-right corner just above the Properties window. If you don't see the Solution Explorer window, select View ⇨ Solution Explorer. You should see Form1.VB listed. Double-click Form1 in the Solution Explorer, and your Design window opens, showing you the mini word processing application you designed in Session 3.

Now you can open the VB code window in which you will actually write your programming. Double-click the button labeled Close. When you want to do some programming for a component, just double-click that component in the Design window, and the code window opens, as shown in Figure 4-1.

Notice that there is a new window with the following code already entered for you:

```
Private Sub btnClose_Click(ByVal sender As System.Object, ByVal e As
System.EventArgs) Handles btnClose.Click


End Sub
```

A *sub* (short for *subroutine*) is a little program within a program. Whatever programming you put between the Sub and End Sub will wait to be activated by some outside event. In this case, you named the Close button btnClose, and this is its Click event. So if this Close button is clicked while this program is running, VB will carry out any instructions that you've written in this Click event. Those instructions are your *programming*.

Sometimes programming is called *coding* and the result is called *code*, but I think that's a rather harsh, and misleading, term. It sounds as if programming is mysterious, even complex. In some computer langauges *mysterious* is the proper adjective, but with Basic, the programming often can be quite clean and clear.

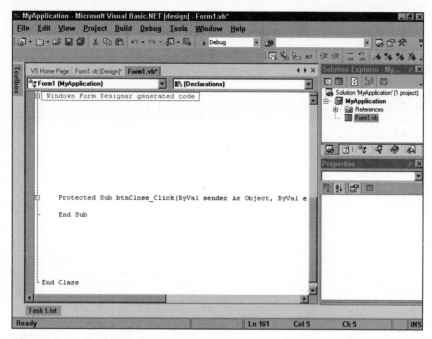

Figure 4-1 *Double-click any component to open the code window on that component's most commonly used event.*

20 Min. To Go

For now, pay no attention to the `ByVal sender As System.Object, ByVal e As System.EventArgs` arguments that follow the `Click` sub. You won't use them here; in fact, you probably won't use them too often. The Sender argument is useful to identify which control in a control array triggered an event, as you will see in Session 19.

Let's try it. Type the command End inside this event, so it looks like the following:

```
Private Sub btnClose_Click(ByVal sender As System.Object, ByVal e As
System.EventArgs) Handles btnClose.Click

    End

End Sub
```

Now press F5 to run and test this application. Click the Close button. What happened? Your application stopped running, and you're back in the VB .NET design environment. In other words, the End command was executed when you clicked that Close button. The program closed, just as if you'd clicked the X in the upper-right corner of Form1, or selected Debug ⇨ Stop Debugging, to stop the program.

Congratulations! Your first programming code — written and successfully tested.

The four basic programming steps

Of course, this wasn't the most demanding programming that you'll come across in your career. As you'll see in the rest of the sessions in this book, there is still more to learn about Visual Basic .NET code. But you now know the fundamental steps of coding in VB:

1. Double-click a component.
2. Decide in which event to write your program code.
3. Write the code.
4. Press F5 to test your code, to see if it does what you expect it to do.

When you double-click a component, VB chooses one of its events to display (often it's the Click event). The chosen event represents VB's guess as to which event you want to use based on statistics. For instance, by far the most common behavior with a Button is that the user clicks it — so when you open a code window by double-clicking a Button, VB shows you that button's Click event.

VB made a good choice. You'll put all of your programming for this application in the Click events of the Buttons. Let's do the programming for the Button captioned New. It's supposed to provide the user with a new, blank document — in other words, it's supposed to clear the TextBox of any text.

You can get to the btnNew_Click event for this button by double-clicking the New button on the Design window. There's also another way. Notice that there are two drop-down listboxes at the top of the code window. Drop the left listbox, as shown in Figure 4-2.

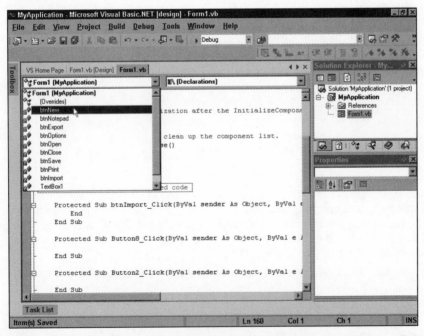

Figure 4-2   *The left listbox displays all of the components on this form. Click any component to get to its default event.*

Click btnNew in the left listbox. Now the code window displays that button's Click event, like this:

```
Private Sub btnNew_Click(ByVal sender As System.Object, ByVal e As
System.EventArgs) Handles btnClose.Click

End Sub
```

You can now program the Click event for the New button. (By the way, if you drop the listbox on the right side, you'll see a list of all the events available to whatever component is currently selected in the left listbox.) Each component has many events you can write programming in, but Click is the most common event. However, if you want to respond, say, to the user making any change to the text in a TextBox, you can use the TextBox's TextChanged event.

Assigning text to a TextBox

You're only interested in reacting to clicks in this application, so what do you do to clear the text from a TextBox when the user clicks the New button?

A TextBox can contain text that the user types into it, but there's another way to add text to a TextBox. You, the programmer, can assign text to the TextBox, like this:

```
TextBox1.Text = "Helloooo!"
```

What you're saying with the equals sign here is something slightly different from what the equals sign means in arithmetic. In arithmetic, when you say $a = b$, you mean that both a and b represent the same number.

What you mean by Text1.Text = "Helloooo!" is "When this line is executed, the contents of this TextBox *will change to* Helloooo!"

You want to remember this distinction: An equals sign used this way in programming indicates *assignment of a new value*, not equality. It means that if this line of programming executes, the text "Helloooo" will be placed (assigned) to this TextBox.

The equals sign is sometimes used in programming to mean what you expect: equality. In a line of programming that tests something, the = symbol really does mean "equals." Here's an example: If X = 12 Then DoSomething. This means that *if* X equals 12, then carry out some job.

When a test is taking place, you'll always find one of the conditional commands — If, While, Select Case, or Until — in the line of programming. Just remember that X = 1 is an assignment of the value 1 to the variable *X*. CheckBox1 = True causes (assigns) that CheckBox to be checked. CheckBox1 = False assigns False (unchecks) to the CheckBox. But IF X = 1, WHILE X = 4, or If CheckBox1 = True are *tests*, not assignments. In these instances, you're actually asking whether or not there is equality, whether or not *X* currently holds the value 1 or 4. Don't panic. We'll go over all this in detail in later sessions.

Whew! We covered quite a bit of ground. Let's slow down a bit now and look at some comparatively simple concepts.

How do you remove all of the text from a TextBox? Just assign nothing — an empty quotation ("") — to the TextBox. Here's the programming that causes the TextBox to empty when the user clicks the New button:

```
Private Sub btnNew_Click(ByVal sender As System.Object, ByVal e As
System.EventArgs) Handles btnClose.Click
TextBox1.Text = ""
End Sub
```

Using Dialogs

10 Min.
To Go

Moving right along, what programming shall we put into the Open button so the user can load a file into the TextBox? Luckily, VB provides controls that display dialog boxes for you — VB does all of the programming required to display the standard Windows Print, File Save, and File Open dialog boxes (and a few others, like Font and Color). So you can use these Dialog controls to display familiar dialog boxes to the user for the Open, Save, and Print buttons on your application.

The Dialog controls are on the Windows Forms tab in the Toolbox. (*Windows Form* is what VB .NET calls a traditional Windows form, to distinguish it from the new VB .NET *WebForm* that is intended for display in an Internet browser.)

Open the Toolbox, click the Windows Forms tab, and then scroll down inside the Toolbox to locate the OpenFileDialog icon. (There are too many controls to display them all at once on the Toolbox, so you must use the little scroll arrows in the Toolbox to see all the controls.)

Double-click the OpenFileDialog icon to place it into your program. Notice that the Design window shrinks and an OpenFileDialog1 "object" is placed in a window below the normal Design window, called the *tray*.

This OpenFileDialog icon (like the Timer icon, some database icons, and a few others) is never visible to the user when the program runs. It just offers features to you, the programmer. So VB .NET displays these "runtime invisible" icons in the tray. They merely serve as a reminders that you've added their features to your bag of tricks.

The programming to display a dialog box and get back the user's response is fairly straightforward. Double-click the Open button on your form and type the following into its Click event:

```
Protected Sub btnOpen_Click(ByVal sender As Object, ByVal e As
System.EventArgs)

        OpenFileDialog1.ShowDialog()

        textbox1.Text = OpenFileDialog1.filename

    End Sub
```

That's all there is to it! You use the ShowDialog command to display the standard Windows Open dialog box. Then your program pauses until the user clicks the Open or Cancel button on the File Open dialog box (or double-clicks a filename). At that point, the dialog box closes, and the next line in your code is executed. That next line assigns the name (not the contents) of whatever file the user selected (OpenFileDialog1.FileName) to your TextBox.

Try it out. Press F5. Click the Open button. You see the typical Open dialog box shown in Figure 4-3.

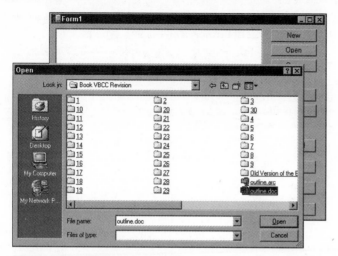

Figure 4-3 *With the help of Visual Basic, you can display this dialog box with a single line of programming.*

Try double-clicking a filename. The dialog box closes, and the name of the file appears in your TextBox. (Actually sucking out the contents of a file and displaying it in a TextBox requires a bit more programming. You'll see how to do that in Session 12, along with how to *save* text to a disk file.)

You can, if you wish, test the filename that the user selects, and react in your programming. Let's assume that for some reason you don't want users to choose a filename that's smaller than 15 characters. You would change the code to this:

```
Protected Sub btnImport_Click(ByVal sender As Object, ByVal e As
System.EventArgs)

    openfiledialog1.ShowDialog()

    If OpenFileDialog1.filename.Length < 15 Then msgbox("too short")

End Sub
```

A msgbox (Message Box) is one of the more useful tools in VB .NET. It displays a simple dialog to the user (see Session 11), but can also be a quick way for programmers to display information to themselves, such as variable values, while a program is being tested (see Session 20). In VB.NET the official "preferred" syntax for the Message Box is:

```
MessageBox.Show("message")
```

I however, do not *prefer* this longer code. The traditional MsgBox("message") style still works just fine in VB .NET, so I'll stick with the classic format.

Notice that the If...Then line of code is quite long. Some VB .NET lines of code are longer than can be displayed in the code window. When you type in a long line of code, it's very important that you simply *keep typing. Do not press the Enter key to move down to the next line.* The VB .NET code window will scroll automatically if you type past the right side.

Put the entire If...Then line on a single line in the code window — don't press Enter to make it two lines. I repeat: This is very important. Beginners often make the error of pressing Enter on a long line of code. VB executes programming one line at a time and considers each line to be a separate, complete statement — just like an English sentence. Breaking a line in half with the Enter key will really confuse VB. And it will let you know when you test the program by throwing up error messages until you repair the line.

You must not break lines of code, any more than you would break a

sentence like this by pressing Enter when typing.

If you must break a line for readability, or because you don't like it to scroll off the code window, there is an optional symbol you can use: the underscore character. But you must precede the underscore with a space, like this:

```
        If OpenFileDialog1.filename.Length < 15 Then _
msgbox("too short")
```

VB will see the space and underscore at the end of the line and understand that you want these two lines to be interpreted as a single "logical" line of code (a single sentence, so to speak).

You'll learn all about the important IF command and the other aspects of this line of code in future sessions. (Hint: < means less than.) For now, let me translate what this line of programming means to Visual Basic: "If the FileName's Length property is less than 15 (in other words, if the filename has fewer than 15 characters), then display the message box to the user."

Select File ➪ Save All to save today's work. Tomorrow morning, in Session 5, you'll finish most of the code to make this word processing application do its job, and also add some nice extra touches to it that users will thank you for.

Done!

REVIEW

In this session, you officially started programming. You learned how to open, and use, the VB code window — the place where you compose and edit programming code. You got your first taste of telling Visual Basic .NET what you want it to do when an event is triggered. Then you saw how to assign text to a TextBox, and discovered the subtle (but significant) distinction between using the equals sign to mean assignment as opposed to equality. Finally, you tried using one of the Dialog controls. I think this set of Dialog controls is so important and useful that we'll return to them and spend all of Session 12 getting to understand them better.

QUIZ YOURSELF

1. What is an event in VB? (See the introductory paragraphs in this session.)
2. What is a .VBPROG file? (See "Using the Code Window.")
3. How would you explain the difference between assignment and equality — the two ways that an equals sign can be used in VB programming? (See "Assigning text to a TextBox.")
4. Why would you add a component to the VB Toolbox? How do you do that? (See "Using Dialogs.")
5. What happens when the following code executes? (See "Using Dialogs.")

```
textbox1.Text = OpenFileDialog1.filename
```

PART

Friday Evening
Part Review

1. Create a user interface with two TextBoxes, two Labels, and a Listbox. Align these components so they look neat, and group them by dragging your mouse around them so you can change all their Font properties at the same time to Arial 11 pt.

2. Create a second form and copy all the components you used in question 1 onto the second form.

3. Explain in a couple of sentences the uses of the Solution Explorer window.

4. What kinds of names does VB provide by default for components. For example, if you add two TextBoxes, what are their default names?

5. The *btn* in the name btnExit is the abbreviation some programmers would use when renaming a Button that shuts down a program. The btn identifies the component as a Button. What are the standard abbreviations for the CheckBox, ListBox, Label, and Menu components?

6. Is it ever possible to design two different projects at the same time in the Visual Basic .NET Editor? If so, why would you do that?

7. Define IDE and RAD. How are they related?

8. What key do you press to start a VB program running in the IDE? How do you stop it?

9. What is the purpose of the TabIndex property?

10. What's the difference between how the equals sign (=) is used in math and in VB .NET programming?

11. How do the VB design window and code window differ?

12. What is the definition of a *sub*?

13. How do you add a component to the VB Toolbox?

14. What do the Dialog components do?

15. How would you define the phrase *logical line*?

16. Write the programming that displays a file open dialog box to the user.

17. Explain what this programming does:

    ```
    If OpenFileDialog1.FileName <> "" Then TextBox1.Text =
    OpenFileDialog1.FileName
    ```

18. What does a pair of double quotes ("") mean in VB programming?

19. What VB command shuts down a running program?

20. If you had to describe the concept of an event in VB to a non-programmer, what would you compare it to?

21. Describe the quickest way to get from the design window to a Button's Click event.

☑ Friday

☑ **Saturday**

☐ Sunday

PART

II

Saturday Morning

Fleshing Out Your First Application

Session Checklist

✔ Understanding the testing process

✔ Employing the Auto Syntax Check and Auto List Members features

✔ Importing and exporting from the Windows Clipboard

✔ Launching a separate application from within VB

**30 Min.
To Go**

Last night you shut down your programmer's workshop with your mini-word processor application only partly finished. Now it's time to finish writing the code that makes most of the buttons do their jobs. (*Most* because some programming — file access and printing — is probably a little advanced for this session. Those topics are covered in Session 12.)

This session also introduces a couple of VB features that may seem like training wheels to expert programmers, but can be lifesavers to a beginner: Auto Syntax Check and Auto List Members.

When you finish this session, you'll have a good overview of the process that produces VB applications: designing, coding, and refining. You'll also find out whether you feel comfortable using those training wheels.

The Testing Process

What about testing your application? Everybody knows that no program of any complexity is ever completely bug-free. After all, teams of the finest programmers available spend years testing major Microsoft applications like Word, yet bugs remain and pop up only after the product is sold to the public. The frequent need for "Service Packs" that fix problems after the sale testifies to the never-ending process of software testing.

A question you need to ask yourself when programming is "Should I test each piece of code as I finish it, or should I wait until I've programmed the entire application?" Recall that several times in Session 4 you pressed F5 to run your application to see what an individual button does when clicked. You had just finished writing a little programming that made that button do what you wanted, but you tested it to be sure that your intentions were, in fact, being carried out. Pressing F5 lets you see what the user will see.

These mini-tests of small pieces of code are so easy to run that many programmers like to check each little piece of programming as they complete it. Others prefer to formally test after all of the coding is complete.

Which approach you choose is purely a matter of personal preference. If you're not sure that you used the right command in a particular event (Sub or Function procedure), go ahead and press F5 to see what happens.

Some programming theorists argue that only when you've finished programming can you test for unintended interactions between perhaps widely separated bits of code. That's true, but there's no reason that you can't run mini-tests while programming, and then also perform larger-scale tests at the end of the programming process. So I guess it's apparent that I favor the test-as-you-go approach. Besides, how can you wait? It's more fun to give it a go right after you finish a piece of programming. And it's a great feeling if some code works the first time you try running it — which sometimes actually happens!

The distinction between frequent testing and waiting until the end is rather like the two ways people use their spell-checkers when word processing. Some people leave the spell-checker on all the time, so it checks each word as it is typed in, and a misspelling is flagged at once. Other people prefer to leave the check-spelling-as-you-type feature off, claiming that they cannot concentrate on the larger issues of logic and organization if they have to stop and respond to every little typo. This kind of writer prefers to wait until the document is finished before running the spell-checker globally.

It's usually up to you, but if you're a beginner, I think you'll probably learn the language faster if you run frequent mini-tests. I also suggest that you use VB's equivalent of the check-spelling-as-you-type feature. VB calls this feature *Auto Syntax Check*. In fact, in VB .NET (at least at the time of this writing) the Auto Syntax Check feature is always on and there's no way to turn it off.

Using Auto Syntax Check

VB .NET features what Microsoft calls *Intellisense*. There are several tools that are included in this category, and you might find them useful.

You can turn *some* of the Intellisense options on and off in the Edit ⇨ Intellisense menu. You can also use the Tools ⇨ Options menu, like this:

1. Choose Tools ⇨ Options.
2. Click the Text Editor folder.
3. Click the Basic Folder.
4. Click the General entry.
5. Click the Auto List Members and Parameter Information checkboxes to select them.

Parameter Information displays the parameters that a procedure — Sub or Function — accepts. For instance, if there's a function in your source code named `ADODataSetCommand1FillDataSet`, as soon as you type that name into the code window and then type a left-parenthesis to begin describing parameters, VB .NET automatically shows you the correct parameters and their data type, as shown in Figure 5-1.

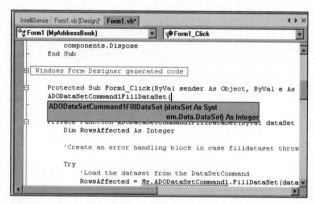

Figure 5-1   *VB .NET can automatically show you the correct parameters and their data types.*

A *parameter* is a piece of data passed to a procedure that the procedure uses to do its job. For example, if you write a function that adds 12 to any number, the number is passed to the function:

```
Function AddTwelve (num as Integer) As Integer

Num = num + 12   'add 12 to the number (num) passed to this function by a caller.

Return num 'send back the answer to the caller

End Function
```

In this example, the parameter that gets passed to this function is num.

> **Just to make our lives more interesting,** *parameters* **are sometimes referred to as** *arguments.* **The distinction is a subtle one: when emphasizing the function, as when speaking of the item(s) in parentheses following a function (such as** num **in the previous example), you use the term** *argument.* **However, if you are emphasizing the caller that is sending information to a function, the term** *parameter* **is used. It's the same distinction as the difference between whether a file is** *uploaded* **or** *downloaded.* **It's the same file; which term you use to describe it depends on which end of the sending process you are.**

Auto Syntax Check watches as you type in each line of code. As soon as you finish a line, it checks the line to see if you mistyped anything, or made some other kind of error such as leaving out something necessary. (VB knows you're finished with a line because you press the Enter key or click the mouse pointer on some other line.)

**20 Min.
To Go**

If the syntax checker has a problem with the line, it underlines the error or errors with a sawtooth blue line (blue by default, anyway). To try this out, type a couple of variable names, neither of which have been previously declared (with Dim). By default VB .NET requires that all variables be declared, so you get a jagged line under each of the undeclared variable names. Figure 5-2 shows what happened when I pressed the Enter key after making two such errors.

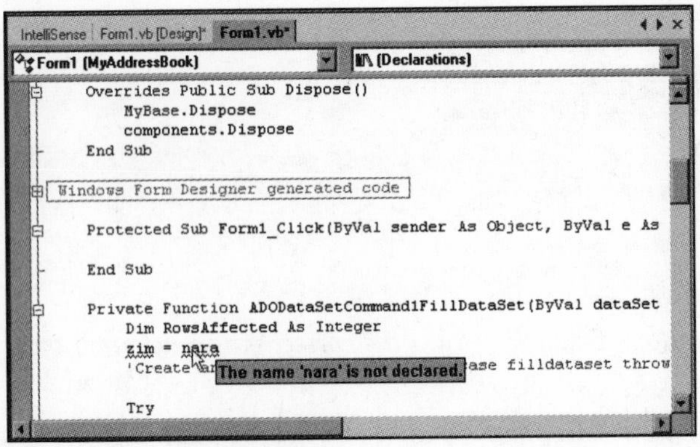

Figure 5-2 *VB .NET helpfully flags errors in your source code, and also describes the problem so you can fix it.*

To see a description of the error, move your mouse pointer on top of the offending (underlined) code. Don't click, just slide the arrow onto the bad part, as shown in Figure 5-2.

To make the jagged blue lines go away, I had to declare the two variable names, like this:

```
Dim RowsAffected As Integer
        Dim zim As String
        Dim nara As String


        zim = nara
```

If you're not clear about the concepts of procedures, arguments, parameters, dim sum, and variables, don't worry — we'll cover them thoroughly in future sessions.

While you're on a roll, give this programming a try:

```
Dim sfd As New SaveFileDialog()
        Dim dlgResponse As Integer
        Dim strFname As String


        sfd.DefaultExt = "txt" '  specifies a default extension
        sfd.InitialDirectory = "C:"

        dlgResponse = sfd.ShowDialog
        If dlgResponse = 1 Then
            strFname = sfd.FileName
            msgbox(strFname)
        End If
```

One more comforting reminder: At this point in the Crash Course, you aren't expected to know which programming commands will accomplish which jobs. For example, when I say it's time to write the programming that displays a Save dialog box, you're not expected to know that you must use the ShowDialog method. You'll learn VB's programming commands throughout the Crash Course and by the end of this book, you will know that ShowDialog can display one of the classic Windows dialog boxes, End shuts down the application, Loop means keep repeating something until I say to stop, and all the rest of them. For now, just relax and go along.

Programming More Events

Let's move closer to finishing up the mini-word processor you started in Session 3. Start VB. (If the New Project dialog box appears, just click Cancel to close it.) Choose File ⇨ Open ⇨ Project, and locate this folder:

```
Documents and Settings\YourPersonalName\My Documents\Visual Studio
Projects
```

Browse your hard drive to find the folder you created in Session 3, and then double-click the file named Project1.VBPROJ to bring in the application. The file dialog box closes when you double-click the .VBPROJ file. At this point, you might see the code window or no window at all, depending on the state of the IDE when you shut down VB.

You want to see Form1, which contains all of your Buttons, so double-click Form1.VB in the Solution Explorer. The Design window opens, showing you the user interface of the application you're building.

When you left this project, you had added an OpenFileDialog control, and written the programming that displays the filename the user selected in the TextBox. Now it's time to use CommonDialog controls to save and to print.

Notice that even though you shut VB down at the end of Session 4 and restarted it just now, VB remembers what you had already done to this project. The state of VB is saved each time you save a project.

Double-click the SaveFileDialog icon in the Toolbox to put it into your project. Now double-click the Save button on Form1. You see the btnSave Click event. The actual VB .NET code for saving a file is a bit advanced for this session, so it isn't covered until Session 12 (but if you're really excited, go ahead and look in that session). Nevertheless, there are other things you can do with the CommonDialog to make life easier for the user.

There are three ways to open a Properties dialog box for a component. You can click the SaveFileDialog1 icon in the Design window (not in the Toolbox) to select the icon, and then press F4. (Pressing F4 ensures that the Properties window is visible.) Or, right-click the SaveFileDialog1 icon in the Design window and choose Properties from the context menu — or drop the listbox at the top of the Properties window — and then click CommonDialog. Now the component's properties are displayed in the Properties window.

For the Save CommonDialog, let's assume you want to automatically add a default file extension of .TXT to whatever filename the user types in. A TextBox's contents are plain, unformatted text, just like Notepad's contents. By changing the FileName property, you cause the CommonDialog to display a default filename. The DefaultExt property represents the extension that is automatically added to whatever filename the user types in when the file is saved. This property is not shown to the user; it's just added during the file save. So type **TXT** in the blank space to the right of DefaultExt in the Properties window (don't use a period).

It's easy to see what the rest of the CommonDialog component's properties do: Just click the Help button, or press F1.

 We are going to put off explaining how to print until Session 12. Printing is not as simple in VB .NET as it was in previous versions of VB.

Using Auto List Members

Try entering this code in a Button_Click event:

```
TextBox1.
```

Aha! As soon as you type the period (.) following TextBox1, you should see the Auto List Members feature sprint into action. A *member* is a property or method of a component (or other object). Technically, events are also considered members.

Anyway, what you should notice at this point is that when you type an object followed by a period (.), you're telling VB that you are going to use a property of that object, or perhaps a method. Objects generally have many properties, and only a few methods. In general, properties are qualities (like size or color), while methods are jobs that the object knows how to accomplish (like the ListBox control knows how to display a new entry if you use the ListBox's AddItem method). We'll look more closely at these categories in Session 30.

The point of Auto List Members is to provide you with a quick reference of all of the properties and methods of the object. Notice in Figure 5-3 that methods are indicated by what looks like a flying purple eraser icon, while the properties icon is a finger poking the sprocket of a cassette tape (or electric outlet or something). I can certainly understand why properties might be symbolized by flying purple erasers, but just how electrocution symbolizes methods is beyond me.

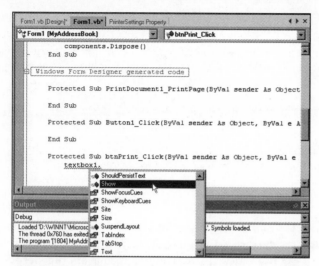

Figure 5-3 *With the Auto List Members feature turned on, you need never wonder which properties and methods are available for your use.*

Importing and Exporting

**10 Min.
To Go**

The Import and Export buttons in your application are supposed to paste text from the Windows Clipboard to the TextBox, or send the text in the TextBox out to the Clipboard. You can bring text in from the Clipboard using this code:

```
Private Sub btnImport_Click(ByVal sender As System.Object, ByVal e As
System.EventArgs) Handles btnImport.Click

        Dim txtdata As IDataObject = Clipboard.GetDataObject()

        ' Check to see if the Clipboard holds text
        If (txtdata.GetDataPresent(DataFormats.Text)) Then

TextBox1.Text = txtdata.GetData(DataFormats.Text)


        End If
End Sub
```

And to export, or save the contents of a TextBox to the Clipboard, use this code:

```
Private Sub btnExport_Click(ByVal sender As System.Object, ByVal e As
System.EventArgs) Handles btnExport.Click

        Clipboard.SetDataObject(TextBox1.Text)
End Sub
```

Running a Separate Application

The Notepad button in your program is supposed to bring up the Windows Notepad utility. You can start a program running in VB with the Shell command. Double-click the Notepad button, and then type this in:

```
Private Sub btnNotepad_Click(ByVal sender As System.Object, ByVal e As
System.EventArgs) Handles btnNotepad.Clicking

        Dim X As Integer
        X = Shell("notepad.exe", AppWinStyle.NormalFocus)

End Sub
```

Recall that in VB .NET — unlike earlier versions of VB — you must declare (Dim) *all* variables. This means that you must declare X using Dim X as Integer before you can use the X. If you really want to avoid this necessity of declaring each variable, put this line up at the top of your programming code window (above any procedures):

```
Option Explicit Off
```

Option Explicit is on by default in VB .NET and it's the Option that demands that each variable be explicitly declared. Option Strict works with Option Explicit, but the Strict option prevents implicit conversion of data. For example, with Option Strict On, this programming (which forces the variable A to be converted to a string data type) would fail to run:

```
Dim A as Integer
A = 1

TextBox1.Text = A
```

Option Strict is off by default. You can turn it on by typing this line at the top of your code window:

```
Option Strict On
```

I suggest that you leave VB .NET's default Option Explicit On. That way, you'll force yourself to get used to programming the new VB .NET way. Also, you'll decrease the number of bugs you have to track down. As for Option Strict, the jury is still out. It forces you to use .ToString rather often to convert numeric variable types into text (string) types before you can display them in TextBoxes or message boxes. You also may have to resort to such programming commands as CType, CInt, and others. Nonetheless, obscure bugs and mathematical imprecision can result from leaving Option Strict turned off. My advice? While you're learning the basics of VB .NET, leave it turned Off. But when you start to work on more sophisticated programs, consider turning it On.

You'll learn more about Option Explicit at the end of Session 14.

Now back to our regular programming. To be honest, I couldn't remember how to use the Shell command when I was writing this session. However, it's simple enough to get answers when you get stuck. Just type the word Shell into the code window, and then type the comma. Two little windows will pop up. The lower window shows you that there are several possible parameters you can pass to this function (items listed within brackets are optional parameters).

Even though it is optional, I wanted to specify that when Notepad starts running, it should be in a normal window. Look at the upper of the two windows that popped out and you will see a list of possible parameters for the second parameter: Style.

If you do not specify a Style parameter, the default Style that is used is rather bad: Notepad runs, but it only appears on the taskbar, not as an opened window the user can see. So you want to use the AppWinStyle.NormalFocus or one of the other choices. Double-click AppWinStyle.NormalFocus in the upper of the two windows to insert it into your source code.

Also, notice that the Shell command is a *function*, which means you must write it in the format X = Shell rather than just using Shell. (You'll find out all about functions in Session 12.)

If you want to see a quick example of how to use the Shell command in your code, click the word Shell in your code window to put your Insertion cursor (that blinking line) on the word Shell. Then press F1 to summon Help. You will immediately find exactly what you need: the full, precise syntax in an example at the bottom of this page of help:

```
RetVal = Shell("C:\WINDOWS\CALC.EXE", 1)
```

You can use X or RetVal or any other name you want for the variable at the start of this line — just don't use a word that's in the VB vocabulary, such as , or If.

The Shell command, like MsgBox and others, is a *wrapper* function. This means that it is a traditional VB command which VB .NET permits you to use, but the same functionality is available using a different VB .NET command (a method). If you want to use the official, "preferred" VB .NET usage, use Process.Start rather than Shell. This example runs Notepad and automatically loads in a text file:

```
Process.Start("Notepad", "c:\wifi.txt")
```

There's still one last button in your mini-word processor project — Options — to write programming for. We'll get to that in Session 6. In that session, you see how to use several kinds of input components — CheckBoxes, OptionButtons, and custom dialog boxes — all of which make life easier for the user of your application.

For now, select File ⇨ Save Project.

Done!

REVIEW

This session took your first application well on its way to completion. You saw how to write code to make the Save and other buttons do their jobs. You also learned how to use the Auto Syntax Check and Auto List Members features to assist you in your programming. Above all, you came away from this session understanding (I *hope*) that you cannot know or remember everything about the Visual Basic language — you must be prepared to press F1 from time to time to summon help. Even Visual Basic crones and geezers who have been using this language from day one back in 1991 need help now and then.

QUIZ YOURSELF

1. Conducting frequent mini-tests on individual events is one approach to testing a program. What is another approach? (See "The Testing Process.")

2. What can Auto Syntax Check do for you? (See "Using Auto Syntax Check.")

3. What can Auto List Members do for you? (See "Using Auto List Members.")

4. What code would you write to export the contents of a TextBox named Text1 to the Clipboard? (See "Importing and Exporting.")

5. How can you avoid having to explicitly declare variables? (See "Running a Separate Application.")

Easy Choices: RadioButtons, CheckBoxes, and Simple Dialogs

Session Checklist

✔ Using more than one form

✔ Grouping RadioButtons within a GroupBox component

✔ The effect of a Cancel button on your programming

✔ Using the Show and Hide commands with forms

✔ Working with namespaces

✔ Understanding CheckBoxes

30 Min. To Go

Computer applications generally involve an exchange, a kind of conversation, between the user and the application. The user clicks buttons, types in data, or otherwise provides information, and the application processes that information.

In previous sessions you worked primarily with a TextBox, Dialog controls, and CommandButtons as user input devices. In this session, you'll see how to use CheckBoxes and RadioButtons to create a custom dialog box that gets information from the user.

Adding a Second Form

You only have one more feature to add to the simple word processor that you've been building since Session 3. What happens when the user clicks the button captioned Options? A dialog box should appear, allowing the user to specify some preferences about how the application behaves. Let's get started adding this final feature:

1. Start VB .NET running. (If the New Project dialog box appears, just click Cancel to close it.)

2. Choose File ⇨ Open Project.

3. Browse your hard drive to find the folder you created in Session 3, then double-click the file Project1.SLN to bring in the application.

   The file dialog box closes when you double-click the .SLN file. At this point, you might see the code window, or no window at all, depending on the state of the IDE when you shut down VB.

4. Double-click Form1.VB .NET in the Solution Explorer to open the Design window.

When the user clicks the Options button, you want to display a small window (in VB .NET, a Windows Form is a window) that includes several options the user can select from. A VB .NET Windows Form application can have as many Windows Forms as you wish. In this case, you'll add a typical dialog for the user to interact with. We will use a second form for our dialog.

Choose Project ➪ Add Windows Form to add a new form to this project (by default, it will be named Form2). The Add Form dialog box appears, displaying the various kinds of form templates offered by VB. Just double-click the first icon, Windows Form — a traditional, ordinary form.

Form2 appears in its own Design window. Stretch it so it's a reasonable size for a typical Windows dialog box. Use the Toolbox to put two Buttons on Form2, and use the Properties window to change their Text properties to **OK** and **Cancel** (the traditional VB Caption property is now called the Text property in VB .NET).

All dialog boxes have these two buttons at the bottom, and some dialog boxes also add a button captioned Apply. The Apply button is used to put into effect the changes the user selects in the dialog box without closing the dialog box.

Now add two GroupBox controls (formerly known in traditional VB as *Frames*) to Form2 by double-clicking them on the Toolbox. The primary use of a GroupBox is to act as a container for a group of RadioButtons. Change the Text property of GroupBox1 to Color and the Text property of GroupBox2 to Border. Your Form2 should look something like Figure 6-1.

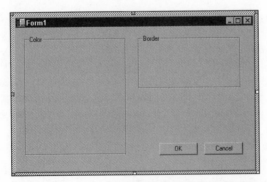

Figure 6-1   *Use GroupBoxes to group RadioButtons.*

Grouping RadioButtons on a GroupBox

RadioButton controls are mutually exclusive within their group. This means that when the user clicks any one of the RadioButtons, none of the other RadioButtons in its group can be selected at the same time. Put another way: Selecting one automatically deselects any previously selected RadioButton in the group. This exclusiveness is useful when you present the user with a set of options, only one of which can be in effect at a given time. (They're called *Radio*buttons because they behave like the buttons on a car radio; press one station button and the previously selected station button is de-selected.)

In this example, you will create a group of buttons that lets the user choose between a 3D or Flat frame around the TextBox. You will then create a second group of buttons that lets the user choose blue, red, green, or black as the text color. Note the mutual exclusivity in these groups. The text is going to be entirely green or red — it cannot be a mixture of those choices. Likewise, the TextBox is either 3D framed or flat, not both.

Now use the Toolbox to add four RadioButtons to the Color GroupBox. Note that you should avoid double-clicking the RadioButtons in the Toolbox — if you do so, they may not be grouped in the GroupBox. Instead, you must use the alternative technique of "drawing" each RadioButton within the GroupBox. To do this, click the RadioButton icon in the Toolbox, and then drag your mouse pointer inside the GroupBox. When you drag your mouse, you will see a solid box that shows what size the component will be, and the mouse cursor changes to a cross.

When you release the left mouse button after dragging, the RadioButton appears within the GroupBox. Repeat this three more times: Click the icon and then drag, so you have a total of four RadioButtons inside the Color GroupBox. Change the Text properties of the four buttons to **Blue**, **Red**, **Green**, and **Black**. If you wish, you can also change each Button's Name property to a name that reflects its purpose. Me, I don't get confused when just using the default names that VB .NET gives controls — as long as I'm working with only a few, simple controls.

Change the Checked (formerly known as *Value* in VB 6) property of the Black RadioButton to True (just double-click the Checked property in the Properties window). This has the effect of selecting this RadioButton (a black dot appears in the button indicating that it's been selected). Black is the default color of the text, so have this button selected when the user first sees this dialog box.

Now repeat this procedure to draw two RadioButtons on the Border GroupBox, and caption them **3D** and **Flat**. Change the 3D button's Checked property to True.

If you *must* double-click grouped controls for some reason, you can. When you double-click the first RadioButton, it will be placed on the form outside the GroupBox. However, if you then drag and drop it into the GroupBox, any additional RadioButtons that you double-click in the Toolbox will join the original one within the GroupBox.

Programming with a Cancel Button

20 Min.
To Go

Now it's time to make the user's choices happen — by writing the programming that changes the text color (the TextBox's ForeColor property does this) or changes the border around the TextBox (use its BorderStyle property).

> Unlike previous versions of VB, you cannot change the Font properties of a control during runtime (by using programming code to do it). You must adjust their size, fontname and so on using the Properties window during design time only. Oddly, you *can* change the color of the font in a TextBox or other control's Text property during runtime by changing the ForeColor property, as we'll illustrate later in this session.

Your first thought is: "OK, I can just put each RadioButton's programming in its Click event, like I did with the CommandButtons on Form1." That would work fine if the only thing you had on this dialog box was a Close or OK button. However, things get a little more complicated when you have that Cancel button.

Cancel means that the user decided to make no changes — even though the user may have clicked some of the RadioButtons before deciding to cancel. Therefore, if you programmed the text to change to blue when the user clicks the Blue RadioButton, you would be jumping the gun.

When there is a Cancel button, you must put all of the programming into the OK button's Click event. OK means make the changes; Cancel means do nothing. So you must write the programming in such a way that nothing happens until (and if) that OK button is clicked. (True, there are other ways to program with a Cancel button — you can memorize all the default settings in effect when the user opens your dialog, and then restore those defaults if the user clicks Cancel. But this isn't *advanced VB .NET*. It's a Crash Course — and so we'll use the more straightforward technique.)

Changing Form1 from within Form2

How do you write this kind of programming? Remember the If...Then command? You simply poll the entire status of all the RadioButtons on Form2. The following programming code is what you should type into the OK button's Click event. You can leave the default name Button1 if you wish.

Whether you change the Name property of components to make them more descriptive is a matter of personal preference. I suggest that you *do* provide descriptive names in large projects or complex forms where it can become hard to keep things straight.

Also notice that I use some "constants" like Color.Blue and Color.Green in the following code. For now, just go along with me on this — trust me. You'll see how to look up VB .NET's built-in constants in Session 10, in the section titled "Understanding Arguments and Parameters."

Here's the code you should type into Form2's Button1 Click Event, to make changes take place in Form1:

```
Private Sub Button1_Click(ByVal sender As System.Object, ByVal e As
System.EventArgs) Handles Button1.Click

        Dim N As New Form1

If RadioButton1.Checked = True Then N.TextBox1.ForeColor =
System.Drawing.Color.Blue
```

```
If RadioButton2.Checked = True Then N.TextBox1.ForeColor =
System.Drawing.Color.Red

If RadioButton3.Checked = True Then N.TextBox1.ForeColor =
System.Drawing.Color.Green

If RadioButton4.Checked = True Then N.TextBox1.ForeColor =
System.Drawing.Color.Black

If RadioButton5.Checked = True Then N.TextBox1.BorderStyle =
System.Windows.Forms.BorderStyle.Fixed3D

If RadioButton6.Checked = True Then N.TextBox1.BorderStyle =
System.Windows.BorderStyle.FixedSingle

Me.Hide()

End Sub
```

Notice that to refer to controls or objects within another form (in this case Form1), you must first declare an object variable to represent that form: `Dim N As New Form1`. (Pay special attention to the necessary New command, required in this situation. Memorize this line of code to prevent future confusion. Most often you create a variable reference without the New, as in: `Dim N As`.)

Now you can adjust properties of the TextBox on Form1 by using `N.TextBox1`. If that TextBox were on the same form as the programming referring to it, you could simply write `TextBox1.ForeColor` rather than `N.TextBox1.ForeColor`. Also notice at the very end, you hide Form2 using the `Me.Hide()` method.

> **In programming, you often find that several lines are nearly identical. Programming can be repetitive, as it is in this example. VB's editor is like a word processor in many ways, and one thing you can do to save time with repetitive coding is to type in the first line:**
>
> ```
> If RadioButton1.Checked = True Then N.TextBox1.ForeColor =
> System.Drawing.Color.Blue
> ```
>
> **Then drag your mouse over it to select it. Press Ctrl+C to copy it, and then press Ctrl+V five times to generate six lines of identical programming beneath it. Then you only need to change the *1* in *RadioButton1* to the correct name for each RadioButton, and change the ForeColors or BorderStyles.**

Understanding Imports

In many VB .NET programs, you'll find that the first few lines in the code window are Imports statements.

The word *import* suggests that something is being added to VB .NET, most probably a whole new set of features (functions in a library that add capabilities, new commands, new properties, and so on). Wrong!

When you import, you are merely saving yourself a little typing. An import brings in a set of *naming* conventions that refer to libraries of functions *already available* to VB .NET. Nothing is actually *imported* in the sense you would think. Just some labels so you don't have to repeat those labels when you write your source code.

For example, in the previous section, you used this code to change the ForeColor of your TextBox:

```
System.Drawing.Color.Blue
```

But if you put this line of code up at the very top of the code window:

```
Imports System.Drawing
```

then you could change color using *fewer words,* like this:

```
Color.Blue
```

By using `Imports`, you don't have to "fully qualify" the reference by adding the "namespace" down in the rest of your source code in this form.

Put another way: if you are going to use the *Color* property (or other features of the `System.Drawing` library) often in a program, you can save typing time by importing the System.Drawing "namespace" as these "imported" lists of names are called. Don't confuse *namespace* with *library* (or as VB .NET now calls them, *assemblies*).

The price you pay is having to figure out which namespace to import for which kinds of functionality. However, over time you become familiar with the primary namespaces and what they contain. Also, VB .NET can sometimes suggest to you which namespace is needed. Type this line into the code window inside a `Click` event somewhere:

```
Open
```

Press Enter. The blue sawtooth line indicates that there is a problem with this code. Pause your mouse pointer on top of the word Open and you'll be told that the Microsoft.VisualBasic namespace might be of help. Then you can go to the top of the code window and type:

```
Imports Microsoft.VisualBasic
```

And see if that helps. It does. The sawtooth line disappears and VB .NET is happy with you.

To see most of the namespaces, type this at the top of your code window:

```
Imports System.
```

(Don't forget the .) As soon as you type the period at the end, the Intellisense Auto List Members feature pops open a listbox of all the namespaces, as shown in Figure 6-2.

Figure 6-2   *Here's how you can see a list of namespaces.*

Then, to see all the members of a particular namespace, just use that namespace in one of your procedures, pausing again at a period. For example, you could add the System.Data namespace at the top of the code window like this:

```
Imports System.Data
```

You could then see the list of all the System.Data properties and methods by typing in this partial line of code:

```
Public Sub New()
c = system.Data.
```

And again, as soon as you type that period following Data, the list of the Data members pops up.

There *are* libraries of functions that you sometimes need to actually *add* to VB .NET. These specialized libraries contain commands that you may sometimes need, but are not among the default group of libraries that are *always* available. To add one of these specialized libraries, you use the Project|Add Reference or Project|Add Web Reference menus. You can also add controls — there are lots of them including perhaps some of your old favorites from VB 6, such as the MSComm control. To add controls, choose Tools|Customize Toolbox. Select the controls you want, and then look for them at the bottom of the Win Forms tab in the Toolbox.

Showing and Hiding Forms

Back to our example. Notice the line at the end: Me.Hide. When the user clicks the OK button, you want Form2 to disappear. The Hide command does just that. In fact, that's all the programming you need to put into the Cancel button's Click event, so type in the following code:

```
Private Sub Button2_Click(ByVal sender As System.Object, ByVal e As
System.EventArgs) Handles Button2.Click

Me.Hide()

End Sub
```

The only thing you need to put into the Options button's Click event on Form1 is the Show command, so double-click Form1 in the Project Explorer, then double-click the button captioned Options on Form1 and type in the following code:

```
Private Sub cmdOptions_Click(ByVal sender As System.Object, ByVal e As
System.EventArgs) Handles cmdOptions.Click

Dim N as New Form2

N.Show

End Sub
```

At this point, why not test your application? Press F5, type some text into the TextBox, and click Options. You see Form2, as shown in Figure 6-3. Click the Red button (notice that the Black default button is automatically deselected the minute you click the Red button). Now click the Flat button. Click OK. The dialog box disappears, and you see that the text has turned red and that the TextBox's frame has gone from a 3D effect to just a simple line.

You can tell when a set of components has been grouped — they all *move* together like Rockettes. Want to see? Choose Debug ⇨ Stop to stop the program from running. Then double-click Form2.vb in the Solution Explorer. Now drag GroupBox1 (the Color box) to move it. Notice that all of the RadioButtons inside it move with it. If one of them doesn't move, it wasn't properly drawn and is merely resting on top of the GroupBox rather than contained by it. To fix that, click the offending RadioButton to select it, press the Del key to delete it, and then look earlier in this session for the instructions on proper component drawing technique.

It's not necessary to use a GroupBox if you're only presenting the user with a single group of RadioButtons. All RadioButtons placed on a form are considered grouped by that form — and they will work together properly just as if you'd contained them within a GroupBox.

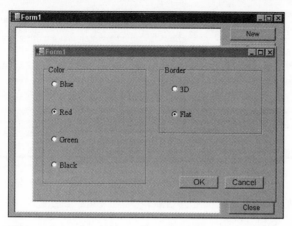

Figure 6-3   *Your Options dialog box in action — everything works as planned.*

Using CheckBoxes

CheckBoxes are quite similar to RadioButtons, except that CheckBoxes are used for nonexclusive choices — things that can be true for all, some, or none at the same time. For example, text can be bold, or italic, or both bold and italic at once. So the user can select a Boldface CheckBox and at the same time select an Italic CheckBox. Selecting one does not automatically deselect the others.

To see how to use CheckBoxes as a way of presenting the user with nonexclusive choices, put two CheckBoxes on Form2. Caption the first one **Boldface** and the second one **Italic** by changing their Text properties in the Properties window. Change their Name properties too, if that's your style.

Now add the following programming just above the Form2.Hide line in the OK button's Click event:

```
If CheckBox1.Checked = True Then
        n.TextBox1.ForeColor = System.Drawing.Color.Black
    Else
        n.TextBox1.ForeColor = System.Drawing.Color.White
    End If

If CheckBox2.Checked = True Then
        n.TextBox1.BackColor = System.Drawing.Color.Blue
    Else
        n.TextBox1.BackColor = System.Drawing.Color.Green
    End If
```

You need to notice some peculiarities about this programming. When you have a multi-line If...Then structure as here, you need to end the zone with End If. Also notice the command Else. This command enables you to specify what VB .NET should do when the If condition is false. What you're saying is: If CheckBox1 is selected, then make TextBox1's forecolor black, or else (if it isn't selected) make it white.

Now Select File ⇨ Save All to save your work.

Done!

REVIEW

You saw how to work with more than one form in a project and then how to group RadioButtons to provide the user with a set of mutually exclusive choices. You worked out the Cancel button problem by putting source code in the OK button rather than in the events of each RadioButton. The mysteries of namespaces were somewhat dispelled. And finally, you learned how to display and hide forms, and also when you should use CheckBoxes as an input device instead of RadioButtons.

QUIZ YOURSELF
---

1. What is the difference between RadioButtons and CheckBoxes? (See "Using CheckBoxes.")

2. What containers can you use to group RadioButtons? (See "Grouping RadioButtons on a GroupBox.")

3. How do you handle it in code when the user clicks a Cancel button on one of your forms? (See "Programming with a Cancel Button.")

4. What is a namespace and what does it do? (See "Understanding Imports.")

5. What's one way to tell if several RadioButtons are grouped together? (See "Showing and Hiding Forms.")

Working with TextBoxes and Their Properties

Session Checklist

✔ Understanding the default TextBox

✔ Common changes to a TextBox's properties

✔ Learning the use of every TextBox property

✔ Understanding that most properties are rarely used

✔ Discovering how to use the Properties window

✔ Changing several properties at once

This session has two purposes: to increase your familiarity with the important TextBox control, and also for you to learn how to use the Properties window.

**30 Min.
To Go**

The TextBox is probably among the most used Visual Basic components — second only to the Button control, I would guess. You already worked with a TextBox in the project you built in previous sessions, but the TextBox is so important that learning some new techniques is worth your time. Recall that a TextBox behaves like a simple word processor, but it does have its limitations. For instance, at any one time it can only display a single font and a single type style (such as italics) for the entire contents. Also, it can display only one size of text at a time. You can change the font, style, and size by changing the TextBox's properties — but the entire contents of the TextBox will change. You cannot change a single word, for example, to italics. It's all or nothing.

> **Note that the RichTextBox control on the Toolbox (which was introduced in Session 3) does not suffer from several of the ordinary TextBox's limitations. You might want to experiment with the RichTextBox if your project has special word-processing needs, or if you expect to exceed the TextBox's 65,535 character (about 10,000 words) limit.**

TextBoxes can be used for both input and output: They can display text or accept the user's typed text. However, if you're merely identifying the purpose of, say, a CheckBox, use a Label instead. A TextBox would be overkill.

Adjusting TextBox Properties

The TextBox is such an important component that you'll spend a good part of this session looking closely at it and its properties. Start Visual Basic, click the Win Forms tab in the Toolbox, and then double-click the TextBox icon in the Toolbox.

After that, there are several steps to clean up some default property settings — which, at least with the TextBox component, aren't usually what you want. (At this point you *cannot* stretch the TextBox vertically to make it higher — that's forbidden right now. Be patient.)

Many Visual Basic components have quite a few properties — just as the TextBox does. However, you usually don't have to change most of them. Each property defaults to its most common value (*in general*; exceptions include the TextBox's notorious default to MultiLine = False). All of VB .NET's controls' Visible properties default to True, rather than False, for instance. This is because you almost always want your components visible to the user. (Some controls, such as the Timer, are used internally by your program and are never made visible to the user. Those few controls have no Visible property at all, of course.)

However, some defaults will be wrong for your project. And a few defaults are nearly *always* wrong for *any project*. One of these infamous defaults is the TextBox's Text property. It defaults to the name of the TextBox (TextBox1, for example), and it's doubtful that any programmer ever wanted to display that to a user. Most often, you'll want the user to see a blank TextBox.

Your first job is to get rid of that default text, which says TextBox1 in the Toolbox. The default should have been a blank, empty Text property, but unfortunately, you're stuck with always having to remove TextBox1 for each TextBox you create. (This has been going on for 10 years, since VB Version 1! With the man-hours wasted, we could have built a second Golden Gate Bridge.)

Note that there are two primary modes in the Visual Basic editor. While you're adding components to a form — or dragging them to change their shapes, or using the Properties Window to change their properties — you are in *design mode*. However, as soon as you press F5, you enter *run mode* and become an "imitation" user who is able to interact with your running application just as a user would. During run mode, you cannot use the Properties window, any more than a regular user could.

Sometimes you'll see a phrase like, "You can't change this at runtime." *Runtime* means the same as what we called run mode in this session (in other words, while the application is running). Similarly, sometimes you'll see a message that says, "Change the property at design time." *Design time* refers to what we call design mode (the application is being worked on in the Visual Basic editor, but is not running). Some properties (such as the Name property) can be changed only at design time. Other properties (such as the Text property) can be changed either during design time or run time. Yet other properties (like the contents of a ListBox) can be changed only during run time — by the programming you write. Every property you see in the Properties window can be set at design time, at least.

It's important to understand that components like TextBoxes start out with all of their properties in one state or another. The Width property, for example, is set to some width, and the Text property contains (or doesn't) some text. In any case, the condition of the properties determines what the user first sees when the application runs, or how the component first behaves.

You don't want users to be greeted with TextBox1 (the default) sitting in your TextBox each time they run your application. So click the TextBox to select it. (Remember that this causes its properties to be displayed in the Properties window. If the Properties window isn't visible, press F4.)

Then click the Text property in the Properties window and drag your mouse across the right column where you see Textbox1 so that you've selected it. Press Del. It disappears.

The second property that you usually have to change is the MultiLine property. By default, it's set to False, which forces all of your text onto the first line, no matter how high the TextBox actually is. Take a look at Figure 7-1.

Figure 7-1   *With the MultiLine property set to the default, there is no word-wrap, and everything typed appears on a single line (as illustrated in the upper TextBox).*

Double-click the MultiLine property in the Properties window and toggle it to True. Now, at last, you can adjust the height of the TextBox because you've made it MultiLine-capable. So, stretch and position the TextBox to make your form look the way you want.

After you've cleaned up the Text and MultiLine properties, you'll still probably want to fix the Font property — it defaults to a small size. I generally change it to a more readable 11-point size. Click the Font property in the Properties Window, and you'll see an ellipsis (. . .), indicating that there is more to see. Click the ellipsis button and you'll then see a dialog box where you can change several qualities of the font. Change it to 11 in the Size list, and then click OK. Notice that the size of the font in the Design window becomes larger. This instant visual response is one of the most widely imitated features that Visual Basic introduced to programming languages.

Now you've got a good, usable TextBox. Remember, if you're going to use more than one TextBox in a project, you can avoid having to set all of these properties for each TextBox. Simply click the TextBox you just finished cleaning up and press Ctrl+C to copy it. Then click the Form and press Ctrl+V to paste a new TextBox with all of the same properties inherited from its parent.

Some Important TextBox Properties (and Many that Aren't)

Now you're ready to dive into the TextBox's properties. I'll discuss each major property in turn. Many of these properties are properties of other components, as well as being properties of forms. For example, the BackColor property is fairly universal — most components have this property so you can change their color. But the main lesson I hope you learn from the following in-depth survey is that the majority of properties are of little use. I'll tell you which ones are valuable, and which ones you can just forget. I'll also mention properties that used to be part of VB, but in VB .NET have either been renamed or eliminated.

Appearing first in the list of TextBox properties is the Bindings property, which is used to attach a control to a database. You'll learn about this property later in the book.

The new AcceptsReturn and AcceptsTab properties describe how VB .NET reacts to the user pressing the Return or Tab keys. Normally, by default, pressing Return moves you down to the next line in a MultiLine-style TextBox. Set AcceptsReturn to False, and pressing return causes a simulated mouse-click on the default button on the form. Set AcceptsTab to True, and a tab (move over 5 spaces) will be inserted into the text. Set it to False, and pressing Tab moves you to the next control on the form, according to the TabIndex property (described later in this section).

The three new Accessibility properties provide features for people with disabilities.

AllowDrop determines whether or not this TextBox permits drag-and-drop operations.

Anchor is a valuable new property. It determines how, or if, a control stretches if the user stretches the form. The default for the TextBox is TopLeft — which means that the TextBox doesn't enlarge or shrink in size if the user drags the form to resize it. Change this property to All, and you'll see the TextBox grow and shrink as the user adjusts the size of the form.

AutoSize determines whether or not the size of the TextBox changes to accommodate any changes in the font or font size.

If you want to, you can change a TextBox's BackColor property to pink or blue or some other color (but it's best to leave it white in most applications). Similarly, you can change the text color by adjusting the ForeColor property. Again, you should probably leave well enough alone. The default black text on a white background is not only more legible, it's also more dignified.

Leave the BorderStyle (formerly Appearance) property alone. It provides part of the 3D framing effect. If you try changing it to one alternative, FixedSingle, you'll turn back time to pre–Windows 95–style user-interface design. If you set it to the third option, None, you'll go back even further in time — regressing all the way to DOS.

The Casing property can be set to force all text to be lowercase, uppercase, or mixed. The CausesValidation property can remain set to True, with no harm done. When set to True, the Validate event will be triggered when the focus shifts from the TextBox to the other component (when the user clicks it or tabs to it). This property only comes in handy with database work — forget about it for now.

ContainsFocus is a new property that tells you whether or not this control (or a child control on it) has the focus (meaning that the next key pressed on the keyboard will be sent to this control). If you want to know whether the control has focus, *whether or not* any of its child controls have the focus, use the Focused property instead.

You can add context menu controls to your form from the Toolbox. A particular context menu control can be assigned to a control by specifying the context menu's name property in the ContextMenu property.

Controls is a new property that represents a collection of any child controls within the current control.

The new Cursor property is what used to be called the MouseIcon property, and it determines what the mouse pointer looks like when it is on top of the TextBox (should you want to change it from the default pointer). I advise against changing this property — unless you're sure you will not confuse the user.

Dock means whether or not you want to cause the control to move to one of several positions within its container (the form). Changing this property also changes the size of the control.

The former DragIcon and DragMode properties are no longer available in VB .NET.

The Enabled property, if set to False, prevents users from typing anything into the TextBox (it is said to be *disabled*). Any text already in the TextBox will appear light gray rather than black to indicate that the TextBox is disabled. Components are disabled when it makes no sense for the user to try to use them. For example, suppose you have several TextBoxes on a form on which the user is supposed to fill in data about himself, and he fills in the TextBox for his age with 44 years. You could then disable a checkbox in which he is supposed to indicate whether or not he is a member of AARP. You have to be over 50 for AARP, so it makes no sense to leave that checkbox enabled. Enabled is often used in programming in response to situations like the one described in this AARP example. The code for this is TextBox1.Enabled = False.

The Focused property is new. It tells you whether the control has the focus (meaning that the next key pressed on the keyboard will be sent to this control).

The Font and ForeColor properties were defined earlier in this session.

The HideSelection property is yet another highly esoteric option. Text can be selected within a TextBox — by programming (as is done by a spell-checker to signal a misspelled word) or by the user dragging the mouse over some text. In either case, the text is highlighted. HideSelection, when set to False, means that selected text in your TextBox remains highlighted, even if the TextBox loses the focus (the user clicks some other form to give it the focus).

I can't really think of a use for this HideSelection property, and, as you've seen in this session, many properties are just like it: highly specialized. I suggest that you not clutter your brain trying to memorize these rare birds. What you do need to remember is that VB contains hundreds of programming features, and if there's something highly specialized you want to do, you probably can. The way to find out how to accomplish your specific goal is to press F1, then click the Search Tab in Help, and type in some words that describe your highly specialized job.

The former Index property is now gone. (It worked with control arrays, which are not supported in VB .NET.)

The Lines property is a collection (an array) of the individual lines of text in the TextBox. Each line is distinct from the previous line because the user pressed the Enter key to move down. You can access the individual lines by using code like this:

```
Dim x as String
X = TextBox1.Lines(2)
```

This example code puts the third line down from the top of the TextBox into variable X. You will learn why (2) represents the *third* line and not the second, and also learn more about arrays, in Session 17.

The Location property, with its *X* (horizontal position) and *Y* (vertical position) attributes, replaces the previous Left and Top properties (although you can still use Left and Top, oddly enough).

You can adjust these X and Y properties in the Properties window, or like this in your programming code to move a control dynamically during runtime. You'll see how to dynamically line up controls when you construct the PDM (Personal Data Manager) application in the last several sessions.

The Locked property is similar, but less drastic, than setting the Enabled property to False. When set to True, Locked permits the TextBox's text to be scrolled, and even highlighted, by the user. It also permits you, the programmer, to change the text: TextBox1.Text = "This new text." The text is not changed to a gray color. However, as when Enabled is set to False, the user cannot edit the text.

The MaxLength property enables you to specify that the user can only enter a particular number of characters into the TextBox. This is useful if you want users to enter information like a zip code, the length of which you know in advance.

The Modified property tells you whether the text has been changed by the user (since the TextBox was created, or since you last set the Modified property to False).

The MouseIcon property is now called Cursor.

The MultiLine property was discussed earlier in this session.

The OLE properties are no longer available.

The PasswordChar property enables you to specify which character should appear visible to the user when he or she types in a password. In other words, if you want to use a TextBox as a password-entry field for the user, you can type in a * symbol as the PasswordChar. If you type in any character as the PasswordChar, the TextBox will display only that character as the user types (for example, **********). You know the routine. (I've always wondered whether this subterfuge is all that necessary — after all, do you have people hovering over your shoulder all the time, just waiting to see your password? I suppose it's better to hide it though — there are lurkers.) Note that the MultiLine property must be set to False for the password feature to work properly.

The new ReadOnly property at first seems baffling. When set to True, the text in the TextBox cannot be changed, only "read." ReadOnly seems rather unnecessary, given that the Enabled property does the same thing. The difference? With Enabled True and ReadOnly False, the text in the TextBox can at least be copied.

The new ResizeRedraw property specifies whether the control should be redrawn when it is resized. In some cases, a graphic or text on a resized control will need to be redrawn to appear correctly.

The new Right property tells you the distance between the right edge of the control and the left edge of its container (usually the form).

For an English speaker, the RightToLeft property has no value and should be left at its default. However, some languages, such as Arabic and Hebrew, run text from right to left. You would set RightToLeft for those languages so vertical scroll bars will appear on the left side of a TextBox.

The Scrollbars property enables you to add horizontal or vertical scroll bars to your TextBox so the user can employ them as a way of moving through text that exceeds the size of the TextBox. However, even without them, the user can always press the arrow keys, the PgUp and PgDn keys, the spacebar, and so on to move around through text that's not shown within the visible opening of the TextBox.

ShowFocusCues is a new property that tells you if the form will currently display one of those visual cues (like the dotted gray rectangle inside a Button control) that indicates which control has the focus.

The ShowKeyboardCues property is new; it tells you if the form will currently display those keyboard shortcuts (underlined letters in the Text property of controls).

The traditional classic pre-VB .NET Height and Width properties are no longer available. They have been replaced with a Size property that includes — what shall we call them? — a pair of "subproperties" named Height and Width. Session 3 covered the TabIndex property — it defines the order in which components get focus as the user repeatedly presses the Tab key to move among them.

The TabStop property, when set to False, removes the component from the TabIndex list. TabIndex is useful because it offers a quick way for the user to move among the input components (TextBoxes, CheckBoxes, and so forth) on a form — all without having to remove his or her hands from the keyboard and reach for the mouse to click a component into the focus. However, there are some components, like a PictureBox, that are not usually employed as user-input devices. So you can set their TabStop properties to False to eliminate them from the TabIndex group. Components such as Labels that can never be used as input devices simply have no TabIndex property in the first place, and are therefore never included in the tabbing.

Sometimes, though, you do want to permit a PictureBox to become part of the TabIndex list so the user can interact with it. How can a PictureBox ever be used as an input device, you ask? A simple example is when the PictureBox is clicked at all, anywhere, something happens (because you put some programming into its Click event). You might display several small PictureBoxes, each containing a different image — perhaps a car, a bus, a train, or a plane. When you click one, a phone number where you can arrange for that kind of transportation is displayed.

Here's a more sophisticated example: Put a map of Italy into a PictureBox in a cookbook application, let the user click on whatever location on the map they choose, and then display a list of recipes typical to the locale that she clicked. (There are x and y coordinates for the MouseDown event that tell you exactly where, on a graphic, the user clicked.)

The Tag property is a kind of Post-It note that you can attach to a component. You can type in some unique text as a way of identifying it when it is passed to a procedure.

There's a new TextAlign (formerly Alignment) property, but it merely offers three alternatives to the traditional left-justify (default). You can center or right-justify the text, but such adjustments are rarely of any use (unless you specialize in wedding invitations, where the centering alignment is always the necessary style).

There used to be a ToolTipText property displayed in the Properties window, representing the small help phrase that pops up to inform the user about the purpose of a component when the user pauses the mouse pointer on top of the component. For mysterious reasons, this property has been promoted to become a full control, and now resides on the Toolbar rather than in the Properties window. Unique among all controls — and indeed unique compared to the way properties are typically handled — you must add a ToolTip control to your form, and *then* the other controls on the form have a ToolTip property in the Properties window.

The Visible property determines whether or not the user can see the TextBox. During design time, components are always visible. But during run time, if you set the Visible property to False, the user cannot see the component. When would you want to make a component invisible? There are at least a couple of uses for this property.

Although it's not traditional, Microsoft and other developers recently started employing a new way of interacting with users. For example, if the user clicks a button that's labeled Additional Features, the button is set to Visible = False and is replaced with two or three RadioButtons from which the user can select additional preferences. Those RadioButtons were always sitting there, but their Visible property was False until (or if) the user clicked the button, revealing them.

A second use for Visible is when you want to use a feature of a component, but you don't want the user to see that component. The most frequent use of this trick is to employ an invisible ListBox. ListBoxes can alphabetize. You can assign a list of names to a ListBox, set its Sorted property to True, and it will organize them for you. However, the user never needs to see this ListBox if there's no need for them to interact with it. You just wanted to borrow the alphabetizing capability of the ListBox control.

The WhatsThisHelpID property is no longer available.

The new WordWrap property mystifies me. I cannot imagine why you would ever want to set it to False. Do so, and if the user types a line longer than the width of the TextBox, instead of automatically moving to the line below, the text scrolls off to the left to accommodate the super-long line they're typing. This is the way a TextBox behaves if its MultiLine property is set to False.

Changing Property Values

10 Min. To Go

Notice that the Properties window has two columns ("panes"). On the left is the property name, and on the right are the values, the actual current status of that property.

Adjusting values

Double-clicking in the left pane usually changes the value of the property. For instance, double-click the Visible property and it switches from its default True to False. Double-click it again, and it goes back to True. Properties with more than two possible values usually cycle through their various possible settings as you double-click them.

When you single-click a property, sometimes a button appears in its right pane. A down-arrow button means that you can click it to drop down a list of values for that property. An ellipsis (...) button means that if you click it, a dialog box will be displayed (see Figure 7-2).

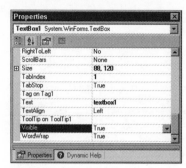 

Figure 7-2   *Drop-down lists and dialog boxes help you quickly change a property's value.*

You might see several kinds of dialog boxes if you click an ellipsis button. When changing the Picture property of a PictureBox, you'll see an Open File dialog box you can use to find a graphics file to fill the PictureBox. The Font property is somewhat unusual because it actually defines several related properties: Font, FontSize, and FontStyle (italics and bold). If you click its ellipsis button, you see a dialog box in which you can select the various font-related properties all at once.

Changing several components at once

There may be times when you want to change the same property for several components at the same time. This was covered in an earlier session, but here's a reminder of how it works: Imagine that you have two RadioButtons, three Labels, and a TextBox on a form. They all need larger fonts so the user can more easily read them. You want to change all of their Font properties from the default 8 to 11. You can do this two ways:

- Click the Font property for the TextBox. Change it to 11. Then click a RadioButton to select it (so its properties fill the Properties window). You'll see that VB has already selected the Font property for you. Whatever property was last selected remains selected, even as you move from component to component. Sometimes, two components don't share a property — in those cases, the default property is selected.

- The fastest way to change a property simultaneously for multiple components is to drag your mouse around the components. This selects all of them (drag handles appear around all selected components). When you do this, the Properties window displays only those properties that all of the selected components have in common (see Figure 7-3). When you change the Font property with several components selected, for example, that property changes for each of the selected components.

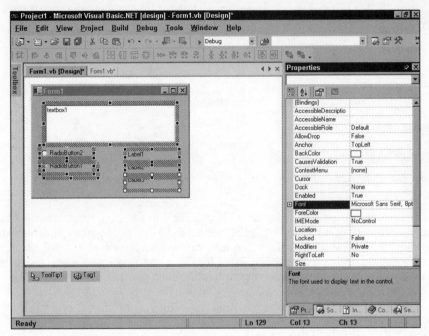

Figure 7-3 *When you select multiple components, the Properties window displays whatever properties they have in common.*

The categorized view

I don't find the feature useful, but some programmers like to click the tab at the top of the Properties window that switches to Categories view. This rearranges the properties into (supposedly) logical groups: Behavior, Appearance, and so on. However, it's really impossible to categorize the highly varied set of properties. To prove my point, the Miscellaneous category is huge — and so very *miscellaneous*. I prefer to leave the list displayed alphabetically. But the view you choose is, as usual, your decision. As I've often said — VB is marvelously flexible.

Done!

REVIEW

In this session, you saw how to work with a TextBox. You learned which of its properties almost always need to be changed from their defaults, and how to use the Properties window to change them. Then — because the TextBox's set of properties are also the properties used with many other components — you learned about their uses and their relative value. You also learned that some are just plain rarely used at all. Finally, you saw how to change the same property in several components simultaneously.

QUIZ YOURSELF

1. Describe the difference between runtime and design time. (See "Adjusting TextBox Properties.")

2. What are two (of the three) TextBox properties that you almost always have to adjust? (See "Adjusting TextBox Properties.")

3. What is the Enabled property used for? (See "Some Important TextBox Properties (and Many that Aren't).")

4. What does the Anchor property do? (See "Some Important TextBox Properties (and Many that Aren't).")

5. If you click an ellipsis button in the Properties Window, what do you see? (See "Adjusting values.")

Labels, ListBoxes, and ComboBoxes

Session Checklist

✔ Adding labels to inform the user

✔ Formatting labels to make them look nice

✔ Watching out when adding new text at run time

✔ Working with ListBoxes and ComboBoxes

**30 Min.
To Go**

L abels are generally used simply to identify the purpose of other components or entire forms. Some components such as Buttons, RadioButtons, GroupBoxes, and CheckBoxes are self-identifying because they have a Text property you use to specify their purpose for the user. However, TextBoxes don't have an exterior caption, so you sometimes need to put a label near them to describe what they do.

Use Labels to Describe Something's Purpose

You might want to identify a whole form with a label, as in Figure 8-1.

Figure 8-1 shows a form the user is supposed to fill in. Two labels are on the form. The top one is in a large, special typeface and titles the form, providing the name of the company. The second label describes the purpose of the TextBox and gives the user instructions. If you want to use various fonts or typesizes, you must use more than one label. As with a TextBox, you cannot mix and match character sizes or styles within a single label.

Notice that the Text property of the form itself was also changed (click on a form and its properties fill the Properties window). The title bar displays the caption (Text) you assign to a form (in this case, "Q & A" rather than the default "Form1" Text property).

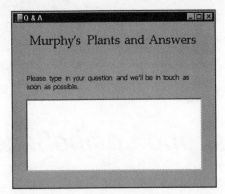

Figure 8-1 *Labels can describe what a form does, and what individual components do.*

Formatting Labels

Labels can be formatted in a variety of ways. You can set their TextAlign property to TopLeft, TopCenter, TopRight, MiddleLeft, MiddleCenter, MiddleRight, BottomLeft, BottomCenter, BottomRight. The AutoSize property, when set to True, causes the label to grow or shrink to fit the text that is inside. This can be useful if you plan to dynamically add text (add it during runtime) without knowing in advance how much text there will be.

There's also a BorderStyle property that puts a simple black line around the label or a 3D sunken frame. This property is nearly always left set to the default None. Labels usually look best unframed, and even the 3D frame can miscue users because sunken objects are supposed to cue the user that the sunken component is an input device, something they can interact with. (True input devices — the box in a CheckBox, the whole TextBox itself, and several other user-input components — appear engraved, a bit sunken into the background, if their BorderStyle property is set to 3D.)

Problem: Adding text during runtime

If you don't plan to dynamically assign text to a label (you aren't going to change its Text property in your programming), go ahead and just stretch the label so it's big enough to display its permanent caption. But if you plan to assign new text at runtime, you've got some questions to answer.

Set AutoSize to True, and the label will expand or contract to hold the new text. It could shoot off the form to the right as you can see in Figure 8-2.

Another problem with AutoSize = True is that your label might cover up any controls located to its right when it expands.

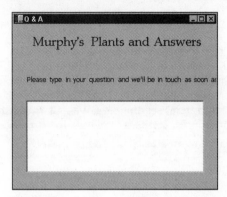

Figure 8-2　*If you add too much text with AutoSize set to True, the Label shoots off the right side of the Form.*

Now, if you leave AutoSize set to False, and if there is too much text to fit inside the label's existing dimensions, the text will truncate, as you can see in Figure 8-3.

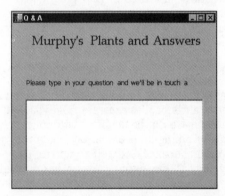

Figure 8-3　*With AutoSize set to False, a label's contents can be cut off.*

Solution: Use a textBox instead

To me, there is only one good solution to this problem: Avoid using a label at all if you must add text to it during runtime. Sometimes you want to display data from a database or other source, and maybe you let a user click buttons to move through the records in that database. Some records may be larger than others (fields such as notes, descriptions, and so forth are not a predictable length the way that a telephone number is). In those cases, I recommend that you use a TextBox, a DataGrid, or some other more flexible control than a label. A TextBox or DataGrid or other database control doesn't need to expand. It will scroll if the contents overflow its boundaries, and you can also provide an optional scroll bar by setting a TextBox's ScrollBars property if you wish. But even without a scroll bar, the user can still use the arrow keys and other keys such as PgDn to see any hidden text.

Using ListBoxes

**20 Min.
To Go**

The ListBox component is used to display a list of information to the user, and possibly elicit a response from the user. The list can be a directory of names of business contacts, a list of books for sale, or whatever. The user can click one of the items, and your programming can detect which item was clicked. Your programming can react to this selection by displaying additional information about the selected item, sending e-mail about the item, ordering the item to send to the user, or other responses. ListBoxes are user-input devices.

Where does the information come from that appears in a ListBox? You can use the VB .NET ArrayList structure:

```
Dim MyArray as new ArrayList

myArray.Add ("key")
myArray.Add ("Name")
myArray.Add ("Address")
```

This holds the list right inside your Visual Basic program. This approach is good for lists that are short and that do not get changed. The data is hardwired in your programming — so changing that data requires that the program itself be modified, then recompiled. But there is no real advantage to using this technique. Why create an ArrayList when you can just use the Add method of a ListBox's Items collection instead, like this:

```
listbox1.items.Add("key")
```

More commonly, though, you'll have a database from which to draw items that you want to display in your list. Data in a database is kept in a file or files separate from your program. Because it's held in an independent file, a database can be modified without requiring that your program itself be modified. Also, manually typing large amounts of data into an ArrayList that is stored within your application is cumbersome, difficult to update (how can different users adjust data that's frozen within your .EXE file?), and causes other problems. So usually you'll avoid the hard-coded ArrayList approach in favor of using a separate data file.

You'll see how to use databases starting in Session 23. For now, though, for purposes of illustrating how the ListBox works, we'll be nasty and avoid involving a database. Let's just use the ArrayList feature to see how to contain data inside a VB program, and then fill a ListBox with that data.

If you wish, you can type in a list of data to be displayed in a ListBox using the Properties window. You can use this somewhat unusual technique, instead of using an ArrayList command, to add short lists of built-in data. To do this, click the elipsis (...) button in the Items property in the Properties window. A String Collection Editor pops open. Type in your data, pressing Enter each time you finish an item. Each item is on a separate line. However, in this session, you'll use the ArrayList command rather than this Items property for your experiments with the ListBox.

The new Form_Load initialization

Start a new VB Windows Application-style project (choose File ⇨ New ⇨ Project, and then double-click the Windows Application icon), and then put a ListBox on Form1. Double-click Form1 so you get to the code window. Now locate the Form_Load event in the code. This is a place where you usually put any of your programming that you want to be executed at the very start, when the application first runs. Put another way: The initialization code is made up of anything you want to happen prior to the user seeing the form. In this example, you want to *populate* (fill) your ListBox with some names before the form is displayed. So type the following lines into the Form_Load event:

```
listbox1.items.Add("Bob")
listbox1.items.Add("Sandy")
listbox1.items.Add("Julie")
listbox1.items.Add("Fred")
listbox1.items.Add("Sam")

End Sub
```

Let's now consider the Add method. In this example, you use the Add command to add each item from your ListBox. As you can see, the technique of adding each name to the ListBox is a bit repetitive, and would be really tiresome if you had a large list to put into an array.

First, let's test this example. Press F5. You should see the list shown in Figure 8-4.

Figure 8-4   *Use the* Add *command to fill a ListBox with data.*

There's another approach you can use involving an *array* object. Arrays are special kinds of variables that contain more than one piece of data. Each piece of data in an array is identified by an index number, as shown in the following example: ItemObj(0) holds Bob, ItemObj(1) holds Sandy, and so on up to Sam in ItemObj (4). Notice that arrays begin counting with an index number of zero. But, just to make things challenging, the System.Obj array must be declared with *(4)*. That 4 represents the upper limit of the array index, *not* the actual number of items you want the array to hold.

Confused? Who can blame you. This problem has been with computer languages forever — those who design computer languages haven't been able to decide between zero-based and one-based lists (or arrays or collections). So, they use *both* approaches! You just have to memorize which approach works with which situation. In VB .NET, it's not too bad. If you do get mixed up and use Dim ItemObj(5) in the following example, you simply get an extra location in your array. In other situations involving arrays, you will see a pretty

understandable error message when you run a program:
`System.IndexOutOfRangeException`. (Don't worry if your understanding of arrays isn't clear yet — they'll be covered thoroughly later.)

Once the array object is created, you can add the contents of the array to the ListBox by using a loop, like this:

```
Private Sub Form1_Load(ByVal sender As System.Object, ByVal e As
System.EventArgs) Handles MyBase.Load
        Dim ItemObj(4) As System.Object

        ItemObj(0) = "Bob"
        ItemObj(1) = "Sandy"
        ItemObj(2) = "Julie"
        ItemObj(3) = "Fred"
        ItemObj(4) = "Sam"

        Dim i As Integer


        For i = 0 To 4
            ListBox1.Items.Add(ItemObj(i))
        Next

    End Sub
```

There is a method named AddRange **that can dump an entire array directly into a ListBox:**

`ListBox1.Items.AddRange (ItemObj)`

If the number of items in a ListBox's list is larger than can be displayed, a scroll bar is automatically added to the ListBox.

Automatic alphabetization

Notice that the items in the ListBox are not alphabetized; they are listed in the order that you added them. Sometimes this is desirable, but usually it's easier for a user if you alphabetize. A ListBox can automatically alphabetize quickly. To alphabetize, change the ListBox's Sorted property to True in the Properties window. Capitalization is ignored.

Removing items from a list

How do you think you remove an item from a ListBox? How about using the Remove command?

It's not all that common, but sometimes you might want to remove (or permit the user to remove) one or more items from a ListBox. You can identify the item you want removed by using its index number or the actual data (such as "Bob"). Each item in the ListBox has a different index number given to it by the ListBox. The ListBox maintains an array (or collection) called *Items*.

Double-click the ListBox in the Design window to get to its `SelectedIndexChanged` event, and then type in the following code to remove Bob:

```
Protected Sub ListBox1_SelectedIndexChanged(ByVal sender As Object,
ByVal e As System.EventArgs)

        ListBox1.Items.Remove("Bob")

End Sub
```

Run this, and then click anywhere inside the ListBox and Bob will disappear. You could achieve the same effect by using the index for Bob, like this:

```
        ListBox1.Items.RemoveAt(0)
```

However, if you want to permit the user to decide what gets deleted, you use the `SelectedIndex` property to find out which item the user clicked, like this:

```
        ListBox1.Items.RemoveAt(ListBox1.SelectedIndex)
```

Press F5. Click any item in the ListBox, and that item will be removed.

Sometimes you want to clear out the entire contents of the ListBox all at once, in preparation for refilling the ListBox with a whole new list. To do that, use the `Clear` command:

```
ListBox1.Items.Clear
```

The Checkbox-Style ListBox

10 Min.
To Go

There is also a CheckedListBox control that works the same way as the ordinary ListBox, except small boxes appear next to each item, as you can see in Figure 8-5. The user gets additional visual cues showing which item or items are currently selected.

Figure 8-5 *The Checkbox-style ListBox indicates selections with checkboxes.*

ComboBoxes, a Variation on the ListBox

The ComboBox is quite similar to the ListBox — it uses the Add, Remove, and Clear methods; both components have a Sorted property that behaves the same way; and so forth. The primary difference is that a ComboBox has a small TextBox at the very top, as you can see in Figure 8-6.

Figure 8-6 *A ComboBox has a TextBox attached to it, where the user can type in new items.*

Sometimes you want to let users add their own items to the list you display. Perhaps you show them a list of travel destinations, but you also want to permit them to type in their own destination if it's not in the list. Another feature of a ComboBox is that user can select from the items in the list by typing only the first letter or first few letters, and then pressing Enter.

A ComboBox only displays one item — the user doesn't see the list unless the down-arrow button is clicked next to the ComboBox's TextBox. The Style property determines a couple of behaviors of a ComboBox. Change the Style to Simple and the drop-down button disappears, though the user can still scroll through the list with the arrow keys on the keyboard.

Change the Style property to the drop-down list style, and the user cannot type something new into the TextBox. In any configuration, a ComboBox's great advantage, in addition to letting users type in a new item, is that it takes up less real estate on the screen than a ListBox. The ComboBox shows only the single default item until the user clicks the drop-down button. The default item, which is the only thing the user first sees, is whatever you've typed into the Text property in the Properties window for that ComboBox.

Done!

REVIEW

All about labels, ListBoxes, and ComboBoxes, this session explored two of the most useful components Visual Basic offers. I say "two" because the ComboBox component is merely a variation of the ListBox. You saw how to format a label and how to add Text to one. You understood when it is best to abandon the label component in favor of the TextBox. Then you discovered how best to take advantage of the ListBox's alphabetizing capabilities, as well as how to add and remove items from the list. Finally, some variations on the ListBox were introduced: the CheckBox-style and ComboBoxes.

QUIZ YOURSELF

1. Should you use the BorderStyle property of a label? Why, or why not? (See "Formatting Labels.")

2. Why do you have to worry if you need to change the Text property of a label during runtime? (See "Problem: Adding text during runtime.")

3. Where do the items displayed in a ListBox or ComboBox usually come from? The user? An array in the program? A database? (See "Using ListBoxes.")

4. How does the user benefit if you employ the CheckBox-style ListBox? (See "The CheckBox-Style ListBox.")

5. Name two advantages offered by a ComboBox. (See "ComboBoxes, a Variation on the ListBox.")

All About Graphics: Adding Pictures to Your Projects

Session Checklist

✔ How to display graphics

✔ How to use a PictureBox

✔ Stretching or shrinking images

✔ Simple animation

✔ Adding graphics to other controls, such as Buttons

✔ Using the GroupBox control to subdivide a form

This isn't really a session; it's more like recess. You'll find out how to use graphics to jazz up your applications, and make them look more professional. It's fast, and it's about the most powerful effect you can achieve in VB in less than ten seconds.

*30 Min.
To Go*

All you do is double-click a PictureBox icon on the Toolbox, click the Image property in the Properties window, find a graphics file, and double-click its name. You're done. What could be simpler?

> **!**
> *Tip*
>
> **Before getting deeper into graphics, you need some actual graphics to work with, right? If you've got picture files on your hard drive, by all means use them. Use Windows's Find utility (WindowsKey+F) to search for .BMP, .JPG or .GIF files.**
>
> **And don't forget: The Internet is loaded with great drawings and photos only a download away.**

Using a PictureBox

Recall that a PictureBox is an all-purpose graphics container. You can use it to display the contents of .BMP, .GIF, .JPG, .EMF, .WMF, or .ICO (icon) graphics files. .EMF and .WMF files are rarely used any more (in fact, they *never were* much used). .ICO files are tiny, symbolic little critters, like the icons on your desktop. .BMP, .GIF, and .JPG files are widely used.

Try displaying a graphic by following these steps:

1. Double-click the PictureBox icon in the VB Toolbox. A PictureBox appears on the form.

2. Click the ellipsis (...) button next to the Image property in the Properties window. VB displays the Open dialog box so you can browse your hard drive for a graphics file.

3. Locate, and then double-click, the name of one of the following graphic file types supported by VB .NET: .BMP (ordinary bitmap), .CUR (cursor), .EMF (older format), .GIF (ordinary bitmap), .ICO (icon), .JPG (popular compressed format — often used on the Internet), or .WMF (a Microsoft format for resizable drawings that never really caught on).

After you double-click a graphics filename in the file browser dialog box, the image will be loaded into your PictureBox control, as shown in Figure 9-1.

Figure 9-1 *Adding drawings or photos to a VB project is a snap.*

You can force the PictureBox to size itself to fit precisely around a .BMP, .JPG, or any graphics format other than the resizable .WMF type — just change the PictureBox's SizeMode property to AutoSize, as shown in Figure 9-2. Also notice the 3D-frame effect around the

PictureBox in the figure. You get a nice frame like that by setting a PictureBox's BorderStyle property to Fixed3D. I suggest you almost *always* take advantage of this sharp-looking BorderStyle, unless you are creating wallpaper or some other specialized situation.

Figure 9-2   *You can add a 3D border and AutoSize the PictureBox to fit the complete image, as shown here.*

Can you stretch (or shrink) a picture? Sure. Set a PictureBox's SizeMode property to StretchImage and feel free to experiment, as shown in Figure 9-3.

Figure 9-3   *PictureBoxes can be freely stretched or shrunk, in four directions.*

Beware of overstretching a graphic

Most graphics become distorted or grainy if you enlarge them too much or stretch them to the wrong shape, as shown in Figure 9-4.

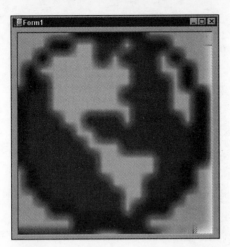

Figure 9-4 *Don't go wild with stretching images, or you'll get ugly results like this.*

Wallpapering

You can repeat images to fill a PictureBox, as shown in Figure 9-5. Change the SizeMode to Normal. Remove the Image (right-click the Image property in the Properties window, and then choose Reset). Now click the BackgroundImage property and choose a smaller graphic, such as the .ICO of the earth used in the figure. Use wallpapering with discretion — a subtle, pale background is more pleasant than a loud, busy pattern.

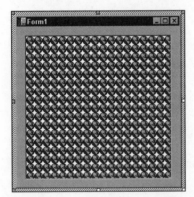

Figure 9-5 *You can fill a PictureBox with repeated images, like this.*

Centering

One final visual effect for a PictureBox: centering. In Figure 9-6, the SizeMode property has been set to CenterImage, and the BackgroundImage property is the same as it was in Figure 9-5.

Figure 9-6   *Combining centering with a BackgroundImage allows you to create elaborate frames of any kind.*

Form Images and Special Gradient Effects

You can add graphics to the BackgroundImage property of a form, as shown in Figure 9-7.

20 Min.
To Go

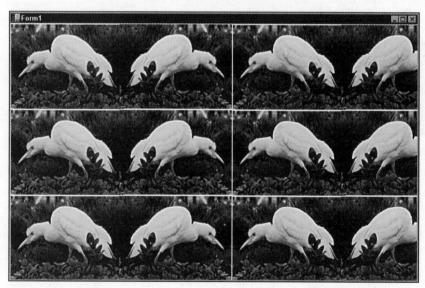

Figure 9-7   *Wallpapering can be applied to forms as well as PictureBoxes.*

One use for form images (as well as the BackgroundImage properties of PictureBoxes, buttons and other controls) is to improve on the traditional and rather tired battleship gunmetal gray that's been behind Windows controls for over a decade.

One of the best ways to avoid dull-looking forms and controls is to use metallic shading. It's subtle and conservative enough for any business application, yet considerably more attractive than plain gray.

Several VB controls, including buttons and forms, have a BackgroundImage property. You can put gradients onto these controls or a form by merely loading in a gradient .BMP graphic. You can make your own gradients with Adobe Photoshop, Picture Publisher, or most any photo-retouching program. It's easy to create gradients. Here's how to do it.

The best metallic gradient is a gradual shift between two shades: white and the typical Windows gray (the light 25-percent gray often used as the default BackColor; the same gray that's used on the VB Button and many other controls). Another, somewhat more powerful, effect can be achieved by using the darker 50-percent gray that's typically used to shadow buttons and other controls.

To capture a gray that will fit in with VB's (and the Windows) color scheme, put a button on a form, and then press Alt+PrnScr to capture the form to the Clipboard. Then open a photo-retouching program like Adobe Photoshop. From its Edit menu, choose Paste to bring in the form.

All retouching programs have a "color picker" tool. It usually looks like an eyedropper. Use it to select the color of the Button's shadow, thereby placing that color into the main color selection (as illustrated in Figure 9-8).

Figure 9-8 *Use the dark shadow around a button to become the base for the gradient.*

Change the alternate color (sometimes called *backcolor* or *secondary color*) to white. If you don't want to use the picker, adjust the main color directly to shadow gray by setting RGB to 75 percent each or to white by setting RGB to 100 percent each. If you're specifying colors in CYMK rather than RGB, the percentages for gray are 25 percent for the first three and 0 percent for K.

Now copy the button or form or whatever you're going to put the gradient in. Paste that picture into your graphics program. Drag your gradient so that the gray shadow is strongest in the lower-right corner and the white is strongest in the upper-left corner. Use the linear gradient option (not circular, radial, or some other type), as shown in Figure 9-9.

Figure 9-9　*This illustrates how you can use a copy of the target button to correctly size your gradient.*

Save the results to disk as a .BMP file for importing into the BackgroundImage property of the button. Switch to VB .NET and load the Gradient.BMP into the BackgroundImage property of the button, as shown in Figure 9-10.

Figure 9-10　*Add gradient backgrounds to forms, buttons, or other controls.*

Figure 9-10 illustrates how metallic gradients look on a form and on buttons. Also try creating subdivisions of a form by putting a PictureBox or two on the form, loading separate gradients into the form and the PictureBoxes, and then placing other controls on top.

Another useful technique involves arranging your controls the way you want them on a form and then pressing Alt+PrtScrn to capture the form. Paste it into a graphics application, and you can then create effects like drop shadows around the controls. When you're finished, save the result as a .BMP file and load it into the form's BackgroundImage property. Now you can use drop shadows or whatever effect you want to incorporate.

Although the BackgroundImage property will not interfere with items in the foreground, such as Text captions, you can also add text effects in your graphics application if you wish. For the OK and Cancel captions on the buttons previously shown in Figure 9-10, I added drop shadows around the text, as shown in Figure 9-11.

Figure 9-11　*Let your imagination guide you. These captions and buttons have drop shadows that were added in a graphics program.*

Most graphics programs of any sophistication have drop shadow Wizards — and drop shadows are among the most effective visual effects. Microsoft even added a drop shadow that follows the mouse pointer in Windows 2000.

Animation

**10 Min.
To Go**

You can achieve animation in various ways. One way is to turn on and off the Visible properties of two or more superimposed graphics (using a VB Timer control). Yet another animation effect, illustrated in the following example, merely rearranges superimposed graphics, as you would by putting different cards on top of a deck. If a set of PictureBoxes are all the same size and in the same place on a form, they act like a deck of cards, and the PictureBox that's on top (and therefore visible to the user) at any given time is governed by each PictureBox's *ZOrder*.

In this next example, each time you click the form, the ZOrder of a PictureBox switches between (on top) and (on the bottom). Because there are two PictureBoxes of the same size and in the same position, this has the effect of toggling them.

You can use the SendToBack or BringToFront methods to adjust ZOrder during runtime.

Start a new VB .NET Windows-style project. Put two PictureBoxes on a form, and then change their Image properties using the Properties window to fill each of them with a different graphic file. Add one button to the form.

Type the following code into the Form_Load event, which causes PictureBox2 to be in the same position, and the same size, as PictureBox1:

```
Private Sub Form1_Load(ByVal sender As System.Object, ByVal e As
System.EventArgs) Handles MyBase.Load
        PictureBox2.Left = PictureBox1.Left
        PictureBox2.Top = PictureBox1.Top
        PictureBox2.Height = PictureBox1.Height
        PictureBox2.Width = PictureBox1.Width

End Sub
```

Then type this into the Button1_Click event to produce the animation:

```
Private Sub Button1_Click(ByVal sender As System.Object, ByVal e As
System.EventArgs) Handles Button1.Click
        Static toggle As Boolean

        toggle = Not toggle

        If toggle Then
            PictureBox2.BringToFront()
        Else
            PictureBox2.SendToBack()
        End If

End Sub
```

You can manipulate the positions of any number of superimposed controls by merely using their BringToFront and SendToBack methods. You can make them overlap each other in various ways.

The previous code used a variable named toggle, declared with the Static command. Session 13 explains the idea of scope, but it's worth briefly noting now that ordinarily when you define a variable in a procedure (between the Sub and End Sub, or Function and End Function), that variable is *extinguished* when VB moves out of the procedure. The variable loses its value and that value cannot be retrieved. Such variables are called *local* (as opposed to *global* variables, which retain their contents during execution in *any* procedure within the form where the global variable is declared).

However, if you use the Static command to declare a variable in a procedure, the variable *retains* its value even when execution of the program leaves the procedure. Each time you click the Button in this example, execution enters the Button1_Click procedure, and then execution leaves this Click procedure after switching the ZOrder of Picture2. Because the variable toggle is defined as Static, the variable "remembers" whether it holds True or False (the only two values that a Boolean variable type can hold). Remember: if you have a local variable that must retain its contents, declare it with the *Static* command.

The Not command switches the value in the variable toggle between True and False — just like flipping a light switch up or down. If toggle holds the value True, then when the line toggle = Not toggle is executed, the contents of toggle switch to False (and vice versa).

Graphics everywhere

In addition to PictureBoxes, Buttons, and Forms, several other controls also have an Image or BackGroundImage property. If a control has one of these properties, you can add graphics to it if you wish, as visual cues regarding the status or purpose of the control. Among the most popular controls with Image properties are the LinkLabel, Label, CheckBox, and RadioButton.

Shapes and Zones

You may have noticed the GroupBox control on VB's Toolbox. Session 6 showed how to use this control to group RadioButtons. The GroupBox has a second specialized role: subdividing a form.

If you have a relatively complicated form, you can organize it visually by using the GroupBox to visually group related items. This can assist the user in understanding what you are showing. Typically, an options or preferences dialog box includes various sections that lend themselves to discreet zoning, as you can see in Figure 9-12.

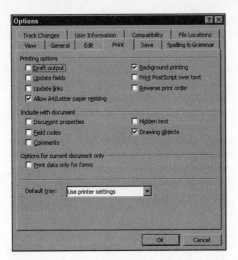

Figure 9-12　*Subdivide a complex window into logical zones.*

The figure shows a dialog box from Microsoft Word with four groups of options, separated by four lines. These visual cues help the reader more quickly understand the contents of a complicated form. However, notice that I used two lines closely spaced together in Figure 9-12, creating a 3D effect. These lines (one white, one medium gray) create a 3D etched effect — as if some sharp object had carved a line into the default Windows light gray background.

You can reproduce this etched effect easily with the GroupBox control in VB. To create these kinds of attractive etched divider zones, add some GroupBoxes to your form, as shown in Figure 9-13.

Figure 9-13　*Use GroupBoxes to zone a form into logical categories.*

To reposition a control on a form with great precision, click the control to select it, and then hold down the Ctrl key while repeatedly pressing (or holding down) the arrow keys. (The best, most precise way to resize a control is to select it by clicking it, then hold down the Shift key while pressing arrow keys. Alas, this feature isn't yet working at the time of this writing. Perhaps

it will work by the time you read this book.) If you're having problems precisely positioning a control on a form, you probably have the Snap-to-grid feature turned on. Choose Tools ⇨ Options, and then click the HTML Designer folder to open it. Click Display. Then deselect the Snap-to-grid option.

Note that you can optionally identify a zone enclosed by a GroupBox by captioning it with its Text property. Or, if you prefer, delete the Text property to get a solid frame, as shown in the GroupBox on the bottom in Figure 9-13.

Done!

REVIEW

In this session, you learned how to add visual effects — such as animation, photos and divider lines — to your applications. You now know how to use graphics to liven up an application, and to provide the user with visual cues as to the purpose of a button or a group of options.

QUIZ YOURSELF

1. Name two graphics file types that can be used in VB .NET projects. (See "Using a PictureBox.")
2. How can you stretch a .BMP graphic? (See "Using a PictureBox.")
3. Describe a technique that adds shadows to controls. (See "Form Images and Special Gradient Effects.")
4. What is a gradient? (See "Form Images and Special Gradient Effects.")
5. Can you add graphics to any other controls beside PictureBoxes and forms? (See "Graphics everywhere.")
6. Name the two uses for a GroupBox control. (See "Shapes and Zones.")

Using the New Menu Editor

Session Checklist

✔ Understanding the MainMenu control

✔ Creating sets of menus

✔ Renaming menu events

✔ Providing programming for menu items

✔ Understanding parameters and arguments

✔ Working with constants

**30 Min.
To Go**

Visual Basic .NET makes the job of adding menus to your projects quite straightforward. It's an improvement over the somewhat clumsy techniques used in previous versions of VB.

You add a control from the Toolbox and then just type in the various menus and submenus you want to add to a form. Then, to make the menus actually *do* something when the program runs, you double-click any of the menu items on the Form and, as usual, you're taken down into the code window where you can then add whatever programming is needed.

The MainMenu control, as it's called, merely leaves behind shell structures (a Click event Sub for each menu item). It's up to you to fill in the programming code that, for example, actually saves a file if the user clicks your Save As option in your File menu. Fortunately, several of the most common menu options — File Open, Save, Print, Print Preview, Page Setup, Color, and Change Fonts — can be handled rather easily with the CommonDialog controls, as you'll see in this session and again in Session 12.

The Basic Menus

Nearly all Windows programs include at least the basic four standard menus: File, Edit, Window, and Help. The File menu generally contains disk file operations and a print option.

The Edit menu includes text-manipulation commands (cutting, pasting, selecting all, and searching). The Window menu includes options for arranging or sizing the window the user works with, and the Help menu is self-explanatory. Of course, you can add any menus that you choose, to let your users exploit all of the features of your application.

Go ahead and give the MainMenu control a try. Choose Start ⇨ New ⇨ Project and type in the name **Menu**. Double-click the Windows Application icon. Then double-click the MainMenu icon in the Toolbox, as shown in Figure 10-1

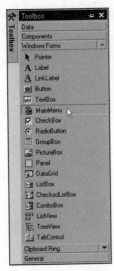

Figure 10-1   *This control makes creating a menu structure a snap.*

The tray opens below your form, displaying a MainMenu icon. Also, you see a box at the top left of the form that says, "Type Here." Go ahead. Click the Type Here box with your mouse to select it, and then type the word **File**, as shown in Figure 10-2.

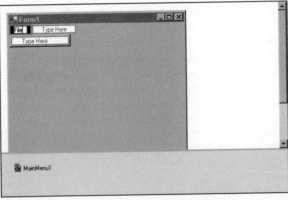

Figure 10-2   *As soon as you label a file item, surrounding empty squares open up inviting you to label them, too, if you wish.*

The menus across the top are *root menus*. They are usually visible. Most of the time, their only job is to drop down a menu — to reveal their set of submenu items. Each submenu item has a Click event where you put the programming for the response if the user chooses that menu item.

Secondary menus

Type the word **Save** in the box just below the one you labeled File. Notice once again that various adjacent empty boxes open up. Click the box to the right of Save, and type in **Text 1**. Then in the box under Text 1, type **Text 2**, so your form looks like the one shown in Figure 10-3. These two options will give the user the option of saving the text in TextBox1 or TextBox2.

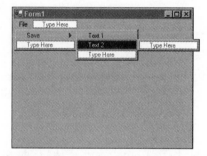

Figure 10-3   *Continue typing in menu items until you've created the menu structure you want.*

Notice in Figure 10-3 that VB .NET automatically adds a right-arrow symbol when you create secondary menu items. This kind of menu item pops out to the right, providing various options. In this case, you're offering the user a choice between saving TextBox1 or TextBox2 in your application.

What this section calls submenus and secondary menus are technically referred to as *child menus.* **And every child (or group of child menus) has a parent. Notice that when clicked, parent menu items usually** *do nothing except display their child (or children).* **So you usually don't write any programming code in the parent menu's event — you write your code in the child item events. (You** *could* **write some code in a parent menu's Click event, to start some process in the background, but this is rare. Also, be aware that if you do want to use a parent menu's Click event, that parent cannot have any child menus under it or the parent's click event will never fire, no code will be executed in it.)**

Separator bars

To make life easier for users, many menus include separator bars to segregate the menu items into logical categories. Click the Debug menu in VB .NET, and you'll see several separators.

The options at the top are grouped together because they specify which debugging windows will be visible. The second set of options, just below the separator bar, has to do with the running debugging process. The third set involves breaking (stopping) the executing program, and other jobs.

To see how to add a separator bar, click File on your form, and then click your other menu items until you see Text 1 and Text 2. You're going to put a separator between these two items. Right-click Text 2, and you'll see a context menu. Choose Insert Separator. Notice that you select the item *just below* where you want the separator bar to be inserted. Also notice that a visible bar appears in your menus. Click the form to close your menus. Then click File in your form again to reopen the menus. The separator bar should now be visible on the menus, as shown in Figure 10-4.

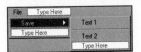

Figure 10-4   *Separator bars divide menus into logical zones.*

Right-click one of the menu items to see the context menu again. Notice that you have many familiar tools you can use when creating menus: cut, copy, paste, delete, redo, and undo.

Fixing the names

Double-click the Save item in your menu system to get to its Click event in the Code window. You'll see that VB .NET has provided this Click event:

```
Private Sub MenuItem2_Click(ByVal sender As System.Object, ByVal e As
System.EventArgs) Handles MenuItem2.Click

End Sub
```

If you are creating a menu system of any complexity, you'll doubtless want to use descriptive names for the events. MenuItem2, MenuItem3, and so on just aren't that descriptive.

Click the Form1.vb(Design) tab on the top of the Design window to get back to the form editor. Right-click the Save item in your menus, and then choose the Edit Names option in the context menu. You see a transformation: Not only does each menu item now have the label section that you've already filled in, but it also has a section enclosed in brackets showing the default name that VB .NET gave to the Click events.

Type **mnuTextBox1** as the name for the Text 1 item, as shown in Figure 10-5.

Figure 10-5   *You edit the menu Event names like this.*

Note the optional *mnu* prefix that I added to remind myself that the Event responds when the user clicks a menu item. Go ahead and fill in the other two of your menu item names in a similar fashion: **mnuSave** and **mnuTextBox1**.

Now right-click mnuSave on the form and choose the Edit Names option once again. This deselects (deactivates) it so you again see only the labels.

Checks and dots

Sometimes it's useful to visibly indicate to the user which menu option is currently in effect. As you saw in the option menu you just worked with, a check symbol was displayed next to the Edit Names option while that feature was active.

You can provide this same cue for your users. Click the Text 1 menu item to select it. Now press F4 to bring up the Properties window displaying this menu item's properties. Double-click the Checked property to change it to True in the Properties window. This adds a check symbol to Text 1, which lets the user know that if they click the Save menu item, it will be Text 1 that's saved, not Text 2. (You'll program the Text 2 Click event later in this chapter to move the check symbol if the user clicks Text 2 instead of Text 1.)

One typical use for check symbols is to indicate the current status of something such as a font: A group of three font sizes (Small, Medium, and Large) should indicate to the user which of them is currently selected. To do this, you would display a checkmark next to the selected one.

If you prefer a dot rather than a checked symbol, double-click the RadioCheck property in the Properties window.

Adding shortcut keys

While you're in the Properties window, you're going add a shortcut key to your menu items as well. Menu items often have a shortcut key so the user can select the item by merely pressing a couple of keys rather than having to take their hand off the keyboard and click with the mouse. Most menu shortcut-key combinations include the Ctrl key, plus some other key. However, the Shift key is sometimes used. (The Alt key is reserved for keyboard-selection of controls — usually buttons.)

The Shortcut feature allows you to give the user a somewhat faster way to launch frequently used options, such as Save. Almost everyone who uses Windows knows at least some of these shortcuts. If you add an Edit menu to one of your VB .NET programs, you might want to use these classic shortcuts for things that people do frequently from that menu:

Ctrl+X — Cut

Ctrl+C — Copy

Ctrl+V — Paste

Ctrl+Z — Undo

Take a look at Microsoft Word or some other popular application to see which Ctrlkey combinations are traditional for the various common shortcuts. When you assign a Ctrl shortcut, it will appear on the menu on the far right to alert the user that they can activate that option directly, without having to use the mouse at all.

To add a shortcut key, click the Shortcut property in the Properties window, and then click the down-arrow icon next to the Shortcut property to display a list of possible shortcuts. Choose Ctrl+T. You won't see the results right away, but if you press F5, you'll see your form and the shortcut key displayed as shown in Figure 10-6.

Figure 10-6 *It's easy to add checks and shortcuts to your menu items.*

Setting the Enabled property

Sometimes a menu item makes no sense because of the current state of the application. For instance, if the user hasn't yet typed any text into a TextBox, Cut and Copy features on an Edit menu are useless. Typically, an application makes such inappropriate options unavailable to the user, and indicates this to the user by making the menu item text gray (disabled). Clicking a grayed option does nothing. To disable a menu item, you can write some code in the Form_Load event so that the item starts out disabled when the program first runs:

```
mnuCut.Enabled = False
```

But as soon as the user types something into a TextBox in your application, you can enable the Cut feature, with this code in the TextBox's Change event:

```
Private Sub TextBox1_TextChanged(ByVal sender As System.Object, ByVal e As
System.EventArgs) Handles TextBox1.TextChanged

If Text1 <> "" Then
    mnuCut.Enabled = True
Else
    mnuCut.Enabled = False
End If

End Sub
```

What this means is: If Text1 is not (<>) empty ("") then enable the Cut menu item; otherwise (Else), disable (gray) it and make it unresponsive to clicking.

Making Menu Items Work

**20 Min.
To Go**

To create a Save feature, you'll use the SaveFileDialog control. Double-click the SaveFileDialog icon in the Toolbox. (You'll probably have to use the down-arrow icon near the bottom of the Toolbox to scroll down to find the SaveFileDialog icon.)

Now you're ready to go into the code window and provide the programming that makes these menu choices perform tasks for the user. Double-click the Text 1 menu item, and you'll get down into the code window in that item's Click event. You want to work with the Text 1 and Text 2 menu item events, so if you don't see those events in the code window, go back to the Design window and double-click each item to force VB .NET to create their Click events in the code window. (You don't put any code into the Save menu item because its only job is to display the Text 1 or Text 2 submenus.)

> **The technique of double-clicking is not the only way to get VB .NET to create these events. You can also have VB .NET create events by selecting each menu item after dropping the list from the top left of the code window (click the down arrow button), then select the Click event (or whatever other event you want) from the list at the top right of the code window.**

Type this into the mnuTextBox1_Click event:

```
Private Sub mnuTextBox1_Click(ByVal sender As System.Object, ByVal e As
System.EventArgs) Handles mnuTextBox1.Click

mnuTextBox1.Checked = True 'show the user that this item was last used

        Dim s As New SaveFileDialog()
        s = SaveFileDialog1

        s.ShowDialog()
        MsgBox(s.FileName)

End Sub
```

Chapter 12 goes into the details of using the various dialog controls. For now, just press F5 to run this program, and then browse to locate the folder where you want to store the file, and type in a filename. Press the Save button. You'll see a MessageBox like the one shown in Figure 10-7 (though your results will display the path and filename you used when running this test).

Figure 10-7 *The FileSaveDialog control returns a path and filename that you can use to save a file.*

As you can see, whatever path and filename you entered into the FileSave dialog was returned as the FileName property of the FileSaveDialog control. You then write some code to actually save a file using that path and filename (as discussed in Chapter 12).

The Checked property of a menu item can be adjusted in your programming as this example illustrates. When the user clicks Text 1, that menu item displays a check; likewise, if the user clicks Text 2, *it* gets checked. In fact, that's the only difference between the code you write for Text 1 and Text 2, as you can see in boldface here:

```
Private Sub mnuTextBox2_Click(ByVal sender As System.Object, ByVal e As
System.EventArgs) Handles mnuTextBox2.Click

MnuTextBox2.Checked = True 'show the user that this item was last used

        Dim s As New SaveFileDialog()
        s = SaveFileDialog1

        s.ShowDialog()
        MsgBox(s.FileName)

End Sub
```

Providing Context Menus

One popular form of menu is the context menu. You right-click an application's editing window (or a toolbar or some other feature) and out pops a menu of frequently used features relevant to that item.

To create a context menu feature for your VB .NET application, you can use the ContextMenu control on the Toolbox. It works much the same way as the MainMenu control described earlier in this chapter.

However, you may rarely need to use the ContextMenu feature in VB .NET because the control for which a context menu is likely to be of most use in your applications is the TextBox — and the TextBox control *already has a built-in context menu.*

So you lucked out. You don't have to write any code to get useful things to happen when your user right-clicks a TextBox in one of your applications — the functionality has been built in. Figure 10-8 shows the various features available when a user right-clicks a TextBox in a running VB .NET application.

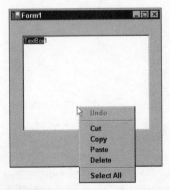

Figure 10-8 *The TextBox has a built-in context menu, and the features it offers are already programmed for you by Microsoft.*

Understanding Arguments and Parameters

**10 Min.
To Go**

Now let's switch to a somewhat more abstract topic, but an essential one. Sometimes an event has *arguments* — items in parentheses that provide information about whatever triggered the event. For example, a MouseDown event occurs when the user clicks the mouse over a PictureBox. That event's arguments include information about which mouse button was pressed (left, middle, or right), and the coordinates where the mouse pointer was within the PictureBox (described in *X* and *Y* positions) when the click occurred. There is additional information in these arguments as well. Here's an example of how you can extract information from a PictureBox's MouseDown event:

```
Private Sub PictureBox1_MouseDown(ByVal sender As Object, ByVal e As
System.Windows.Forms.MouseEventArgs) Handles PictureBox1.MouseDown

    MsgBox("Button:" & e.Button & "  X:" & e.X & "  Y:" & e.Y)

    If e.Button = MouseButtons.Left Then MsgBox("LEFT BUTTON")

End Sub
```

As you can see, the e argument contains lots of information from MouseEventArgs (*Args*, get it?).

Arguments tell you, the programmer, information about the event. You can find out which built-in information is available by typing in some source code, as you can see in Figure 10-9.

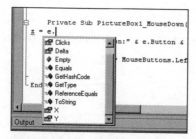

Figure 10-9 *Type in an object followed by a period (.), and you'll get a list of possible constants or properties.*

In this example, typing **e.** triggers VB .NET's (very helpful — *essential* in fact) auto-completion *intellisense* feature, which you'll come to rely on in your VB .NET programming.

This same feature also works when you type:

```
Mousebuttons.
```

as in the following line:

```
If e.Button = MouseButtons.Left Then MsgBox("LEFT BUTTON")
```

Go ahead and try it. Put a PictureBox on a form and try these examples to get a feel for using the intellisense features. If you don't see any drop-down lists (as shown in Figure 10-9), it means you've been bad and turned off these features in the VB .NET Options menu. Choose Tools ⇨ Options ⇨ Text Editor ⇨ All Languages, and then select (check) the options under Statement Completion.

Just to make life a little more confusing, *arguments* are often referred to as *parameters*. Purists insist there is a difference between these two terms, but in practice people use them interchangeably.

Technically, the items listed in parentheses following a procedure declaration (such as an event declaration) are called arguments. However, the items listed in parentheses following *a call* to a procedure are called parameters. The programmer is said to *pass parameters* to a procedure. Here's how it works:

```
Public Sub DoubleIt(ByVal X As Integer)
    MsgBox(X * 2)
End Sub
```

This is a procedure declaration, and therefore the X in the first line (the declaration line) here is, technically, referred to as an *argument* of the DoubleIt procedure. Then you *call* (use) this procedure, like this:

```
Private Sub Form1_Load(ByVal sender As System.Object, ByVal e As
System.EventArgs) Handles MyBase.Load

    Dim x As Integer = 12
    DoubleIt(x)

End Sub
```

In this case, you're calling the DoubleIt procedure and *passing a parameter* to that procedure.

Using Constants

VB .NET includes many *constants* — predefined values for such things as colors, keypresses (KeyF10 = 121, for example), and other elements used in programming. In the preceding section, you saw that there are several constants for the MouseButtons object (such as different values indicating Left button, Middle button, and so on).

It's best in VB .NET to use the *names* of the built in constants. Although the constants do have numeric values you could use, your programs will be far easier to read and deal with if you stick with the built-in names.

How do you find these built-in constant names? Again, you rely on the intellisense lists that VB .NET will display to you while you're writing a line of programming. For example, there's a slew of constants associated with the Color object in VB .NET. So, for example, to choose one of these colors for the BackColor property of a form, type part of the line until you get to the dot (.), as shown in Figure 10-10.

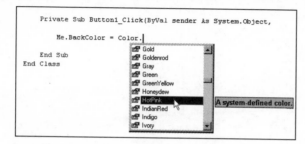

```
Private Sub Button1_Click(ByVal sender As System.Object,

    Me.BackColor = Color.|

End Sub
End Class
```

Gold
Goldenrod
Gray
Green
GreenYellow
Honeydew
HotPink   A system-defined color.
IndianRed
Indigo
Ivory

Figure 10-10 *Use VB .NET's intellisense to provide you with a list of constants from which to choose.*

Some people like to use the VB.NET Object Browser utility instead of (or in addition to) intellisense. Press F2, then open the various namespaces in the left pane to see if you can find the object that interests you. For this example, you would look for System.Drawing.Color.

Done!

REVIEW

This session was mostly about menus — which ones to offer the user, and the easy way to create them. That easy way is to use the VB .NET MainMenu control and let it provide the procedures that you later fill in with code. You also saw how to create and modify menus using the visual cues provided by the MainMenu control. Finally, you learned the uses of arguments (otherwise known as parameters) and constants in programming.

QUIZ YOURSELF

1. What kinds of menu items do not require that you write any programming for them? (See "Secondary menus.")
2. Describe a parent menu's purpose. (See "Secondary menus.")
3. How do you insert a separator bar into a menu? (See "Separator bars.")
4. What two effects result from setting the Enabled property to False? (See "Setting the Enabled property.")
5. Why do VB .NET programmers like to use constants? (See "Using Constants.")

PART

II

Saturday Morning
Part Review

1. What do the Parameter information and Auto List Members features do?
2. What does this line of code do:

   ```
   X = Shell("notepad.exe",  AppWinStyle.NormalFocus
   ```

3. How do you add a second form to a project, and why would you?
4. OptionButtons are often grouped together within a GroupBox component. Why group them?
5. How do CheckBoxes differ from OptionButtons?
6. If you set a component's Enabled property to False, what happens?
7. A ToolTip does what?
8. What happens in the Properties window if you drag your mouse to select several components at once on a form?
9. What is the purpose of a Label component?
10. Labels have an AutoSize property. What does it do and why would you use it?
11. Is it possible to superimpose the text in a label on top of a background graphic in a form?
12. How do you request that a ListBox alphabetize its contents?
13. What command do you use to delete an item from a ListBox?
14. If you want to display data in multiple columns in a ListBox, how do you accomplish that?
15. List two ways that a ComboBox differs from a ListBox.

16. What does a PictureBox do?

17. What does this code do:

```
PictureBox1.Image = Image.FromFile("C:\Graphics\MyDog.jpg") ?
```

18. There's a control in VB .NET that makes it easy to design menus for your projects. What's the control's name?

19. Sometimes a menu item makes no sense in the current state of the application. If the user hasn't typed any text into a TextBox yet, for example, Cut and Copy features on an Edit menu are useless. Typically, an application makes such inappropriate options unavailable to the user, and cues the user by making the text gray (disabled). What code do you write to disable a menu item named mnuNew?

20. What are built-in constants?

PART

III

Saturday Afternoon

Talking to the User with Dialog Boxes

Session Checklist

✔ Working with the MsgBox feature

✔ How to use arguments

✔ Adding buttons and icons

✔ Getting information from the user

✔ Text responses from an InputBox

✔ Using Auto Quick Info and Auto List Members

**30 Min.
To Go**

VB offers many ways for you to communicate with the user. You can display text in Labels, TextBoxes, or the Text properties of other components. You can display pictures in PictureBox components, or as wallpaper in the background of a form. You can ask the user to respond to CheckBoxes or to fill in TextBoxes.

But how do you display *temporary* messages? Brief warnings, for example, which alert the user that he has entered a zip code instead of a telephone number or some such thing?

Communicating via a Message Box

The most common approach is to use a MsgBox to display information, or an InputBox to get an answer back from the user. (You can get back some kinds of information from a MsgBox — such as which button the user clicked — but the InputBox can send back a text answer typed in by the user.)

You've seen them hundreds of times. The simplest version is a basic message box that says "Printing" or "File Not Found," and there's an OK or Cancel button the user can click to close the box (see Figure 11-1). Sometimes these little informational windows are called *dialog boxes*.

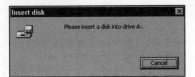

Figure 11-1 *Message boxes are common Windows tools you can use to inform the user of something.*

The message box shown in Figure 11-1 is displayed by Windows Explorer if you select Drive A when it's empty.

You could create a similar message with this code:

```
Private Sub Form1_Load(ByVal sender As System.Object, ByVal e As
System.EventArgs) Handles MyBase.Load

    MsgBox("There's no diskette in Drive A:")


End Sub
```

When you're practicing or testing programming, it's often a good idea to put your code into the `Form_Load` **event, just temporarily. This event is triggered when the form is loaded (instantiated, brought into existence), so it automatically executes its code when you press F5 to test your project.**

The `MsgBox` command has three *arguments* you can specify: the message (called the *prompt*), the buttons, and the title.

The syntax (proper arrangement of elements) shown in VB .NET Help looks like this:

```
MsgBox(prompt[, style] [, title])
```

Notice that any arguments listed within brackets are not required. So with the `MsgBox`, you must provide a prompt (the message), but it's up to you if you want to also specify style and a title.

Pay attention now. All hands on deck. Here's an important point about arguments. If you omit an optional argument, *you must still include its comma*. That's how VB .NET can tell that you mean to include a title, for example, rather than style. For instance, to specify a prompt and title, but no style, the middle comma is still necessary, like this:

```
MsgBox("My Prompt", , "My Title")
```

This results in the dialog box shown in Figure 11-2.

Figure 11-2 *Add a title to the title bar, if you wish.*

Understanding Arguments

**20 Min.
To Go**

You need to understand the term *argument*. An argument is information that you provide to a sub or its close cousin, the function. Often there is more than one argument. In such a case, commas separate the two or more arguments, and the group of arguments is referred to as the *argument list*. In the phrase *Bring food, put it on the table, wrap it,* the sub or function is the action *Bring* and the argument list is *table, wrap.* (Section 13 discusses arguments in more detail.)

For now, just note that Visual Basic reads arguments in order. You must be careful to ensure that the arguments are in the proper order.

Unless you specify otherwise, the title bar of the message box will default to "Error." Often, that's just fine.

Adding buttons

The second argument of the MsgBox command combines several different qualities into a single argument. You can use it to specify the kind of buttons and icons it has, which button is the default, right-aligned text, right-to-left text (Middle-Eastern style), and whether the message box halts only your VB program — or all running applications — until the user closes the message box. (This program-halting behavior is called *modality*.)

How can one argument describe several conditions? You can add several conditions together, and use them within the *button argument space*. Here's how. Type this into the Form_Load event:

```
msgbox("msg",
```

As soon as you type the comma, VB .NET displays a list of possible values. Double-click *msgboxstyle.information* in the list. It appears in your code. Now type a bit more (shown here in boldface, using the + operator to add a second button item):

```
msgbox("msg",MsgBoxStyle.Information + msgboxstyle.
```

When you type the period (.), the list appears again, in abbreviated form. Now double-click OKCancel in the list to include it in your code. Now you've specified two qualities for your message box (in the single button argument). You'll see OK and Cancel buttons, along with the Information icon.

Perhaps you're asking *why* a single argument is used to specify multiple qualities? It would be easier to read and maintain programs if each specified condition (button, icon, default, alignment, and modality) were a separate argument. This would add extra arguments to the MsgBox argument list, but so what?

The answer is the same as it is for all the Y2K problems — in the early days of computing, memory was expensive and scarce. So various ways of conserving memory — shortcuts like using a single argument to define several conditions — were popular.

How does it work? Without getting into binary arithmetic, all you have to know is that to include an element, you simply use the + symbol to add its value to any other elements you want included.

Take a look at Table 11-1. It shows you all the buttons, icons, defaults, and modalities available. Use the items in this table to build the second argument in a MsgBox.

Table 11-1 *MsgBox Buttons, Icons, Defaults, Modalities, and Alignments*

Constant	Description
OKOnly	Displays the OK button only.
OKCancel	Displays the OK and Cancel buttons.
AbortRetryIgnore	Displays the Abort, Retry, and Ignore buttons.
YesNoCancel	Displays the Yes, No, and Cancel buttons.
YesNo	Displays the Yes and No buttons.
RetryCancel	Displays the Retry and Cancel buttons.
Critical	Displays the Critical Message icon.
Question	Displays the Warning Query icon.
Exclamation	Displays the Warning Message icon.
Information	Displays the Information Message icon.
DefaultButton1	The first button is the default.
DefaultButton2	The second button is the default.
DefaultButton3	The third button is the default.
ApplicationModal	The VB application will not respond until the user reacts to the message box by clicking one of its buttons, or closing it by pressing the X button in the upper right corner.
SystemModal	*No* application will respond until the user reacts to the message box by clicking one of its buttons, or closing it by pressing the X button in the upper right corner.

If you specify nothing for the second argument in a MsgBox, there will only be an OK button and no icon. The OK button will be the default (the one activated if the user presses the Enter key), and the modality will be Application modal.

Remember that you can pick one option from each of the major categories shown in Table 11-1, and then add them together with the + operator.

Working with data types

You can also define arguments by assigning values to variables first. Let's say that you want Yes, No, and Cancel buttons on your message box, and you also want the Warning Message icon.

First, you should import a *namespace* that includes the constants you're adding together (yesnocancel + exclamation). This means you should type in this line at the top of the code window where the other Imports statements are:

```
Imports Microsoft.VisualBasic.MsgBoxStyle
```

You can add the arguments together and assign them to the variable Style, like this:

```
Private Sub Form1_Load(ByVal sender As System.Object, ByVal e As
System.EventArgs) Handles MyBase.Load

        Dim Style As Integer
        Dim msg As String

        Style = YesNoCancel + Exclamation

        msg = "There is no diskette in A: Do you want to insert a
diskette?"

        MsgBox(msg, CType(Style, MsgBoxStyle))

    End Sub
```

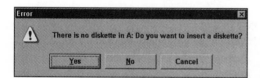

Figure 11-3 *You can add icons and extra buttons to your message boxes.*

That CType command is new in VB .NET. It handles one of the issues you must deal with in .NET. Essentially, it permits you to convert a variable (or expression) into a variety of other types: date, object, class, or interface. Don't trouble your pretty head about this right now. As with so much else in VB .NET, just memorize the technique (or remember that you can look it up in this book's index).

The problem is the MsgBox Buttons attribute (the one you're using the variable style to describe). It is a peculiar, highly specialized data type. (The prompt and title attributes are ordinary string variables, so you can just declare them as String, and use them in the attribute list without further ado.)

But if you attempt to use the Buttons attribute as an Integer type, VB .NET gives you this error message:

```
Option Strict disallows implicit conversions from System.Integer to
Microsoft.VisualBasic.MsgBoxStyle
```

In English, VB .NET is saying this: "I *know* it's really an integer type (it's a whole number), but the buttons argument requires a bit of special handling. So, you've got to convert it from an integer type into a MsgBoxStyle type before I'll work with it."

The format for the CType command is:

```
CType(expression, typename)
```

So, to transform your "expression" (your variable) *style* from an Integer type into the MsbBoxStyle type, you use this code:

```
CType(Style, MsgBoxStyle)
```

Note that you can convert common types by using a small set of commands, such as CInt or CString, which convert into an integer or string, respectively:

```
Dim n As String
    Dim z As Integer
    N = "45"
    Z = CInt(N)
```

This example converts n from a String (text) type into an Integer type. However, the handful of commands like CInt cannot cover all the possible types in VB .NET. As you've seen, even that little table of constants defining the message box button argument is its own "class" or something. So it's a *type* of its own. And there are thousands of such classes. That's why the CType command exists — to handle all those thousands of types that derive from classes.

Take a five minute break if your head is spinning.

Recall that VB .NET permits you to use the classic MsgBox function, but also contains a replacement for it: the MessageBox object. It has 12 different ("overloaded") variations of its argument list. As is often the case with new VB .NET commands, you gain in flexibility, but you pay the price of having to write longer code. Here's an example showing you how to use the MessageBox object:

```
MessageBox.Show("Message",
System.Windows.Forms.MessageBoxButtons.YesNoCancel,
MessageBoxButtons.YesNoCancel, MessageBoxIcon.Question,
MessageBoxDefaultButton.Button2, MessageBoxOptions.RightAlign)
```

If you want to use the MessageBox object, you can type MessageBox.Show(**in the code window, and as soon as you type the left parentesis, VB .NET's intellisense feature will kick in and show you all 12 variations.**

Getting Information Back

So far so good. But if you're using several buttons, it usually means that you want to know which button the user clicked. Then your program can respond to the user's selection. Let's say that if he or she clicks the Cancel or No button, your program won't do anything (see this kind of MsgBox in Figure 11-3), but if he or she clicks the Yes button, the user wants your program to retry saving something to Drive A. Therefore, your program needs to know which button was clicked.

To do this, you must use MsgBox as a function. A function's syntax is different from a Sub (subroutine). You must provide a variable in which the function can store the value it gives back: Variable = FunctionName

Unlike subs, a function returns a value (an answer). You don't always make use of the returned value, but in this case, you do. You want to know if the user clicked the Yes button. Here's how to cast MsgBox as a function. You'll use the variable name Response, although you can use any word that's not in VB's vocabulary (it can't be a VB command, such as For or MsgBox — these words are reserved for VB's own use and cannot be used as names for your variables).

```
Response = MsgBox(msg, CType(Style, MsgBoxStyle))
```

Now you can test the value in the Response variable, and if it's Yes, you can either react right away in that same procedure where the MsgBox is, or you can send back the Response to the caller (the procedure that called the procedure where the MsgBox is), like this:

```
Return Response
```

For this example, you're going to set up the program to react immediately:

```
Dim msg as stringDim Style As Integer, Response As Integer

        Response = MsgBox(msg, CType(Style, MsgBoxStyle))
        If Response = 7 Then MsgBox("They clicked No")
```

How you know that 7 means the No button was clicked? There's another table of MsgBox codes — Table 11-2 shows the constants and values that the MsgBox function returns for the various buttons that can be displayed.

Table 11-2 *The MsgBox Return Values for Clicked Buttons*

Constant	Value	Button Caption
OK	1	OK
Cancel	2	Cancel
Abort	3	Abort
Retry	4	Retry
Ignore	5	Ignore
Yes	6	Yes
No	7	No

Displaying an InputBox to Get Text Back

There is a variation on the MsgBox called the InputBox, and you can use it pretty much the same way as MsgBox. InputBoxes are built to return information from the user — their primary value is that they include a built-in TextBox so that the information your program gets back is a piece of text rather than information that tells you which button was clicked (as happens with a MsgBox).

This offers you more flexibility when getting information — the user types in his or her response, so there can be many different responses, not just the limited number of buttons they can click in a message box. Also note that an InputBox has only OK and Cancel buttons. If the user clicks Cancel, an empty text string is returned "". You can find out if an empty string was returned by using programming such as this:

```
Dim Response As String

        Response = InputBox("What is your Area Code?")

        If Response = "" Then
            MsgBox("You pressed Cancel or refused to type anything in.")
        End If
```

The InputBox function requires a prompt, but the rest of its arguments — Title, Default, X, and Y — are optional.

```
InputBox (prompt [,  title] [,  default] [,  xpos] [,  ypos] )
```

The default argument is text that you can display in the InputBox, if you have a good guess regarding what the user will likely type. This saves the user time. If the useragrees with your default text, she just clicks OK. She doesn't have to type anything, because you displayed what she would have typed.

The X and Y coordinates enable you to enter numbers to specify where on your form you want the InputBox to appear. Just leave that alone and let the box appear in the middle of the screen — that's the usual Windows behavior. In rare cases, you might want to move it to expose something on the form the user should see while responding.

Here's an example. You'll leave out the title, but you will provide a default, the contents of Text3, and a TextBox. Say that the user typed a two-letter last name into Text3, and you're suspicious that's not a correct last name:

```
Protected Sub Button1_Click(ByVal sender As Object, ByVal e As
System.EventArgs)

        Dim Response As String

        Response = InputBox("Please retype your last name...you entered
only two letters and few last names are that short.", , TextBox3.Text)

TextBox3.Text = Response


End Sub
```

You put a TextBox (named TextBox3) and a button on a form. Then the above code was placed inside the Button's click event. You display the contents of the TextBox (that the user had typed in as their last name) as the default text in the InputBox (see Figure 11-4). Then, whatever the user types into the InputBox is sent to the TextBox.

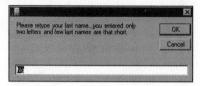

Figure 11-4 An InputBox is similar to a MsgBox, but the InputBox returns text.

Exploiting Auto Quick Info and Auto List Members

Some people find the Auto Quick Info and Auto List Members features of VB's help system quite useful. I promised in the last session that I'd introduce you to these features in case you like them. You've actually seen Auto List Members before, in Session 5, but it's worth another look here in conjunction with Auto Quick Info.

I'll use the MsgBox function to illustrate these features. Go to the VB code window and type this:

```
Result = MsgBox("You left the Quantity field empty.", vbOKCancel)
```

As soon as you type result = msgbox and then press the spacebar and type the left parenthesis, Auto Quick Info does its job — a box pops out, listing all of the arguments that can be used with the MsgBox command. The Auto Quick Info box is shown in Figure 11-5.

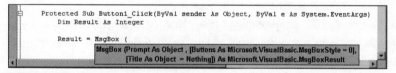

Figure 11-5 Auto Quick Info shows you the argument list, and its variable types.

Then, after you continue and type a message, and then type a comma and press the spacebar, out pops a listbox, allowing you to select a constant. This is the position in a message box's argument list where its *button* (or *style*) property is defined. The Auto List Members feature is shown in Figure 11-6.

You might find the Auto List Members and Auto Quick Info features helpful. That list of constants is pretty intelligent. And the Quick Info can remind you of the argument list and (sometimes, not always) the variable types required.

If these auto features are not working in your code editor, it means they are not selected in Tools ⇨ Options. Turn them on by opening the Text Editor folder, then choose the General section in the Options window.

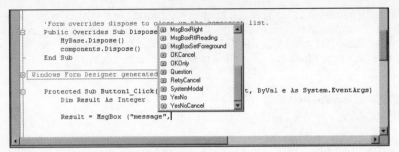

```
        'Form overrides dispose to clean up the component list.
        Public Overrides Sub Dispose    ☒ MsgBoxRight
            MyBase.Dispose()            ☒ MsgBoxRtlReading
            components.Dispose()        ☒ MsgBoxSetForeground
        End Sub                         ☒ OKCancel
                                        ☒ OKOnly
       Windows Form Designer generated  ☒ Question
                                        ☒ RetryCancel
        Protected Sub Button1_Click(    ☒ SystemModal        t, ByVal e As System.EventArgs)
            Dim Result As Integer       ☒ YesNo
                                        ☒ YesNoCancel
            Result = MsgBox ("message",
```

Figure 11-6 *Auto List Members shows you various constants you can use for the button property of the MsgBox object.*

 The word *member* in VB .NET means a property, method, or event of an object. Session 30 covers objects and their members.

Done!

REVIEW

This session is all about communicating with the user via dialog boxes. You saw how to display a MsgBox and the arguments you can use to create variations on the standard MsgBox. Then you saw how to use a variable to get information back from the user. Finally, you worked with the MsgBox's cousin, the InputBox, and also experimented with VB .NET 's Auto Quick Info and Auto List Members options.

QUIZ YOURSELF

1. Why use the Form_Load procedure to test parts of your program? What's the advantage? (See "Communicating via a Message Box.")
2. What is an *argument* in VB programming? (See "Understanding Arguments.")
3. If you have more than one argument, what punctuation do you use to separate them? (See "Understanding Arguments.")
4. What's the main reason you would use an InputBox rather than a MsgBox? (See "Displaying an InputBox to Get Text Back.")
5. Describe the difference between Auto Quick Info and Auto List Members (See "Exploiting Auto Quick Info and Auto List Members.")

Using the Dialog Controls

Session Checklist

✔ Understanding the purpose of Dialog controls

✔ Using Dialog control properties

✔ How to find properties

✔ Learning the six tasksthat Dialog controls assist with

✔ Offering file access to the user

✔ Changing colors

✔ Selecting font properties

In this session, you'll fully explore one of the more useful groups of user-interaction controls available in Visual Basic .NET.

30 Min. To Go

The main purpose of the Dialog controls is to provide predictable, standardized dialog boxes. The user shouldn't have to figure out how to use a different File Open dialog box in each different application. All Windows applications should use the same dialog box for common jobs (such as file access or printing) and regular customizations (choosing fonts and colors).

As a side benefit, when you use the Dialog controls, your Visual Basic programs will look more professional and polished.

Microsoft has created standard Dialog controls to assist you with six common user-input tasks: Open, Save, Font, Color, Print, PrintPreview, and PageSetup. Every user except a novice will already know how to interact with these Dialog controls — where the buttons are, what the options are, and so on. Plus, the bonus for you is that you can avoid a lot of programming by simply using the handy Dialog controls.

Note that these dialogs are "modal" like a message box. In other words, once you display one of these dialog boxes, it halts your VB program until the user responds and closes the dialog box. (If you are using *multithreading*, the other threads will not be halted. Multithreading is a topic way beyond the scope of this book.)

After the user closes the dialog box, your program gets back information about what the user did, perhaps which file was selected, or which color. In each case, your program can query a property of the Dialog control to find out what the user wants to happen.

Displaying a Graphic

For example, let's say you want to allow your user to choose a graphics file to display in a PictureBox. First, you display the Dialog OpenFile dialog, then after the user closes the dialog, you query the OpenFileDialog object by using its FileName property. Here's the simplest version of this process:

1. Start a new Windows Application-style VB .NET project (File ⇨ New ⇨ Project). Name it **commondiag**.

2. Double-click the OpenFileDialog icon in your Toolbox to add it to your program. You will have to click the Windows Forms tab on the Toolbox, and then click the down-arrow icon at the bottom of the Toolbox to scroll down until the Dialog controls become visible.

   During program design the Dialog icons are on a tray below your form, but will not be seen by the user when the program runs.

3. Double-click the PictureBox icon in the Toolbox to add a PictureBox to the form.

4. Use the Properties window to change the PictureBox's BorderStyle property to Fixed3D. It looks better.

5. Double-click the Button icon to add a button to the form.

6. Now type the following code into the Button's Click event:

```
Private Sub Button1_Click(ByVal sender As System.Object, ByVal e As
System.EventArgs) Handles Button1.Click

    OpenFileDialog1.ShowDialog()

    PictureBox1.Image = Image.FromFile(OpenFileDialog1.FileName)

End Sub
```

When you press F5 to run this code and then click the Button, you see the dialog box shown in Figure 12-1.

Figure 12-1 *The file-opening dialog box looks as it does in all other contemporary Windows applications.*

Then, when the user double-clicks on a graphics file, the PictureBox is filled with the graphic, as shown in Figure 12-2.

Figure 12-2 *The results are in — your PictureBox is filled with the user's graphic selection.*

Of course, this example is bare-bones. You would want to include some error-trapping code (the new VB .NET Try command) in case the user goofs up (such as trying to load a .DOC file instead of a .BMP file or one of the other graphics files that VB .NET can handle (.ICO, .GIF, .JPG, or .WMF files). Try and error-trapping in general are covered in Session 20, so you'll leave that alone for now.

Loading Text

You've just seen in the previous example how to load a graphics file. How about loading and saving text? It's not as simple as you might hope.

You can use the following code to open a disk file containing text, and put it into a TextBox. Put a TextBox and a Button on a form. Then, in the Button's Click event, type this code that will put a disk file's contents into the TextBox:

```
Private Sub Button1_Click(ByVal sender As System.Object, ByVal e As
System.EventArgs) Handles Button1.Click

Dim strFileName As String = TextBox1.Text

        If (strFileName.Length < 1) Then
            MsgBox("Please enter a file path and filename in the TextBox")
            Exit Sub
        End If

        Dim objFilename As FileStream = New FileStream(strFileName,
FileMode.Open, FileAccess.Read, FileShare.Read)

        Dim objFileRead As StreamReader = New StreamReader(objFilename)

        TextBox1.Text = "" ' empty the TextBox

        While (objFileRead.Peek() > -1)
            TextBox1.Text += objFileRead.ReadLine()
        End While

        objFileRead.Close()
        objFilename.Close()
End Sub
```

To go the other way, to save the contents of a TextBox to a disk file, add another Button to your form, and caption (change its Text property) **Save.** Then type this into the Button's click event:

```
Private Sub Button1_Click(ByVal sender As System.Object, ByVal e As
System.EventArgs) Handles Button1.Click

        Dim strText As String = TextBox1.Text

        If (strText.Length < 1) Then
            MsgBox("Please type something into the TextBox so we can save
it.")
            Exit Sub
        Else
            Dim strFileName As String = "C:\MyFile.txt"
            Dim objOpenFile As FileStream = New FileStream(strFileName,
FileMode.Append, FileAccess.Write, FileShare.Read)
            Dim objStreamWriter As StreamWriter = New
StreamWriter(objOpenFile)

            objStreamWriter.WriteLine(strText)

            objStreamWriter.Close()
            objOpenFile.Close()
        End If
End Sub
```

This is rather lengthy and roundabout code, but it makes VB.NET compatible with the other .NET languages, which use these "streams" to read and write data.

Using Dialog Properties

**20 Min.
To Go**

Often, you'll want to set some Dialog properties to make the behavior of a dialog box more helpful to the user, before you display it.

Notice that many properties can be used two ways:

- You can "read" properties to get information, such as which filename the user double-clicked in the OpenFile Dialog. (See the previous code for an example.)
- You can "set" (sometimes called "write to") a property in your code to change that property while the program is running to modify the behavior, appearance, or some other quality of an object. (This is the same as adjusting a property in the Properties window, except that you do it with code, while the program runs, rather than during design time.)

Often, it's unimportant which of these two ways you choose to set a property. Of course, if you want to change a property sometime during the execution of the program — other than right at the start in the Form_Load event — you'll have to do it in code.

Let's try setting the Filter property of the OpenFile Dialog so that the dialog box only displays graphics files that a PictureBox can accept. This Filter property has two features. First, you provide a text description that the user sees in the dialog's "Files of Type" listbox. These descriptions can be phrases such as "Bitmap Files" or "GIF Files" or whatever description you decide to provide. The user can click one of these descriptions to see only those kinds of files displayed in the dialog box. The second element is the actual file extension, such as .EXE or .GIF. You pair these elements, separating them with the | symbol.

Change the code in step 6 in the previous procedure to add the code shown in boldface:

```
OpenFileDialog1.Filter = "Bitmap Files|*.BMP|JPEG
Files|*.JPG|Icons|*.ICO|GIF Files|*.GIF"

OpenFileDialog1.ShowDialog()
PictureBox1.Image = Image.FromFile(OpenFileDialog1.FileName)
```

Now the dialog will display only the graphics files. Press F5 and try it.

There are many properties you can set for the various Dialog windows, prior to showing a dialog box to the user. But how do you know what properties are available to you? That's the topic of the next section.

How to Find Properties

You can always put your insertion cursor (the flashing vertical line that shows where you are typing) on top of a word like OpenFileDialog1 in your source code. (Do this by clicking the word, or by moving the insertion cursor with the arrow keys.) Now press F1. VB .NET will display a help screen, as shown in Figure 12-3.

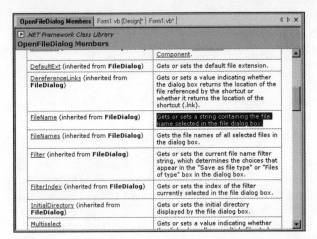

Figure 12-3 Help is often your first choice when trying to find out which properties exist for a control, and how to use those properties in your programming.

The help screen for OpenFileDialog says that the FileName property:

```
Gets or sets a string containing the file name selected in the file dialog
box.
```

This tells you that the FileName property can let your program know ("gets") which file-name the user selected when the OpenFileDialog was displayed. To see more details about how to use the FileName property, click the FileNames link, as shown in the left column of Figure 12-3.

You might wonder what use it would be to *set* the FileName property (Help does say "gets or sets"). If you think about it for a minute, you might realize that sometimes a dialog will include a default (suggested) filename that the user can either accept or replace. To do what the previous sentence just mentioned, insert the following line of code before using the ShowDialog command:

```
OpenFileDialog1.FileName = "Tests.Bmp"
```

Then, when this dialog is displayed, it will show Tests.Bmp as a default filename in the File name field of the OpenFile dialog.

Intellisense

You can also rely on your old friend Intellisense (auto-statement completion) to show you a list of available properties. In the code window, type this:

```
OpenFileDialog1.
```

As soon as you press the period key, a list pops up that shows all the properties and methods available to the OpenFileDialog1 control, as shown in Figure 12-4.

Figure 12-4 *Auto-statement completion displays a complete list of all properties and methods.*

The properties have an icon of a small hand holding perhaps a deed (an electric socket or maybe it's a "property deed," get it?) and methods have an icon displaying what looks like a flying purple book (???). For a discussion of the sometimes-blurry distinction between properties and methods, see Chapter 27.

Available Dialog Controls

Depending on which of the Dialog controls you use, a different dialog window is displayed, waiting for user input:

```
OpenFileDialog.ShowDialog
SaveFileDialog.ShowDialog
FontDialog.ShowDialog
ColorDialog.ShowDialog
PrintDialog.ShowDialog
PrintPreview.ShowDialog
PageSetup.ShowDialog
```

You can give any of these dialogs a title of your choosing. Just set the Title property before using the ShowDialog method, like this:

```
OpenFileDialog1.Title = "Please choose a graphics file."
```

Without assigning a title, the default title is not very descriptive. For the OpenFile dialog the default is "Open."

If you want to let the user choose multiple files (by holding down the Shift or Ctrl key while clicking) in the OpenFile dialog, set this property:

```
OpenFileDialog1.Multiselect = True
```

Then in your code you can find out which filenames were selected by using the FileNames property (which is an array):

```
Dim i As Integer

        For i = 0 To OpenFileDialog1.FileNames.Length - 1
            MsgBox(OpenFileDialog1.FileNames(i))
        Next
```

Every one of the several Dialog controls has a Title property and ShowDialog method. However, they differ in which other properties they have. For instance, the Font dialog box has a Color property, which tells your VB program the color the user selected for text.

The Font dialog box also has MaxSize and MinSize properties to allow you to set a font-size range beyond which the user cannot choose. On the other hand, the two file-access dialog boxes have no font properties, but do have the InitialDirectory property, which allows you to specify which folder on the hard drive will be displayed as the default. Each dialog box has its own appropriate properties, as do all objects in VB.

Saving Files with SaveFile

The SaveFile dialog works nearly the same way as the OpenFile dialog. The primary difference is that the user is saving a file rather than loading one.

Here's an example that illustrates how to set the various properties, and then save the contents of a TextBox to a file. Add a TextBox to your form, and then erase any code in your Button's Click event in the code window. Now, it is essential that you go to the top of the code window and type in this line:

```
Imports System.IO
```

Without this Imports line, VB .NET will not understand the meaning of the FileStream and other elements you'll be using to save this file.

Then type this into the Button Click event:

```
Private Sub Button1_Click(ByVal sender As System.Object, ByVal e As
System.EventArgs) Handles Button1.Click

        SaveFileDialog1.Title = "Save the contents of the TextBox"
        SaveFileDialog1.FileName = "TextBox1.txt"
        SaveFileDialog1.InitialDirectory = "C:\"
        SaveFileDialog1.DefaultExt = ".txt"
        SaveFileDialog1.Filter = "Text files (*.txt)|*.txt|All files
(*.*)|*.*"

        SaveFileDialog1.RestoreDirectory = True

        If SaveFileDialog1.ShowDialog() = DialogResult.OK Then
            'actually save the file:

            Dim strText As String = TextBox1.Text

            If (strText.Length < 1) Then
                MsgBox("Please type something into the TextBox so we can
save it.")
                Exit Sub
            Else
                Dim strFileName As String = SaveFileDialog1.FileName
                Dim objOpenFile As FileStream = New
FileStream(strFileName, FileMode.Append, FileAccess.Write, FileShare.Read)
```

```
          Dim objStreamWriter As StreamWriter = New
StreamWriter(objOpenFile)

          objStreamWriter.WriteLine(strText)

          objStreamWriter.Close()
          objOpenFile.Close()
      End If

   End If

End Sub
```

You often need to test whether the user has pressed the Cancel button in a dialog box. Here's a good way to do that:

```
If SaveFileDialog1.ShowDialog() = DialogResult.OK Then
```

If the user clicks the Cancel button, this `If` test will fail, and the program will skip and ignore any programming code between the `If` and the `End If`. Notice that this line of code both displays the dialog box, and then when the user is finished and closes this dialog box, the code tests `DialogResult.OK` to see if your program should do anything, or should respond to a Cancel by doing nothing.

Before you displayed this dialog box (with the `ShowDialog` command), you set a series of properties. You created a title for the dialog box, and then you suggested a default filename. The user always has the option of changing that suggestion by overtyping in the dialog box. However, after `ShowDialog` executes, the Dialog's FileName property automatically contains the full path of where the file was actually saved, such as `C:\MyFolder\Trips.Txt`. You then use that information to write the code that actually accomplishes the file-saving, as this example illustrates.

Next, you set the DefaultExt property so that if the user doesn't supply a filename extension, .TXT will be appended to their filename automatically. The directory that is first displayed is set to C:\.

The Filter property adds a typical filter. By default, this dialog box will display only those files ending in the .TXT extension when it displays the contents of a disk folder. However, if the user clicks the Save as type field, they can choose to display all the files (*.*).

Finally, as a courtesy, you set the `RestoreDirectory` property to True. Windows always maintains a *current directory*, which is the one displayed by default unless a program specifies otherwise (as you did when you specified the `InitialDirectory`). If the user browses around the hard drive while using the SaveFile dialog box, they are changing the current directory each time they move to a new directory. However, by setting the `RestoreDirectory` property to True, you cause Windows to ignore the user's browsing — and the current directory remains what it was before your dialog box was used.

Saving a File

The actual saving is accomplished by using a C-language style of file-access, involving a *stream* of data (flowing, presumably, between a hard drive and the computer's RAM memory). VB programmers will wonder where their familiar Open, Write, Print, and Close commands have gone. You can still use that old style if you want by adding this at the top of the code window:

```
Imports Microsoft.VisualBasic
```

This adds the *compatibility* feature (allowing you to use various VB 6 programming code commands to VB .NET programs), like this:

```
Open FileName For Output As #1
Write #1, Text1.Text
Close #1
```

However, if you want to know how to save a file using VB .NET-style code, follow the example earlier in this chapter that uses the FileStream and StreamWriter objects. You can simply copy that code into your own projects, modifying it as necessary. As you can see, you create a FileStream object and a "streamwriter" object.

Reading a File

You use a similar syntax to open a disk file and read ("get") its contents into your program:

```
Private Sub Button2_Click(ByVal sender As System.Object, ByVal e As
System.EventArgs) Handles Button2.Click

        Dim strText As String
        Dim strFileName As String = "C:\myfile2.txt"

        Dim objOpenFile As FileStream = New FileStream(strFileName,
FileMode.Open, FileAccess.Read, FileShare.Read)
        Dim objStreamReader As StreamReader = New
StreamReader(objOpenFile)

        strText = objStreamReader.ReadLine()

        objStreamReader.Close()
        objOpenFile.Close()

        MsgBox(strText)

    End Sub
```

I've illustrated the primary differences between the file writing and file reading commands in this example. Pay special attention to this line:

```
strText = objStreamReader.ReadLine()
```

Memorize the fact that you must *assign* the value of (the text in) the file you are reading to your strText variable. However, when you are writing, you *pass* the text as a parameter to the WriteLine method:

```
objStreamWriter.WriteLine(strText)
```

This is typical of the difference in syntax between sending data to a procedure (writing) and getting data from a procedure (reading).

Changing Colors with the Color Dialog Box

The ShowColor Dialog command is quite simple. Here's an example that shows how to use it. Add a ColorDialog control to your form, and then type this into a Button's Click event:

```
Private Sub Button1_Click(ByVal sender As System.Object, ByVal e As
System.EventArgs) Handles Button1.Click

        If ColorDialog1.ShowDialog() = DialogResult.OK Then
            Me.BackColor = ColorDialog1.Color
        End If

End Sub
```

Remember that you cannot refer to your form object like this: Form1.BackColor. That was the VB 6 style of programming. Instead, you must use the *me* object in VB .NET. The user sees the standard Windows color picker dialog box, shown in Figure 12-5.

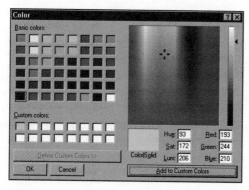

Figure 12-5 *The Color dialog box is another of the familiar Windows Dialogs.*

Here are some properties of the Color dialog box you might want to set:

- To disable the Define Custom Colors button (the user isn't allowed to open the Custom window in the dialog box):

  ```
  ColorDialog1.AllowFullOpen = False
  ```
- To cause a particular color to be selected by default within the color-picker window, change Teal in the following line to whatever color you want to make the default:

  ```
  ColorDialog1.Color = Color.Teal
  ```

Selecting Fonts

When you add a FontDialog to a program, the user gets to specify various aspects of the text. Here's an example:

```
Private Sub Form1_Load(ByVal sender As System.Object, ByVal e As
System.EventArgs) Handles MyBase.Load
Dim n As String

        FontDialog1.MaxSize = 14
        FontDialog1.MinSize = 10

        If FontDialog1.ShowDialog() = DialogResult.OK Then

            n = FontDialog1.Font.Name
            n &= ", Bold:" & FontDialog1.Font.Bold
            n &= ", Italic:" & FontDialog1.Font.Italic
            n &= ", Point Size:" & FontDialog1.Font.SizeInPoints

            MsgBox(n)

        End If

    End Sub
```

Prior to displaying the FontDialog, you first specify a lower and upper limit to the size the user can choose. When the FontDialog is displayed in this example, the user will only see 10, 11, 12, and 14 as font size options.

Max and Min

Although font sizes can be as small as 1 point (a character will be $1/72$ of an inch tall) and as large as 2048 points (and anywhere in between), you can set the Max and Min properties of the Font dialog box to specify a more limited range of permitted font sizes from which the user can select. You specify the limits with an integer that describes the largest or smallest permitted point size you will allow. Then, after the FontDialog has been closed by the user, you look at the FontDialog's properties to figure out which size, font name, and bold or italic preferences the user has selected.

Printer Dialog Controls

Using a printer in a VB .NET application is quite complicated. In previous versions of VB you could simply use a Printer object, but those days are gone. To show you how to use the printer in VB .NET, I've written about that topic in detail in Appendix C, which you will find on this book's CD. The subject is important, but simply too lengthy and intricate a topic to include in a 30-minute session.

Done!

REVIEW

In this session, you zeroed-in on the Dialog controls — perhaps the single most useful VB user-interaction components, next to the TextBox. Why are they so useful? Because they do many things, and the majority of them (printing and file-access excepted) are also very easy to program. You also learned how to work with file-access, color and fonts dialogs, and how to deal with their various properties.

QUIZ YOURSELF

1. What does the DefaultExt property do? (See "Saving Files with SaveFile.")
2. Describe two ways to figure out which properties a Dialog has. (See "How to Find Properties.")
3. How do you display a Dialog to the user? (See "Displaying a Graphic.")
4. Name four of the available Dialog controls. (See "Available Dialog Controls.")
5. Describe what the following code does: FontDialog1.MinSize = 10 (See "Selecting Fonts.")

Making the Most of Procedures

Session Checklist

✔ Understanding procedures

✔ Passing parameters to procedures

✔ Understanding functions

✔ Knowing when to use the argument-passing modes

✔ Single-stepping to see how code executes

30 Min. To Go

In previous sessions, you wrote your programming code in VB's events. This is an excellent way to organize a program into manageable subdivisions. Relatively small units of programming are more easily written, tested, and fixed, and are, in general, easier to understand. It's just natural that a program does things in events — responding to mouse clicks, keypresses, and other stimuli.

So, most of your program's code can usually go into these events. In some VB programs, all code can go into events.

However, sometimes you want to create separate procedures of your own. You'll see why shortly. First, you need to understand the term *procedure*.

Understanding Procedures

What's a procedure? It's a relatively small unit of programming that accomplishes some specific job. Events are procedures.

There are two kinds of procedures: subroutines and functions. Events are subroutines. That's why they begin with the word Sub and end with End Sub. Between the Sub and End Sub lies your programming code, if you choose to write some for that event.

You can also just type in a plain sub of your own that's not part of an event. The reason to create your own sub is that your program might need to accomplish the same task in several events. There's no reason to type in the same code in each of those events. You only need to write it once, in a sub of your own, then call that sub from all of the events that need it.

What if your program needs to display a message box from several different events? You can repeat the code that displays the message box in each of those events. Or you can write a single, standalone sub to do the job.

To see how to make this work, you'll give it a try now. Start a new VB project. Put two CheckBoxes on the form. Now double-click the form to open the code window. Press the down-arrow key and hold it until you're in a blank area in the code window (just above the line that says End Class). You don't want to be in any existing event procedures — you want to type in your own procedure. Type this:

```
Sub ShowThem()
```

Press Enter. Notice that VB understands that you're writing a new sub, so it automatically and intelligently adds this code to complete the procedure structure:

```
End Sub
```

Now, in between the Sub and End Sub, type the following lines of code to display a message box:

```
Sub ShowThem()
```

```
    Private Sub Button1_Click(ByVal sender As System.Object, ByVal e As
System.EventArgs) Handles Button1.Click

        Dim Title, Msg As String
        Dim Response As Integer

        Title = "My Program's Warning"

        Msg = "Did you mean to click that CheckBox?"

        Response = MsgBox(Msg, MsgBoxStyle.Exclamation, Title)

    End Sub
```

You want to use this code in several different events. You wouldn't want to have to put that same code over and over into each of those events, would you? It would waste time, waste space, and make your program harder to read and maintain.

When the user clicks a CheckBox (or any other component), that component's Click event automatically executes any code it holds. But how do you trigger this new ShowThem procedure you wrote? It's not *automatically* part of any event. The answer is — you put a reference to it into all the events that need to use your procedure. You just use its name to trigger it from an event or other procedure.

A CheckBox offers a CheckChanged event that triggers when the user clicks it to select, or deselect, the CheckBox. Locate the CheckBox1_CheckedChanged event and type the following code into it:

```
Private Sub CheckBox1_CheckedChanged(ByVal sender As System.Object,
ByVal e As System.EventArgs) Handles CheckBox1.CheckedChanged

    ShowThem()

End Sub
```

Then locate CheckBox2_CheckChanged and do it again:

```
Private Sub CheckBox2_CheckedChanged(ByVal sender As System.Object,
ByVal e As System.EventArgs) Handles CheckBox2.CheckedChanged

ShowThem()

End Sub
```

Now press F5 and try clicking either of the CheckBoxes.

Great! Your ShowThem procedure works. Wherever in this form that you want ShowThem to do its job, just name it (type ShowThem), and your little procedure will happily oblige and do its thing, displaying a message.

Some programmers like to use the optional Call **command whenever they call a sub or function, like this:**

```
Call ShowThem()
```

This helps remind them of what the line does.

Customizing the Behavior of a Procedure

*20 Min.
To Go*

So far so good, but how about a little customization? What if you want to display a different message, depending on what control the user clicks?

That's easy. You just "pass" the message as a parameter:

```
ShowThem("This message") 'pass a parameter
Sub Showthem (ByVal m as string) 'receive an argument
```

Have you wondered why every procedure's name always has a pair of parentheses following it, even if the parentheses are sometimes empty? These parentheses can be used to enclose an *argument list* that defines which parameters can be passed to this procedure.

In the code where you call a procedure, the passed items are referred to as *parameters*. **But when those** *same passed items* **are specified in the code that defines the procedure, they are called** *arguments*. **This is another one of the little computer programming** *fun things* **that you just have to memorize and live with.**

Next, you'll change the ShowThem procedure to make it more flexible. You'll remove the fixed (hard-coded) message that is stored inside the procedure, and let the caller (the procedure that triggers ShowThem) pass whatever message it wants. The ShowThem sub will display that passed message, rather than a canned one that's already prewritten in the ShowThem sub:

```
Sub ShowThem(ByVal m As String)


    Dim Title As String
    Dim Response As Integer

    Title = "My Program's Warning"

  Response = MsgBox(m, MsgBoxStyle.Exclamation, Title)


   End Sub
```

I'll explain what that As String code means in the next session. (Hint: it tells VB to expect text, rather than a number or some other kind of variable.) Also, just ignore the ByVal for now (it's covered in Session 30).

You can use any name that you wish instead of m *msg*. Take your choice (but remember that you cannot use a VB command such as If or Sub).

If you do change the name in the argument list (between the parentheses), remember to also change it in the second-to-last line where you display the message box. Replace the m that I'm using with your new word.

OK, now the message gets passed to the ShowThem procedure. To pass the parameter, you want to change the calls. Change the CheckBoxes' code to the following:

```
Protected Sub CheckBox1_CheckedChanged(ByVal sender As Object, ByVal e As
System.EventArgs)

ShowThem("This is CheckBox1. Thanks for clicking me!")

End Sub

Protected Sub CheckBox2_CheckedChanged(ByVal sender As Object, ByVal e As
System.EventArgs)

ShowThem("This is CheckBox2. Thanks for clicking me!")

End Sub
```

The only thing you do to pass a parameter is type the passed parameter in between the parentheses. If it's text you're sending you must enclose it in quotes, as illustrated in the previous code.

Press F5 and see what happens when you click either CheckBox. Sure enough, the caller passed information to the procedure.

Do you think it's possible to go the other way? That is, for a procedure to pass information back to the caller? That would be handy in some situations. The procedure could send back an OK code (perhaps the number 1) if all went well, but send back an error code (perhaps 0) if the procedure had a problem carrying out its task. Maybe the procedure was supposed to save some information to the floppy drive, but when it tried, it found that there was no diskette in Drive A.

Sending information back would also come in handy when the procedure does some transforming. For example, what if various events in your program need to round off numbers? You could write a procedure that accepts (gets passed) a number, rounds it off, and then passes it back.

Sending information back *is* possible. In fact, it's the reason that functions exist, as you'll see in this next section.

Understanding functions

Recall that there are two kinds of procedures. One kind of procedure gives feedback, and the other does not. A sub doesn't give any feedback. However, the second kind of procedure, the *function*, does provide feedback. It gives feedback to the caller, the location in your program that called (triggered) the function.

Often, your code doesn't need feedback. If you write a sub that plays a note of music to alert the user that they made an error, that sub doesn't need to provide any feedback to the caller code. It just does its job and that's the end of it.

Sending information back

Sometimes a caller *does* want information back. To see how this works, you'll translate the ShowThem sub into a function. It will pass back to any caller the name of the button that the user clicks to close the message box. Some callers might be simply displaying a warning to the user and won't care which button was pressed. They can just ignore the button code that gets passed back. Other callers might want to react one way if the user presses Cancel and a different way if the user presses OK. For instance, the message "If you want this data saved, press the OK button" requires feedback.

To change your ShowThem sub into a function, all you have to do is replace the word Sub with the word Function, replace End Sub with End Function, and provide an As statement that identifies which kind of variable the Function sends back to the caller, like this:

```
Function ShowThem(msg As String) As Integer
```

```
End Function
```

You probably noticed that as soon as you changed Sub to Function in the top line, VB .NET considerately changed the end line to End Function.

Next, you need to find out which button the user clicked in the message box. (Do you remember from Session 11 how you can get this information back? If not, press F1 and look at the Help information about the MsgBox command.) Here's one way to rewrite the sub so that it will send back the information:

```
Function ShowThem(ByVal ms As String) As String
    Dim Title, Msg As String
    Dim Response As MsgBoxResult
    Dim Style As MsgBoxStyle


    Style = MsgBoxStyle.Exclamation + MsgBoxStyle.YesNo

    Title = "My Program's Warning"

    Response = MsgBox(ms, Style, Title)

    If Response = MsgBoxResult.Yes Then    ' User chose Yes.
        Return "Yes"
    Else    ' User chose No.
        Return "No"
    End If


End Function
```

There are some things to notice in this code. In this example I defined the Response variable as a MsgBoxResult object, and the Style variable as a MsgBoxStyle object. This is a technique you might want to use, if it appeals to you.

The MsgBox assigns a number to the variable named *response* in the code example, but choose your own word if you wish. That variable gets information about which button the user clicked in the MsgBox. How? The MsgBox command is itself a function, and it always returns information about which button was clicked. There are predefined meanings to the returned information (6 means the user clicked the Yes button, for instance). Also, this example added the line of code that uses the command Return, which, as you probably guessed, returns information to the caller (the CheckBox's events).

Consider what happened here. You changed a sub into a function because you wanted information back from it. You added As String to the Function name on the first line, to define which variable type the Function returns. You also added some code that uses the Return command to send back information to the caller.

You don't have to worry about figuring out how to make the MsgBox **function send back information about which button was clicked. It's not a function** *you* **wrote anyway.** MsgBox **is built into Visual Basic — so the code that makes a MsgBox work is hidden from you (and that code includes a Return command to send back the clicked info).** MsgBox **is hard-wired into VB itself. Does VB offer other built-in functions? You betcha — many of them. So many that you're going to spend all of Session 15 exploring them — so you know they're available if you need them. You don't want to reinvent the wheel, if VB has already done the job for you.**

Recall that technically, MsgBox **is not itself a** *function* **built into VB .NET. Instead, MsgBox is now a** *method* **of the Microsoft.VisualBasic.Interaction**

shared class. It provides "encapsulated access" (it's a *wrapper*) to the
MessageBox.Show **function which *is* built into VB .NET. For more details
about using the official VB .NET version of the MessageBox, see the tip at
the end of the section titled "Working with data types" in Session 11.**

**10 Min.
To Go**

How to call a function

You may suspect that because you've changed ShowThem from a sub to a function, you have
to change how you call it from elsewhere in the program. You called the sub like this:

```
Protected Sub CheckBox1_CheckedChanged(ByVal sender As Object, ByVal e As
System.EventArgs)

ShowThem("This is CheckBox1. Thanks for clicking me!")

End Sub
```

You call both subs and functions the same way, with one exception: a sub never returns
any information, so you cannot call it using an equals sign (=) the way you call a function.
(Code like x = ShowThem is only used when calling a function, which places information in
that *x*.)

Do you know what to change to transform a sub call to a function call? Take the following steps:

1. Add a variable = to the call (to get back the information the function sends).
2. Add an As command to the Function line at the top to define the variable type
   returned by the function.
3. Add a Return statement to send the information back to the caller.

Now you'll add a little code that will display the results when you test this program. This
is how CheckBox1_ CheckedChanged should be changed:

```
Protected Sub CheckBox1_CheckedChanged(ByVal sender As Object,
ByVal e As System.EventArgs)


        Dim ButtonClicked As String

        ButtonClicked = ShowThem("This is Check1. Thanks for clicking
  me!")

        If ButtonClicked = "Yes" Then MsgBox("They clicked Yes")


End Sub
```

Press F5, and then click CheckBox1 to trigger the code.

Watching and Stepping

Single-stepping is a technique you can use to see your program execute in slow motion. This technique will let you watch as your program moves from line to line in your code. You'll also see the effect of calling, and then returning from, a function.

Single-stepping is a good way to see your program's *flow*, as its path of execution is sometimes called. Single-stepping is also often the best way to figure out why things are not working as you hoped they would.

If your program is still running, select Debug ⇨ Stop Debugging to stop it. Now, instead of pressing F5 to run it at normal speed, press F8.

First, you'll notice that the code window is displayed and the Sub New line (the first line that executes in any VB .NET Windows-style program) has a yellow arrow next to it, as you can see in Figure 13-1.

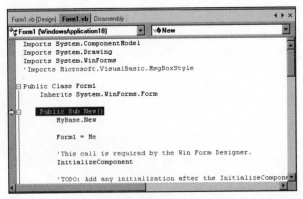

Figure 13-1 *Single-stepping is an excellent way to watch how a program runs.*

The yellow arrow shows you the next line that will be executed. Press F8 again. (If you had itchy fingers and already pressed it, choose Debug ⇨ Stop Debugging, and then press F8 to restart the program. This is a controlled experiment. You have to maintain self-control.)

When you press F8 this second time, the Sub New line is executed and the program again halts, showing you where execution will resume (when you press F8 yet again). In other words, every time you press F8, one line of code gets executed, and then the program halts and waits.

Repeatedly press F8 until you get to the End Sub line (ending the Sub New). At this point, after your form has been "instantiated" as they call it, the form is displayed as usual.

Now try clicking a CheckBox. Instead of displaying a MessageBox, you are dropped back down into the code window where you can single-step through the event and your ShowThem function called by that event.

Press F8. You now go to the second line of code in the CheckedChanged event. When you get to the line that triggers your ShowThem function, what do you think will happen next?

Press F8 until program jumps out of the CheckedChanged event and lands at the ShowThem event. Much of the time in VB .NET, a program executes a line, goes to the next line, executes it, goes to the next line, and so on — moving down through a procedure in a linear fashion. Sometimes, however, the program jumps somewhere else, to a different procedure, as is happening now.

Press F8 several times to see what happens, but stop after you've pressed F8 on the line that begins If Response. Now try something new: Move your mouse pointer until it rests on the word Response. A small window opens and displays the contents of that variable, as is shown in Figure 13-2.

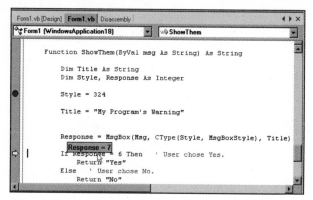

Figure 13-2 *Move your mouse pointer onto any variable or constant, and you can see its current contents.*

Done!

REVIEW

By now, you know all (well, a lot) about the mysteries of procedures — those little "programlettes" within a large program. You saw that putting small, individual tasks into small packages called *procedures* makes your program easier to read, test, maintain, and debug. The techniques for passing information to, and back from, procedures became part of your programmer's arsenal in this session. You also found out when to use functions and when to use subs. Finally, the great single-stepping feature of VB showed you in slow motion just exactly how your program's execution flowed from line to line, but sometimes jumped to a different procedure.

QUIZ YOURSELF

1. What are the two kinds of procedures? (See "Understanding Procedures.")
2. How do you pass information to a procedure? (See "Customizing the Behavior of a Procedure.")
3. Can you send information from a procedure back to the line of code that called the procedure? (See "Sending information back.")
4. Do you call a function the same way you call a subroutine? (See "How to call a function.")
5. What key do you press when you want to single-step through your program? (See "Watching and Stepping.")

Understanding Variables and Scope

Session Checklist

✔ Visualizing the two kinds of data: text and numeric

✔ How to name and create variables

✔ Manipulating variables and their values

✔ Using Option Strict to discipline yourself

**30 Min.
To Go**

Computers process information in much the same sense that a Cuisinart processes food: You put some carrots, cabbage, and mayo in — they get transformed, chopped up — then you take the result out and yell "SLAW!" at the top of your voice.

Likewise, with a database program, you type in a list of names and phone numbers. Then the program processes them to give you a list, say, of all the people having birthdays this month.

Two Kinds of Data

It's called data processing, or information processing. But no matter how huge the database program, or how sophisticated the graphics program, all computer programs process only two categories of information: strings or numbers.

A *string* is characters strung together: "Don Wilson", "b", and "454-5001 ext. 23" are all strings. *Text* is another word for *string*. When you assign some literal text to a string variable, the text is enclosed in quotation marks:

```
Dim MyVariable As String
MyVariable = "This is Tuesday."
```

If there's enough memory in your computer and an application permits large strings, you can hold the entire phone book in a single string if you wish. By contrast, "" is an empty string.

As you see from the example, a string can be a single character, really huge, empty, or anything in between. It can contain letters of the alphabet, symbols like * or @, and even digits like "2".

Note, however, that a *digit* is not the same as a true *number*. A digit is just a character (string) representation. You cannot do math with strings. You *can* concatenate strings: `Print "fluor" & "ide"` will display fluoride. `Print "2" & "3"` displays 23. You cannot multiply or subtract or do other math on strings. (VB prefers that you use the & symbol to concatenate strings and reserves + for adding numbers. It will usually accept + with strings, but it doesn't like it.)

You've seen how to work with strings now. Numbers are the other kind of data, and they operate inside the computer just as they do in real life: You can do all kinds of math with them. Programmers sometimes store numbers as strings, though, if they don't expect that they'll be doing math with them. Your zip code, "27244", and phone number, "336-555-0123", make better sense stored as strings. You're never going to multiply them, are you?

What's more, some kinds of numeric information cannot be stored as a numeric variable. You can't store a phone number as a numeric variable if you want to include those hyphens in it. Symbols like that must be stored in a string. If you left the quotation marks off of this phone number, 336-555-0123, Visual Basic would think you wanted to subtract real numbers, and would calculate the value, -342. Always remember to enclose strings in quotation marks. An integer is a numeric variable type. Here's how a phone number is misunderstood if you try to use it as an integer numeric type (the hyphens are thought to be minus signs):

```
Dim n As Integer

    N = 336 - 555 - 123
    msgbox(n)
```

Understanding Variables

Variables are a way of storing information — sometimes quite briefly (they can *vary* as their name implies). Nonetheless, we are talking about storing data when we discuss variables. Here's how it works. The computer asks you to type in how much you're willing to pay for a new TV. You oblige and type in **299**. What happens then? The computer must remember that information. It stores the information in a *variable*.

Each variable has a name that the programmer gave it. Usually, programmers like to use memorable variable names, something easily recognized, like TopTvPrice. Underscore characters are allowed, so some programmers make the name even more readable this way: Top_Tv_Price. After the user types in **299** (called a *value*), the program assigns the value to the variable. Let's assume that the user types the answer into TextBox1:

```
Dim TopTvPrice As Integer

TopTvPrice = TextBox1.Text
```

Your source code assigns the value to the variable.

The contents of the TextBox, the value, is copied into the variable TopTvPrice.

Recall from Session 11 that there is a great debate raging among programmers about just how much power a computer language should have to *change a variable type all by itself*. The TopTvPrice variable in this example started out being declared an integer type, but when VB .NET saw that you wanted to assign *text* (a string type), it *automatically* changed the type to accommodate you. Some languages — such as C — forbid permitting languages to change type. If you prefer to be strict about data type conversions, type Option Strict On at the very top of the code window. With that option on, VB .NET will display an error message if you try to assign a string to a variable declared As Integer. With Option Strict on, you could use the Val command to get a numeric variable from text.

How to name variables

You must observe several rules when making up a name for a variable (otherwise, Visual Basic will protest):

- It must start with a letter, not a digit.
- It cannot be one of Visual Basic's own command words, like For or Dim.
- It cannot contain any punctuation marks or spaces.

How to create a variable

20 Min. To Go

In previous versions of VB, when you needed to use a variable in a program, you could simply type in a name for it, and voila, the variable will come into existence. This is called *implicit declaration*. VB .NET frowns on this kind of thing. VB .NET wants all variables explicitly declared, and their variable type specified in that variable declaration, like this:

```
Dim UsersAge as Integer
```

That's the VB .NET default. However, if you're a rebel and want to use implicit declaration, you can type this at the *very top* (above the Imports statements) of your code window:

```
Option Strict Off
```

Here's an example of implicit declaration. Perhaps your program displays an InputBox that asks the user how old he or she is. The variable you want to put his or her answer (the value) in can be named UsersAge (I know, I know; it should be User'sAge, but you can't use punctuation in variable names):

```
UsersAge = InputBox ("How old are you?")
```

As soon as the user types **44**, or whatever, and closes the InputBox, the value 44 is assigned to the variable UsersAge. The value is stored. When your program later wants to process that data, it knows where to look. It merely uses the variable name. Let's say you want to find out if the user is eligible for AARP (the < symbol means less than):

```
If UsersAge < 50 Then MsgBox ("You're too young to join AARP, pup.")
```

Notice that you use the variable name as you would any other number in this programming. When the program executes, whatever number the user typed in is compared to 50.

There's a second way to create a variable — many programmers swear by it and VB .NET defaults to it. It's called *explicit declaration*. You use the Dim command to explicitly declare the variable:

```
Dim UsersAge As Integer
UsersAge = InputBox ("How old are you?")
```

If you're going to use several variables in the procedure, Dim each of them:

```
Dim UsersAge, UsersHeight As Integer
Dim UsersName, Nickname As String
```

Notice that you can combine several declarations on a single line, as long as they are the same variable type. That's why the As String variable names are not declared in the same line as the Integer types in the preceding code example.

VB .NET also permits you to declare a variable, *and* assign a value to it on the same line:

```
Dim UsersAge As Integer = 21
```

You only need to use Dim at the start of the line, and then just separate the variable names by commas. Now do you see one reason why you can't use punctuation in variable names? Visual Basic uses various kinds of punctuation to mean various things in a line of code. Recall that the single-quote symbol (') means that you're making an annotation, and VB should ignore everything following the ' on that line. The * means multiply, & means concatenate text, and so on.

Notice that the line of code beginning with Dim ends with an As clause that specifies the variable's or variables' type.

One reason that using an explicit declaration is so highly regarded is that when you look later at the code you wrote and you're trying to figure it out, you can see a list of all the variables right there at the top of the procedure, or at the top of a class if you want the variable to apply to the entire class — not just a single procedure. (There's a second reason for using Dim — Option Explicit — which is covered at the end of this session.)

There are nine fundamental variable types in VB .NET, but thousands of objects that you can use as *types*. You'll get to know fundamental types later in this session. For now, just note that each declared variable must be explicitly typed (*typed* here means given a data type, not pressing keys on the keyboard).

Although Dim is the most commonly used, there are seven additional declaration commands: Static, Public, Protected, Friend, Shared, Protected Friend, and Private. These additional commands specify either *scope* (from how many locations in your program can the variable be accessed) or *lifetime* (how long the variable holds its value — only while the procedure within which it is declared is executing, or while the entire program is running).

Manipulating Variables

Variables hold only one value at a time. But the value can change as necessary (hence the name *variable*). For example, you could write the following code (although it would make no sense to do so):

```
Dim TVShow as String
TVShow = "Barney"
TVShow = "Five-0"
```

When this program executes, VB assigns the text Barney to the variable TVShow, but immediately dumps that value and replaces it with Five-0. When a new value is assigned to a variable, the previous contents of that variable simply no longer exist.

You can assign literal values ("Barney" or 299, as illustrated previously), but you can also assign one variable to another. When you assign a variable to another variable, the variable on the left of the equals sign (=) gets the value held in the variable to the right of the =. At this point, both variables contain the same value. This is like making a copy of the value. In this next example, the contents (the value) in the variable PopularShow are copied into the variable MyTVShow:

```
MyTVShow = PopularShow
```

One practical and common use of copying one variable into another was illustrated earlier in this chapter with this line:

```
TopTvPrice = TextBox1.Text
```

Properties are similar to variables. What do I mean by this? Am I saying that the Text property of a TextBox is a variable? No, but in many ways it behaves like one. Properties *are* a bit different from ordinary variables: They're predefined by the people who created the component, and they usually have a default value. Also, in some situations they cannot be changed, merely read (queried). However, you can usually change them (assign a new value to them), either during design time in the Properties window, or at runtime with your programming code, or both: Command1.Height = 55. The values in properties usually can vary.

Communicating Across Forms

You can also assign variables to other forms in your project. Some VB .NET programs use more than one form. If you need to write code in, say, Form1 that modifies a Label in Form3, declare a variable that stands for Form3, and then attach that variable name to the front of the component's name, like this:

```
Dim Frm3 as New Form3
Frm3.Label1.Text = "Press this button to see the list"
```

Some More Efficiencies

Sometimes you want to concatenate or otherwise combine two variables. Say you want to personalize your program, so you first ask the user to type in his or her name, and then use that variable along with another variable to create a complete sentence:

```
Dim Msg, Result As String
     Result = InputBox("Please type your first name.")
     Msg = "Thank you, " & Result
     MsgBox(Msg)
```

There are sometimes ways to shorten code. If you're one of those people who is always looking to conserve variable names, you can reuse Result like this, without even needing that second variable Msg:

```
Dim Result As String
     Result = InputBox("Please type your first name.")
     Result = "Thank you, " & Result
     MsgBox(Result)
```

Or if you're one of those people who are really, really conservative, and always want to save space and condense code, you can do it like this:

```
Dim Result As String
     Result = InputBox("Please type your first name.")
     Msgbox("Thank you, " & Result)
```

As this illustrates, a variable can be part of what's assigned to itself. One use for this technique is illustrated in the previous example: You want to preserve the contents of the variable (Result), but add something to the contents ("Thank you"). To illustrate this same principle with a numeric variable, perform the following math equations using the variable name:

```
A = 233
A = A + 1
```

Now A holds 234.

Saving time with +=

VB .NET introduces a new construct when you are adding a variable's current contents to some new value like the previous example. You can avoid repeating the variable's name by combining + with =, for instance. Here's how this trick works — instead of:

```
A = A + 1
```

You can now use:

```
A += 1
```

This condensation has several variations:

- A *= 4 (The value currently in variable A is multiplied by 4 and assigned to A.)
- A -= 1 (Decrement the value currently in variable A.)

Here's an example:

```
Dim Brother as String
Brother = "Tom"
Brother += " and Bob"
```

Now Brother contains Tom and Bob. This technique, which avoids repeating the variable name (Brother = Brother + " and Bob" as in the traditional VB approach) is wildly popular with C and C-derivative language programmers. See if it appeals to you. It does come in handy to avoid repeating a really lengthy variable (or object) name, which sometimes happens in VB .NET.

There are usually several ways to code, and your personal style will emerge over time. Notice how I always seem to use Result or Response as the variable names with the InputBox command? It's just a little habit of mine — you can use Reaction, Retort, Reply, or Rejoinder, just as long as it begins with an *R*. Just kidding! You can use Answer, Users_Input, or whatever. You know the rules for thinking up variable names — you can use pretty much any word, or even a nonsense word like *jaaaaakaa*. But it's best to make your variable names descriptive of what the variable holds.

A note on arrays

Recall that I said that a variable can hold only one value at a time. Sometimes, though, it's useful to collect a whole group of values together in one package. There is a special way to group values: You give them one name, but each is given a unique index number.

This collection of values is called an *array*. An important feature of arrays is that you can use their index numbers as a way of working with the values in sequence. This is particularly useful in loops like For...Next where you keep incrementing a counter variable each time through the loop. (You will find out about For...Next in Session 17.) That counter can access each value in the array by using the index numbers. (The term *counter variable* is merely a description of what that variable is doing in the code. It's still just another ordinary variable. There's nothing odd about it.)

For example, if you want to manipulate the names of five people coming to dinner this Friday, you can create an array of their names:

```
Dim guests(4) As String
```

This creates five "empty boxes" in the computer's memory, which serve as spaces for five values. However, instead of five unique individual variable names, the values share the same name, guests, and each value is identified by a unique index number from 0 to 4:

```
guests(3) = "Bill Hitch"
MsgBox(guests(3))
```

Arrays *must* always be declared (Dim). You cannot implicitly create an array the way you can with an ordinary variable, even if you use the Option Strict Off command. Session 17 discusses arrays more thoroughly. We'll look at the various numeric data types, and the important issue of *scope* in Session 18.

Forcing Yourself to Declare Variables

Recall that you can turn off the requirement that all variables be explicitly declared (by using the Option Strict Off command). But be warned that many programming teachers insist that all variables be officially, explicitly declared. One reason they do this is so that you can easily see which variables are in use — without having to search the code for them. A second reason to require the declaration of variables is that it prevents a common source of error. Consider this code:

```
TempString = "Tex"
TempString = TemString & "as"
MsgBox (TempString)
```

You probably think that this code displays a message box with the word Texas in it. No, it only displays as. Can you see why? One of those variable names is misspelled. That's very easy to do. (TemString, the typo made when this code was typed in, contains nothing. So when you add nothing to "as", you're left with "as") However, with Option Strict in force (the VB .NET default), VB will alert you if you make this common kind of mistake.

With Option Strict on, if you try running the example code, VB .NET will respond by highlighting the first instance of TempString and telling you "The name TempString is not declared." So go ahead and declare it:

```
Protected Sub Button1_Click(ByVal sender As Object, ByVal e As
System.EventArgs)

        Dim TempString As String


        TempString = "Tex"
        TempString = TemString & "as"
        MsgBox(TempString)

End Sub
```

Now when you run this code, VB shows you the typo, as you can see in Figure 14-1.

You never intended to have a variable named TemString, and with Option Strict turned on, VB .NET shows you the typo. VB .NET flags any undeclared variables.

Well, time's up! We'll return to the subject of variables later in Session 18, where you'll learn more about numeric variables, and the important issue of *scope*.

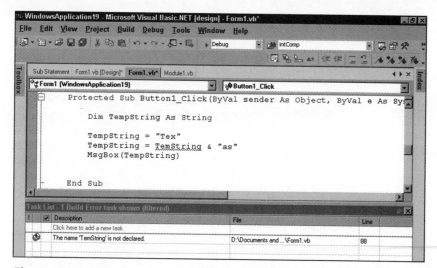

Figure 14-1 *When you use the Option Strict feature, VB .NET will point out any typos in variable names.*

Done!

REVIEW

This session was all about variables — one of the most important tools in a programmer's arsenal. You saw that variables are divided into two primary categories:

- Strings that can be alphabetized and concatenated, but are not numbers and can't be manipulated mathematically (even if the string holds a series of digits that *look* like real numbers).
- Real numbers that can be manipulated mathematically.

You also discovered the naming conventions and the various ways that variables can be copied and typed. Finally, the Option Strict command was introduced.

QUIZ YOURSELF

1. Which kind of variable uses quotation marks around its value? (See "Two Kinds of Data.")
2. Would the word *Function* make a good variable name? (See "How to name variables.")
3. Why can properties be considered variables? (See "Manipulating Variables.")
4. How do you change properties across forms? (See "Communicating Across Forms.")
5. Name one reason that many programming teachers insist that all variables be officially, explicitly declared. (See "Forcing Yourself to Declare Variables.")

Understanding VB .NET's Built-In Functions

Session Checklist

✔ Learning to use literals, constants, and expressions

✔ Using the string functions

✔ Converting data and querying data types

**30 Min.
To Go**

I n Session 13, you saw how to work with event procedures, as well as subs and functions that you yourself create. In this session, you'll see how to tap into several collections of built-in methods and functions that are provided by VB .NET. This session doesn't cover every method or function, but it does survey the ones you're most likely to need.

This session is something of a reference so we'll leave out figures. You should come away from this session with a sense of the variety of tools VB .NET contains to help you get things done in your own applications.

You perhaps suspected that the InputBox and MsgBox commands were, in fact, functions. Both can return information to your program. (Recall that the key distinction between a function and a sub is that a sub doesn't return anything.) You were correct in your suspicions.

Where previous versions of VB used functions, VB .NET often uses *methods* — behaviors that are built into objects. In VB .NET everything is an object, even a string variable. So, you shouldn't be surprised that to find the length of a string in VB 6 you used the function Len(*String*), but now in VB .NET you use the method *String*.Length. Fortunately, the old functions like Len still work in VB .NET, so usually the approach you choose — function or method — is up to you. However, in the case of strings, I suggest you make the leap to using the new VB .NET methods, and especially familiarize yourself with the new StringBuilder. They are usually quite clearly superior to the various string functions available in previous versions of VB. And the StringBuilder can do things — such as replacing all instances of a substring — for which there is no VB 6 equivalent at all. VB .NET has many other methods and built-in functions. Knowing they exist will save you the trouble of writing special functions yourself when you want to get a particular job done.

VB .NET's methods and functions fall into six fundamental categories: string; numeric; data conversion and data-testing; formatting; financial; and date and time. We don't have space or time to go into the formatting, financial or data and time methods and functions in this session. Nevertheless, I suggest you look at the Supplementary Notes for Session 15 on this book's CD where those topics are covered. They are not absolutely essential, but you do want to know that they are available in the language when you need them.

Understanding Literals, Constants, and Expressions

Before plunging into the various methods and built-in functions, let's pause for a bit to deepen your understanding of variables. Sometimes you provide a variable to a function, like this:

```
Dim Msg As String
Dim Response As Integer
Msg = "Hello"
Response = MsgBox(Msg)
```

Literals

Other times you might use a literal (you type the actual value itself instead of using a value stored in a variable):

```
Response = MsgBox("Hello")
```

Literals can be strings or numeric. String literals are enclosed in quotation marks.

Constants

A constant is a number that cannot change while your program runs, like pi or the address of the White House. You may recall that VB .NET contains many built-in constants (Blue is a built-in constant, located in the VB .NET System.Drawing.KnownColor enumeration), but you can also define your own constants, like this:

```
Const WHITEHOUSE As String = "1600 Pennsylvania Ave."

msgbox(WHITEHOUSE)
```

You can also use Public or Private to govern the scope of a constant, like this:

```
Public Const MyString As String = "1600 Pennsylvania Ave."
```

To give a constant enough scope so that it's available to your entire program, define it with the Public command.

Constants can hold strings or numbers. By convention, constant names use all uppercase letters. VB .NET doesn't care if you use uppercase or lowercase, but it helps programmers to recognize a constant.

Some programmers like to use constants. They argue that one good candidate to be a constant is something like the state sales tax. Say it's 7 percent. Rather than putting 1.07 several places in their program, they define a constant instead:

```
Const STATESALESTAX As Single = 1.07
```

Now they can use this in their programming:

```
GrandTotal = TotalPurchases * STATESALESTAX
```

Which is easier to understand than this:

```
GrandTotal = TotalPurchases * 1.07
```

And a constant can also make it easier to modify your program later. If the sales tax changes in the future, you don't have to go through your entire program looking for all occurrences of 1.07 and adjusting it to 1.08 or whatever. Instead, you only have to modify that single line in the application where the constant is defined.

To me, whether you use constants or not depends on your situation. If you write lengthy programs that can benefit from them, go ahead. If you write programs that might need to be maintained later by you or by other people, constants are yet another way to clarify the meaning of your code.

Expressions

Recall that when you call a function, there is often an argument list — one or more variables, or literals, that you "pass" to the function, enclosed in parentheses. The function can make use of these arguments.

Usually, you can also use an expression as part of the argument list for a function. An *expression* is a compound entity that VB .NET evaluates at runtime. An expression can be made up of literals, variables, or a combination of the two:

```
Response = MsgBox ("Hello" & MyVariable)
```

If someone tells you she has a coupon for $1 off a $15 Bach CD, you immediately think $14. In the same way, at runtime, VB .NET reduces the items in an expression into its simplest form. A numeric expression results in a single number (after the expression is evaluated).

When an intelligent entity — like you or VB .NET — hears an expression, the entity collapses that expression into its simplest form. In other words, if you type **15 – 1** into one of your programs, when the program runs, Visual Basic reduces that group of symbols, that expression, to a single number: 14. Visual Basic simply evaluates what you've said and uses it in the program as the essence of what you are trying to say.

Here is a list of items you can use in an expression:

- A numeric or string variable
- A variable in an array
- A literal (numeric or string)
- A function that returns a number or string
- A numeric constant, like `Const Pi As Long = 3.14159265358979`
- Any combination of the above

Manipulating Strings

The new VB .NET StringBuilder is an excellent tool which can manipulate text in many ways. It effectively replaces a variety of traditional VB string-manipulation functions, it is easier to use, more flexible, and faster. What's not to like? There are also some new VB .NET methods of the string object (such as Length which replaces the tradtional VB Len function).

Chr (number)

This traditional VB function returns the character represented by the ASCII code. In computer languages, all characters (which include the uppercase and lowercase letters of the alphabet, punctuation marks, digits, and special symbols) have a numeric code from 0 to 255 (though this is changing to a larger set of numbers to accommodate most of the world's languages).

The computer works exclusively with numbers. The only purpose of text, from the computer's point of view, is to facilitate communication with humans. When you type in the letter **a**, the computer "remembers" it as the number 97. When that character is printed on the screen or on paper, the computer translates 97 back into the visual symbol we recognize as *a*.

Chr can be useful when encrypting messages, or to solve specialized character-displaying problems, as the following example illustrates.

To display quotation marks to the user, you must define a variable containing the code for the quotation mark, which is 34:

```
Dim quot As String

    quot = Chr(34)
    MsgBox("We're selling " & quot & "wood." & quot)
```

Another common use of Chr is to force a carriage return (linefeed); in other words, to simulate pressing the Enter key to move down to the next line in a TextBox. There is no way to type the Enter key into a string, so you must define the two character codes that simulate it, like this:

```
Dim cr As String = Chr(13) & Chr(10)
TextBox1.Text = "Hi" & cr & "How are you all!"
```

Or, instead of Chr(13) & Chr(10), you could use the built-in constant for these two characters, like this:

```
Dim clrf As String = ControlChars.CrLf
```

You may have noticed that a couple of examples in this session have used a condensed format when declaring a variable. You can, if you wish, both declare the variable, and assign a value to it, right on the same line:

```
Dim clrf As String = ControlChars.CrLf
```

This is a handy shortcut for the following:

```
Dim clrf As String
Clrf  = ControlChars.CrLf
```

You're probably muttering to yourself, "Well, if they defined a constant called ControlChars.CrLf to solve this problem, why didn't they just go the whole way and really solve it by simply defining *CrLf* so I, the programmer, don't have to go to the trouble? Life isn't always fair, so stop muttering. You could use this tactic, and avoid having to create your own variable:

```
TextBox1.Text = "Hi" & ControlChars.CrLf & "How are you all!"
```

IndexOf or InStr

If you want to find out the location of one piece of text within larger text, you can use either the traditional VB InStr function, or the new VB .NET IndexOf method.

**20 Min.
To Go**

Using IndexOf

The VB .NET IndexOf method can tell you where (in which character position) one piece of text is located within a larger text string.

This capability remarkably handy when you need to *parse* (locate or extract a piece of text within a larger body of text) some text. IndexOf can enable you to see if a particular word, for example, exists within a file or within some text that the user has typed into a TextBox. Perhaps you need to search a TextBox to see if the user typed in the words **New Jersey,** and if so, to tell them that your product is not available in that state.

IndexOf is the equivalent VB .NET method that replaces the traditional VB InStr function. Here's an example that finds the first occurance of the letter *n* in a string:

```
Dim s As String = "Hello Sonny"
Dim x As Integer
x = s.IndexOf("n")
MsgBox(x)
```

IndexOf is case-sensitive. To specify the starting character position, add an integer to the argument list, like this:

```
x = s.IndexOf("n", x)
```

What if you want to know whether there is more than one instance of the search string within the larger text? You can easily find additional instances by using the result of a previous IndexOf search. IndexOf, when it finds a match, reports the location — the character position within the larger text — where the match was found. Here's an example that reports how many times it finds the word *pieces* in some text:

```
Private Sub Form1_Load(ByVal sender As System.Object, ByVal e As
System.EventArgs) Handles MyBase.Load

        Dim quot, MainText, SearchWord As String
        Dim X, Y, Z As Integer


        quot = Chr(34)

        MainText = "Masterpieces are built of pieces."
        SearchWord = "pieces"

        Do
            X = Y + 1
            Z = Z + 1

    Y = MainText.IndexOf(SearchWord, X)
     Loop Until Y = -1

        MsgBox("We found " & SearchWord & " " & Z - 1 & _
            " times inside " & quot & MainText & quot)


    End Sub
```

In this example, the loop continues to look through the MainText until the IndexOf method returns a -1 (which indicates that the SearchWord was not found any more). The variable Z is used to count the number of times there's a successful hit. The variable X moves the pointer one character further into the MainText (X = Y + 1). You can use this example as a template any time you need to count the number of occurrences of a string within another, larger string. (Don't worry about the Do...Loop structure — it's covered in a future session.)

Using InStr

The traditional VB InStr format is:

```
InStr([start, ]string1, string2[, compare])
```

InStr is case-sensitive by default — it makes a distinction between *Upper* and *upper*, for example. InStr tells you where (in which character position) string2 is located within string1.

To use InStr in the previous "Masterpiece" example, you only need to change these two lines:

```
        Y = InStr(X, MainText, SearchWord)

    Loop Until Y = 0
```

To merely see if, in the previous example, a string appears at all within another one, you can use this technique:

```
If InStr("Masterpiece", "piece") Then MsgBox "Yep!"
```

Which translates to: If "piece" is found within "Masterpiece," then display "Yep!"

ToLower or LCase(String)

Sometimes you want to capitalize text in some new way. For example, you can use the ToLower method to remove any uppercase letters from a string, reducing it to all lowercase characters. *AfterWord* becomes *afterword*. Likewise, there's also a ToUpper method that raises all of the characters in a string to uppercase.

The VB .NET ToLower method replaces the traditional VB LCase function, and VB .NET's ToUpper replaces the traditional UCase function.

These methods or functions are used when you want to ignore the case — when you want to be case-insensitive. Usually, ToLower or ToUpper are valuable when the user is providing input and you cannot know (and don't care) how he or she might capitalize the input. Comparisons are case-sensitive:

```
If "Larry" = "larry" Then MsgBox "They are the same."
```

This message box will never be displayed. The *L* is not the same. You can see the problem. You often just don't care how the user typed in the capitalization. If you don't care, just use ToLower or ToUpper to force all the characters to be lowercase or uppercase, like this:

```
Private Sub Form1_Load(ByVal sender As System.Object, ByVal e As
System.EventArgs) Handles MyBase.Load

        Dim reply As String
        Dim n As Integer

        reply = InputBox("Shall we proceed?")

reply = reply.ToUpper

        Dim x As Integer


        If reply = "YES" Then
            MsgBox("Ok. We'll proceed.")
        End If


    End Sub
```

Notice that in this example it now does not matter how the user capitalized *yes*. Any capitalization will be forced into uppercase letters, and we in turn compare it to a literal that is also all uppercase.

Substring or Left(String,Number)

If you want to retrieve only a portion of a string — the first three letters, say — you can use the VB .NET equivalent of the traditional Left or Right string functions: the SubString method:

```
Dim n As String = "More to the point."

        n = n.Substring(0, 4)
        MsgBox(n)
```

The first number inside the parentheses specifies the position to start at, with zero meaning the first character. The second number (4 here) specifies how many characters you want to extract. The result of this code puts the characters *More* into the string variable *n*.

Or to get a string from the right side, this retrieves all characters from the 12th character to the end of the string:

```
n = n.Substring(12)
```

The traditional Left function works similarly; it returns a portion of a string, the number of characters defined by the Number argument. Here's an example:

```
Dim n As String

        n = Microsoft.VisualBasic.Left ("More to the point.", 4)
        MsgBox(N)
```

There's also a Right function. Both Left and Right require the Microsoft.VisualBasic qualifier, which was not necessary in previous versions of VB.

Length or Len(String)

The VB .NET Length method tells you how many characters are in a string. You might want to let the user know that their response is too wordy for your database's allotted space for a particular entry. Or perhaps you want to see if they entered the full telephone number, including their area code. If they have, their number will have to be at least ten characters long. You can use the less-than symbol (<) to test their entry, like this:

```
        If TextBox1.Text.Length < 10 Then
```

Or to use the traditional Len function:

```
        If Len(TextBox1.Text) < 10 Then
            MsgBox("Shorter")
        End If
```

The Trim Method or LTrim(String)

The VB .NET Trim method can remove any leading or trailing space characters from a string. The uses for this method are similar to those for ToUpper or ToLower: Sometimes people accidentally add extra spaces at the beginning or end of their typing. Those space characters will cause a comparison to fail because computers can be quite literal. *"This"* is not the same thing as *"This"*, and if you write code If " This" = "This", and the user types in *"* **This** *"*, the computer's answer will be no. Also, some data formats require a particular string length. The Trim method

Here's an example that removes four leading spaces:

```
Dim s As String = "    Here"
s = s.Trim
MsgBox(s & s.Length)
```

Trim, LTrim (and its brother RTrim) are the traditional VB space-removal functions.

Substring, StringBuilder, or Mid

When you want to manipulate text, you'll likely find VB .NET's StringBuilder a highly useful tool. But before considering its various benefits, let's look at one more use for the VB .NET Substring method.

You'll probably find yourself using the Substring method surprisingly often. It can extract a substring (a string within a string) from *anywhere* within a string.

```
Dim s As String = "1234567"
MsgBox(s.Substring(2, 4))
```

Running this code results in 3456. You asked to start at the third character and to extract the 4 characters following it. VB .NET brings us many improvements over traditional VB, and some degradations. In my view, this example illustrates one of the degradations: Notice that to start with the *third* character in this string, you must specify *2* as your Substring argument. This nonsense is because the Substring method begins counting characters with zero (the *first* character — as we humans think of it — must be described in VB .NET here as the *zeroth* character). Of course, in human language (and consequently human thinking processes), the zero means *absence, non-existence*. So we never think of the first item in a list as being the *zero* item. Nor should we have to think this way in computer languages either. And, in previous versions of VB we didn't have to. The VB 6 Mid function does the same thing as the VB .NET Substring method in this example. Mid begins counting characters with 1, as we humans do. Somebody who worked on designing VB .NET thinks we should start counting with zero, as in: "This is my zeroth time visiting Greece, I'm so glad I got to vacation here! Next year I'm coming back for my *first* visit!"

The traditional VB Mid format is:

Mid(String, StartCharacter [, NumberOfCharacters])

The Mid function works like this:

MsgBox(Mid("1234567", 3, 4))

There are numerous string methods in VB .NET. Here are some additional methods you might want to familiarize yourself with — just so you know they exist if you ever need them: Compare, Concat, Format, Chars, EndsWith, Insert, LastIndexOf, PadLeft, PadRight, Remove, Replace, Split, StartsWith.

Numeric Functions

Most of the numeric functions have to do with trigonometry. If you need them, you know where to look: VB .NET's Help feature. Press F1, and then use the Index tab to search VB .NET Help for Atn, Cos, Exp, Len, Log, Sin, or Tan. See the Supplementary Notes for Session 15 on this book's CD for information about the ABS function — it can come in handy sometimes.

Data Conversion: The "C..." Functions

Sometimes, you want to force a variable to be a certain type, usually because you want to achieve a high level of precision, or because you are using Option Strict. A string can be coerced into a numeric type, or an integer can be made into a floating-point type — pretty much any type can be converted into any other type.

10 Min. To Go

You can force variables to become particular types by using these functions: CBool (Boolean, true or false), CByte (byte, 8-bits, 0-255), CChar (char, 0 to 65535), CDate (date), CDbl (double), CDec (decimal), CInt (integer), CLng (long), CObj (object), CShort (-32,768 to 32,767; fractions are rounded), CSng (single), CStr (string), Fix (removes the fractional part of a number), Int (rounds down to the next lowest integer — even 1.9 becomes 1), Hex (changes to hexadecimal base), and Oct (changes to octal base).

Here are the primary uses for these "C . . ." functions:

- For the greatest possible precision and the greatest possible range, use the Decimal type. You can transform other variables into the Decimal type with the CDec function. The special Decimal numeric type provides this enormous range: plus or minus 79,228,162,514,264,337,593,543,950,335 for numbers with no decimal places. For numbers with a decimal, the Decimal type provides this enormous precision: plus or minus 7.9228162514264337593543950335. The smallest possible fraction is 0.0000000000000000000000000001.

- Use CInt (for simple integers) or CDbl (for large numbers with fractions) if you want to change a string variable type into a numeric variable. Use cStr to force real numbers to become text digits (characters rather than computable numbers).

- The CDate command might seem to duplicate the behavior of the DateValue and TimeValue functions, but there is a difference. DateValue converts a number to the date format; TimeValue converts to the time format; CDate converts both date and time. (DateValue and TimeValue are discussed in more detail later in this session.)

The Formatting Functions

The Format functions are multipurpose tools. They can be used to add commas to numbers to separate the thousands, display a number in scientific notation or as a percent, display time and dates in various formats, and so on. See the Supplementary Notes for Session 15 on this book's CD for further information about these sometimes useful tools.

The Financial Functions

If you're an accountant, or otherwise heavily into the mathematics of business, you should know that VB .NET includes a generous supply of accounting and business functions for you. It can do what financial calculators can do. See the Supplementary Notes for Session 15 on this book's CD for further information about these functions.

Date and Time Functions

After the embarrassment of riches you've noticed in the other categories in this session, do you think VB .NET is stingy with functions that manipulate and display dates and time? Of course not. Here are the main date and time functions you'll likely want to use in your programming:

- Today — Gives you the current date.
- TimeOfDay — Gives you the current time.
- Now — Gives you both the date and time.

See the Supplementary Notes for Session 15 on this book's CD for further information about these often-useful functions.

Done!

REVIEW

This session introduced you to the close cousins of variables: *literals* and *constants*. Then you were introduced to a compound structure known as an *expression*. You then went on a cook's tour of many of the major built-in functions that VB .NET generously offers. There's no point in reinventing the wheel if VB .NET itself already contains the solution.

QUIZ YOURSELF

1. How does a literal differ from a variable? (See "Literals.")
2. Name two benefits of using constants. (See "Constants.")
3. What is the ToLower method useful for? (See "ToLower or LCase(String).")
4. How do you find out how many characters are in a string variable? (See "Length or Len(String).")
5. Which command gives you both the date and time? (See "Date and Time Functions.")

The Big Operators: Comparison, Math, and Logical

Session Checklist

✔ Learning about expressions

✔ Understanding what operators do

✔ Using comparison operators

✔ Working with arithmetic operators

✔ Learning about the specialized logical operators

✔ Solving the problem of operator precedence

**30 Min.
To Go**

This session shows you how to use *operators*. Operators are used in expressions to compare two elements (like two variables), to do math on them, or to perform a "logical" operation on them. The plus sign (+), for example, is an operator in the following example: 2 + 4. The greater-than symbol (>) is an operator in this example that says n is greater than z: n > z.

Understanding Expressions

Recall that expressions are not limited only to variables. Expressions can also be built out of literal numbers, literal strings, numeric variables, string variables, numeric variables in an array, a function that returns a number or string, a constant, or any combination of these.

An expression is looked at and evaluated by VB during runtime. This evaluation produces a result. It might be that the expression is True, or it might produce the number 6, or some other result that the expression yields, such as the expression "A" & "sk", which produces the result "Ask".

An expression must contain at least two elements, separated by an operator. For example, the expression "A" > "B" asks if the literal letter A is greater alphabetically than the letter B, which is untrue, so this expression evaluates to False.

However, an expression can contain more than two elements. For example, 1 < 2 And 3 < 4 uses three elements and evaluates to True because the number 1 is less than 2 and the number 4 is greater than 3. However, if any part of a compound expression is false, the whole expression evaluates to False. For example, the following expression is false: 1 < 2 And 3 > 4. (You'll get to the And operator later; it's one of the so-called "logical" operators.)

Comparison Operators

Often, you need to compare two values, and then your program reacts based on the result of the comparison. Say, for example, the user has typed in his or her age, and you want to respond to the age in your code:

```
Dim usersage As Integer

Dim Msg As String

If UsersAge < 50 Then
    Msg = "You "
Else
    Msg = "You do not "
End If

Msg += "qualify for reduced term insurance."

MsgBox(Msg)
```

The *expression* in this code is UsersAge < 50. This particular expression uses one of the *comparison* (also called *relational*) operators: the less-than symbol (<). The line of code means: *If the value in the UsersAge variable is less than 50, then show the "You qualify..." message. Otherwise (Else), show the "You do not qualify..." message.*

The eight comparison operators

Table 16-1 lists the eight comparison operators used in VB .NET.

Table 16-1 *Comparison Operators*

Operator	Description
<	Less than
<=	Less than or equal to
>	Greater than
>=	Greater than or equal to
<>	Not equal
=	Equal

Is	Do two object variables refer to the same object?
Like	Pattern matching

It's easy to remember the meaning of the < and > symbols. The large end of the symbol is the greater, so A > B **means A is greater than B.** A < B **means A less than B.**

You can use the comparison (also known as relational) operators with text as well. When used with literal text (or text variables), the operators refer to the alphabetic qualities of the text, with the value of Andy being less than Anne.

The Is operator is highly specialized. It tells you if two object variable names refer to the same object (more on this in Session 30). It can be used with arrays that keep track of controls or forms.

The Like operator lets you compare a string to a pattern, using wildcards. This operator is similar to the wildcards you can use when searching, using the symbols * or ?. In the Windows search utility or in Explorer, for instance, you can see all files ending with .DOC by typing ***.DOC**.

Working with the Like operator

Use Like to compare strings, as follows:

```
Dim Msg, A As String

A = "Rudolpho"

If A Like "Ru*" Then Msg = "Close Enough"

MsgBox(Msg)
```

This results in the message being displayed. The Like operator can be used to forgive user typos. When testing for Pennsylvania, you could accept Like Pen* because no other state starts with those characters, so any misspellings the user makes further on in this word can be ignored.

20 Min. To Go

The following example uses the Like operator to compare against a single character in a particular position. (Notice that the two logical lines are placed on a single physical line here, separated by a colon. You can use a separate line for MsgBox(A), but it's so short, I just stuck it onto the end of the other code. If you do put two or more logical lines together, remember that the colon is necessary to separate them.)

```
Dim A As Boolean

A = "Nora" Like "?ora" : MsgBox(A)
```

This results in True.

Note that many expressions evaluate to True or False, and therefore the expression returns a *Boolean* answer. So, you must declare a Boolean variable to receive that answer, as in the previous example. Here's another example:

```
Dim A As Boolean

        A = "Nora" Like "F?ora" : MsgBox(A)
```

This results in False, because the first letter in Nora isn't *F*, the third letter isn't *o*, and so on.

You can also use Like to compare when you don't care about a match between a series of characters, like this:

```
If "David" Like "*d" Then
```

This code results in Match. "D*" or "**D*d" or "*i*" will all match "David".

Or you can use the following to match a single character in the text against a single character or range of characters in the list enclosed by brackets:

```
If "Empire" Like "??[n-q]*" Then
```

This code results in Match, because the third character in Empire, *p*, falls within the range n-q. You can also use multiple ranges such as "[n-r t-w]".

Or you can use the following to match if a single character in the text is not in the list:

```
If "Empire" Like "??[!n-q]*" Then
```

This code results in No Match (the ! symbol means "not").

Using Arithmetic Operators

Arithmetic operators work pretty much as you would expect them to. They do some math and provide a result. Table 16-2 lists the arithmetic operators used in VB .NET.

Table 16-2 *Arithmetic Operators*

Operator	Description
^	Exponentiation — the number multiplied by itself (for example, 5 ^ 2 is 25 and 5 ^ 3 is 125)
–	Negation — negative numbers (such as –25)
*	Multiplication
/	Division
\	Integer division — division with no remainder, no fraction, no decimal point (for example 8 \ 6 results in the answer 1). Use this if you don't need the remainder.

Mod	Modulo arithmetic (explained in the text following this table)
+	Addition
–	Subtraction
&	String concatenation (This & is still supported in VB .NET, but is no longer necessary. It was used in previous versions of VB with variant variable types. VB .NET has no variants, so you can use + for both numeric addition as well as concatenation.)

Use the arithmetic operators like this:

```
If B + A > 12 Then
```

The modulo (Mod) operator gives you any remainder after a division, but not the results of the division itself. You just get the remainder. This is useful when you want to know if some number divides evenly into another number. That way, you can do things at intervals. For instance, say you wanted to print the page number in bold on every fifth page. Here's how you could code that:

```
If PageNumber Mod 5 = 0 Then
    FontBold = True
Else
    FontBold = 0
End If
```

Here are some more Mod examples:

- 15 Mod 5 results in 0.
- 16 Mod 5 results in 1.
- 17 Mod 5 results in 2.
- 20 Mod 5 results in 0.

The Logical Operators

The logical operators are sometimes called *Boolean* operators because technically they operate on individual *bits* (and a bit can only be in two states: true or false, on or off). But whatever you call them, the logical operators are most often used to create a compound expression. The logical operators you'll use frequently are And, Or, and Not. They allow you to construct expressions like this:

```
If BettysAge > 55 And JohnsAge > 50 Then
```

The And operator means that both comparisons must be true for the entire expression to be true.

Similarly, Or allows you to create an expression where only one comparison must be true for the entire expression to be true:

```
If TomsMother = Visiting Or SandysMothersAge > 78 Then
```

The Not operator is good for switching a toggle back and forth, like this:

```
Protected Sub Button1_Click(ByVal sender As Object, ByVal e As
System.EventArgs)

    Static Toggle As Boolean

    Toggle = Not Toggle

    If Toggle Then MsgBox("See this message every other time you
click")


End Sub
```

The Static command preserves the contents of the variable Toggle (Dim would not). The Boolean variable type is the simplest one: It has only two states: True or False. It can be flipped back and forth like a light switch. This line, Toggle = Not Toggle, means: *If Toggle's value is False, make it now True. If it's True, make it False.* You'll be surprised how often you use this technique in your programming.

Table 16-3 gives you a complete list of all the logical operators, some of which have esoteric uses in cryptography and such.

Table 16-3 *Logical Operators*

Operator	Description
Not	Logical negation
And	And
Or	Inclusive Or
Xor	Either but not Both

10 Min. To Go

Here's an example of a logical operator at work:

```
If 5 + 2 = 4 Or 6 + 6 = 12 Then MsgBox("One of them is true.")
```

One of these expressions is true, so the MsgBox comment will be displayed. Only one or the other needs to be true.

Here's another example:

```
If 5 + 2 = 4 And 6 + 6 = 12 Then MsgBox ("Both of them are true.")
```

This is false, so nothing is displayed. *Both* expressions, the first and the second, must be true for the printing to take place.

VB .NET offers two new operators — AndAlso and OrElse — which differ technically from the way that the And **and** Or **logical operators work, and how expressions using them are evaluated. The purpose of this is to attempt to prevent some esoteric, yet possible, errors. If this is important to you, see the entry titled "AND, OR, XOR, and NOT" in Appendix C on this book's CD.**

Operator Precedence

When you use more than one operator in an expression, which operator should be evaluated first? Clearly, a simple expression is unambiguous — 2 + 3 can only result in 5.

But sometimes a complex expression can be solved more than one way, like this one:

```
3 * 10 + 5
```

Does this mean *first multiply 3 times 10, resulting in 30, and then add 5 to the result*? Should VB evaluate this expression as 35? Or, does it mean add 10 to 5, resulting in 15, and then multiply the result by 3? This alternative evaluation would result in 45.

Expressions are not necessarily evaluated by the computer from left to right. Left-to-right evaluation in the previous example would result in 35, because 3 would be multiplied by 10 before the 5 was added to that result. But remember that complex expressions can be evaluated backwards sometimes.

Visual Basic enforces an *order of precedence*, a hierarchy by which various relationships are resolved between numbers in an expression. For instance, multiplication is always carried out before addition.

Fortunately, you don't have to memorize the order of precedence. Instead, to make sure that you get the results you intend when using more than one operator, just use parentheses to enclose the items you want evaluated first. Using the previous example, if you want to multiply 3 * 10, and then add 5, write it like this:

```
(3 * 10) + 5
```

By enclosing an operator and its two surrounding values in parentheses, you tell VB that you want the enclosed items to be considered as a single value and to be evaluated before anything else happens.

If you intended to say add 10 + 5 and then multiply by 3, move the parentheses like this instead:

```
3 * (10 + 5)
```

In longer expressions, you can even nest parentheses to make clear which items are to be calculated in which order, like this:

```
3 * ((9 + 1) + 5)
```

If you work with these kinds of expressions a great deal, you might want to memorize Table 16-4. But most people just use parentheses and forget about this problem. If you're interested, the table lists the order in which VB will evaluate an expression, from first evaluated to last.

Table 16-4 *Arithmetic Operators in Order of Precedence*

Operator	Description
^	Exponents (6 ^ 2 is 36. The number is multiplied by itself *X* number of times.)
−	Negation (negative numbers like −33)
* /	Multiplication and division
\	Integer division (division with no remainder, no fraction)
Mod	Modulo arithmetic
+ −	Addition and subtraction
The relational operators	Evaluated left to right
The logical operators	Evaluated left to right

Given that multiplication has precedence over addition, the ambiguous example that started this discussion would be evaluated in the following way:

```
3 * 10 + 5
```

So, the result would be 35.

Done!

REVIEW

This session is all about *operators* — ways to take two or more elements (like two variables) and combine, modify, compare, or otherwise manipulate them. You saw how you can compare numbers in various ways (such as greater-than or equal) or text (alphabetically, or find similarity with the Like command). Then you explored all the various arithmetic operators. Finally, you experimented with logical operators such as And, Not, and Or to create longer, more complex expressions: with Not to toggle a value; with And to read a bit; and with Xor to toggle a bit. Finally, you saw how to use parentheses to specify the order in which the parts of a complex expression should be evaluated.

QUIZ YOURSELF

1. What operator would you use if you wanted to ask, "Is A less-than or equal-to B?" (See "The eight comparison operators.")

2. Explain the code If N Like "T*" in plain English. (See "Working with the Like operator.")

3. Which arithmetic operator allows you to specify intervals? (See "Using Arithmetic Operators.")

4. What is concatenation and what operator do you use to accomplish it? (See "Using Arithmetic Operators.")

5. Why does operator precedence matter, and what's the easy way to solve the precedence problem? (See "Operator Precedence.")

PART

III

Saturday Afternoon Part Review

1. Define the purpose of an argument.
2. Can you leave out an argument in an argument list?
3. What is the difference between a subroutine and a function?
4. Name four of the Dialog controls.
5. Which two Dialog controls work directly with the Print Dialog control?
6. How do you send information back from a function?
7. What is stepping and what is it good for?
8. Do you call a function the same way you call a subroutine?
9. What are the two fundamental kinds of variables?
10. What does the term *value* mean when used with variables?
11. Name two rules you must observe when making up a variable's name.
12. What does *implicit* variable creation mean?
13. Name three of the five commands that are commonly used to create a variable.
14. How many values can a variable hold at one time?
15. Are properties variables?
16. What is the default variable type in Visual Basic .NET?
17. What is unique about the Boolean data type?

18. Define the concept of scope.
19. What is an expression?
20. What is an operator?

PART

IV

Saturday Evening

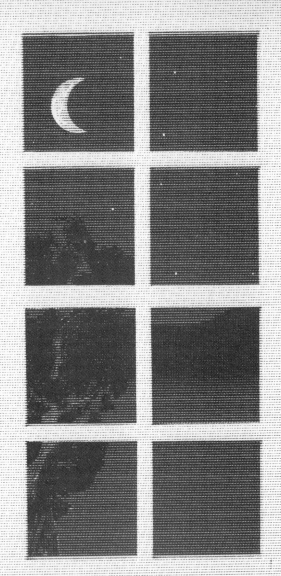

Arrays and Looping

Session Checklist

✔ How to create and manipulate arrays

✔ Understanding For ... Next loops

✔ Learning to use Do...Loops

**30 Min.
To Go**

N ow for some heavy-duty programming. By that, I don't mean to imply that it's hard to learn, it's just that looping is a common and important programming technique.

Because we often use arrays within loops, we'll take a look at arrays first.

Understanding Arrays

An *array* is a set of variable values that have been grouped together. Once inside an array structure, the variables share the same text name, and are individually identified by an index number.

Because numbers can be manipulated mathematically (and text names cannot), putting a group of variables into an array allows you to easily and efficiently work with the entire group. You can manipulate the items in the array by using *loops*, such as For...Next and Do...Loop structures.

Numbers and names

Arrays can be extremely useful to a programmer. For example, if you want to remember all of the trips you have taken, you can create an array to hold the names of each place you visit:

```
Dim PlacesVisited(500) As String
```

This creates 501 "empty boxes" in the computer's memory, which serve as spaces for text (String) variables that name the trips taken. (It's 501 rather than 500 because the first space, the first "empty box" is given the index 0.)

However, instead of 501 unique individual variable names for each of these 501 variables, the variables in this cluster share the single name PlacesVisited, and each box is identified by a unique index number from 0 to 500. (You decide that 501 is probably large enough for your purposes, vacation-mad though you are.)

To fill this array with the names of the places you've visited, assign the names just as you would assign them to normal variables, but just use the index number to distinguish them. You can tell an array from a regular variable because arrays always have parentheses following the array name. The index number goes between these parentheses, like this: MyArray(122).

Also, even if you use the Option Strict Off feature, unlike variables, arrays must *always* be formally declared with Dim, ReDim, Private, Public, Static or the other commands that declare variables or arrays. You cannot implicitly just start using an array. You must use one of the declaration commands to declare the array. It's not possible to just use code like this: PlacesVisited(1) = "St. Louis", with no previous declaration of the PlacesVisited array.

Here's one way to put the names of places you visit into an array:

```
PlacesVisited(0) = "St. Louis"
PlacesVisited(1) = "San Diego"
PlacesVisited(2) = "Richmond"
PlacesVisited(3) = "Jordon"
PlacesVisited(4) = "Montana State Park"
```

Now the array is partly filled with data. The process of filling an array can be accomplished in several ways: by having the user type in the array items, by reading the data from a disk file, or as you did, by directly filling the array with pieces of information (literals) in the programming itself.

Now that you have the first few cells of the array filled, you can manipulate it in ways that are much more efficient than when using ordinary variables. What if you wanted to know if a particular place had been visited? You could loop through the array, like this:

```
Dim I As Integer
    Dim PlacesVisited(500) As String

    PlacesVisited(10) = "St. Louis"
    PlacesVisited(21) = "San Diego"
    PlacesVisited(32) = "Richmond"


    For I = 0 To 499
        If PlacesVisited(I) = "Richmond" Then MsgBox("Yes, ") _
            & PlacesVisited(I) & " has been visited."

    Next I
```

This session provides examples that you can test by putting them within a `Button_Click` event, or putting them up near the top of the code window just following the line:

```
'TODO: Add any initialization after the InitializeComponent() call
```

In other words, to get this example to work when you press F5, either type it into the initialization section of your code, or add a Button to your form, and then put the example code within that Button's `Click` event, press F5, and click the button:

```
Protected Sub Button1_Click(ByVal sender As Object, ByVal e As
System.EventArgs)

        'Put the example code here.

    End Sub
```

You are not going to repeat the `Button1_Click....End Sub` code for each example.

 Notice that in the previous example, the loop counts from 0 to 499, rather than to 500. It's my hope that some day computer languages will stop perpetuating this oddity. For now, you just have to remember that arrays start with a zeroth cell, so when you create a loop, you must loop up to a number *one less than the declared size* of the array. In other words, if you `Dim MyArray(4)`, you must loop `0 To 3`. This bug-causing "feature" of arrays results in counterintuitive phrases that have bothered programmers for years, like listing December as the *11th* month of the year, as you'll see shortly.

Using line breaks

Notice how the `MsgBox` line in the previous example ends with a space character followed by an underscore (_). This is how you can force a line break in VB. VB executes lines of code one at a time, so you must never press the Enter key until you have completed the line of code, or used the space-underscore (_) to indicate that the line continues just below (that there has been a "line break").

Also, you cannot put a line break within a string (between quotation marks). You cannot do the following, for instance, and break the text *Toronto* in two:

```
"Toron _
to" Then
```

To return to the subject at hand: The key to the utility of arrays is that you can search them, sort them, delete from them, or add to them using *numbers* to identify each value, instead of using individual text variable names. Index numbers are much easier to access and manipulate — for groups of data — than text labels.

Why arrays are efficient

Still not convinced? Here's another example. Suppose you want to figure out your average electric bill for the year. You can go the cumbersome route, using an individual text variable name for each month:

```
JanElect = 90
FebElect = 122
MarElect = 125
AprElect = 78
MayElect = 144
JneElect = 89
JulyElect = 90
AugElect = 140
SeptElect = 167
OctElect = 123
NovElect = 133
DecElect = 125
YearElectBill = JanElect+FebElect+MarElect+AprElect _
    +MayElect+JneElect+JulyElect+AugElect+SeptElect+ _
    OctElect+ NovElect+DecElect
```

Or, you could use an array to simplify the process:

```
Dim I, MonthElectBill(12) As Integer

        MonthElectBill(0) = 90
        MonthElectBill(1) = 122
        MonthElectBill(2) = 125
        MonthElectBill(3) = 78
        MonthElectBill(4) = 144
        MonthElectBill(5) = 89
        MonthElectBill(6) = 90
        MonthElectBill(7) = 140
        MonthElectBill(8) = 167
        MonthElectBill(9) = 123
        MonthElectBill(10) = 133
        MonthElectBill(11) = 125
```

```
For I = 0 to 11
    Total = Total + MonthElectBill(I)
Next I
```

By grouping all of the variables under the same name, you can manipulate the variables by their individual index numbers. This might look like a small savings of effort, but remember that your program will perhaps have to use and manipulate these variables in several different ways in several different contexts. You'll also probably have to save them to disk. If they're in an array, you can save them with a loop like this:

```
Dim I, MonthElectBill(12) As Integer

        MonthElectBill(0) = 90
        MonthElectBill(1) = 122
        MonthElectBill(2) = 125
        MonthElectBill(3) = 78
        MonthElectBill(4) = 144
        MonthElectBill(5) = 89
        MonthElectBill(6) = 90
        MonthElectBill(7) = 140
        MonthElectBill(8) = 167
        MonthElectBill(9) = 123
        MonthElectBill(10) = 133
        MonthElectBill(11) = 125


        Open(1, "C:\Teset.Txt", OpenMode.Output)

        For I = 0 To 11
            Print(1, MonthElectBill(I))
        Next I


        Close()
```

If they're not in an array, you need to do this:

```
Print(1, JanElect)
Print(1, FebElect)
Print(1, MarElect)
Print(1, AprElect)
Print(1, MayElect)
Print(1, JneElect)
Print(1, JulyElect)
Print(1, AugElect)
Print(1, SeptElect)
Print(1, OctElect)
Print(1, NovElect)
Print(1, DecElect)
```

Unless you have put this group of variables into an array, you'll have to access each by its text name every time you deal with the group in your program. That's quite inefficient.

 These previous two examples use VB 6 code for the file-saving part of the source code. File access in VB 6 is much simpler than the code you must use in VB .NET (see Session 12). I use VB 6 here so you can focus on the topic: arrays.

Declaring an array

Recall that arrays must be formally declared. They can be created by using one of eight declaration commands: Dim, ReDim Static, Public, Protected, Friend, Protected Friend, or Private. (These are the same declaration statements you can use when declaring a variable.)

All seven of these commands create arrays in the same way: by dimensioning the new array. This means that the computer is told how much space to set aside for the new array (how many values it will contain), and also the variable type that the array contains.

You'll use the Public command in the following examples, but the Private, Dim, ReDim, and Static commands follow the same rules.

To create space for 50 text variables that share the label Names and are uniquely identified by index numbers ranging from 0 to 49, type the following in a module:

```
Public Names(50)
```

Multidimensional arrays

Arrays can be more complex. You can create arrays that you might visualize as similar to a spreadsheet with multiple columns and rows. You could use this as a way to associate related information such as places visited, the length of the trip, and the date of the trip. This is similar to providing several fields (columns) for different information about each item of data (record).

VB allows you to create as many as 60 dimensions for a single array! But few programmers can visualize, or effectively work with, more than two or three dimensions.

A two-dimensional array is like a graph, a database table, a crossword puzzle, or a spreadsheet: cells of information related in an *x,y* coordinate system. A three-dimensional array is like a honeycomb — it not only has height and width, it also has depth. Most people check out at this point, not being able to visualize a 3-D array.

A model of a four-dimensional array cannot be physically constructed, so there simply is no example of one to try to visualize. (You might think of it as a set of several identical honeycombs, if you're brave.) Go beyond four dimensions, and you've gone past physics into an abstract domain that would challenge Leonardo. (Well, maybe not Leonardo.)

Anyway, to make a two-dimensional array, program something like this:

```
Public PlacesVisited (500, 3) As String
```

This means that there will be potentially 500 PlacesVisited, and each of them can have three associated additional values.

Here's how to retrieve the data about the fourth trip. Its name would be stored in PlacesVisited(3,1), its length, say, would be in PlacesVisited(3,2), and its date would be in PlacesVisited(3,3). So, you can display the information about the date of the fourth trip using the following code: MsgBox (PlacesVisited(3,3).

Same as when declaring a variable, if you do not specify a data type for an array, the data type of the elements defaults to the *object* type.

Understanding ReDim

The ReDim command works only with arrays and is mainly used to resize them while a program runs. It's not often used. If you are interested in it, see the Supplementary notes for Session 17 on this book's CD.

Going Round and Round in Loops

Often a job requires repetition until a result is achieved: Polish your boots until they shine, add spoonfuls of sugar one at a time until the lemonade tastes good, and so on. The same kind of repetition is often needed in computer programs.

Using For...Next

The most common loop structure is For...Next. Between the For and the Next are the instructions that get repeatedly carried out. The number of times the computer will execute the loop is defined by the two numbers listed right after the For:

```
For I = 1 To 4
    A = A + I
Next I

MsgBox (A)
```

In this example, the loop's counter variable is named I. (There's something of a tradition to use the name I in For...Next loops in programs.) But the important thing to understand is that the counter variable is incremented (raised by 1) each time the program gets to the Next command. The Next command does three things: It adds 1 to the variable I; it checks to see if I has reached the limit set in the For statement (4 in this example); and it checks to make sure the limit has not been exceeded. Then Next sends the program back up to the For statement to repeat the code one more time. Any code within the loop is executed each time the loop cycles.

The answer displayed by the MsgBox is 10. Try single-stepping through the execution of this loop (press F11 repeatedly) and pause your mouse cursor over the counter variable I and also over the variable A each time you go through the loop. You'll see that the first time through I is 1 (the code says 1 To 4, so the counter starts with 1). The variable A is empty, but as soon as its line of code is executed, it contains the value of I (plus whatever was in A). The second time through the loop, A has a 1 in it, but the value of I is 2, so A then contains 3. The third time through the loop, 3 is added to 3, resulting in 6. Finally, the last time through the loop, I has a value of 4, which, added to 6, becomes 10. The program then exits the loop and displays the MsgBox.

You can use literal numbers to specify the start and count:

```
For I = 1 to 20 'literal
```

Or you can use a variable. Perhaps you want to allow the user to decide how many copies of a document should be printed. Here's how:

```
Numberofcopies = InputBox("How many copies?")

For I = 1 To Numberofcopies

'print the document

Next I
```

Notice the convention of indenting the code inside a For...Next loop. This graphically illustrates the loop. VB .NET by default automatically indents various code structures for you as you type the lines in.

**10 Min.
To Go**

Using the Step command

There is an optional command that works with For...Next called Step. Step can be attached at the end of the For...Next line of code to allow you to skip numbers, to step past them. When the Step command is used with For...Next, Step alters the way the loop counts.

By default, a loop counts by one:

```
Dim i As Integer

        For I = 1 To 12
            Debug.Write(I)
        Next I
```

This results in 1 2 3 4 5 6 7 8 9 10 11 12.

I prefer to use the MsgBox to display results in many cases — as you've doubtless noticed in the example code in this book. However, it isn't practical in the preceding example to display 12 message boxes — that would be rather clumsy and slow. So, instead, the example illustrates a technique favored by some programmers: the Debug command. In previous versions of VB you would use Debug.Print, but this has been changed in VB .NET to Debug.Write or Debug.WriteLineThe results of a Debug.Write command appear in the VB .NET Output window.

When you use the Step command, you change the way a For...Next loop counts. It can count every other number (Step 2):

```
For I = 1 to 12 Step 2
    Debug.Write (I)
Next I
```

This results in 1 3 5 7 9 11.

Or you can Step every 73rd number (Step 73), count down backward (For I = 10 to 1 Step -1), and even count by fractions (Step .25).

Nesting loops

For...Next loops can be nested, one inside the other. At first, this type of structure seems confusing (and it often is). The inner loop interacts with the exterior loop in ways that are instantly clear only to the mathematically or spatially gifted. Essentially, the inner loop does its thing the number of times specified by its own counter variable multiplied by the counter variable of the outer loop. Got it?

In some confusing programming situations, you have to simply hack away, as programmers say. In this case, you might have to try substituting counter numbers (and maybe moving code from one loop to the other) until things work the way they should. *Hacking* to a programmer means the same thing as adding spices means to a cook — messing around until the desired result emerges.

In this example, the Chr variable, defined as character code 13, inserts a carriage return — moving the Debug.Write down one line in the Output window each time the *cr* executes. Alternatively, you could use the Debug.WriteLine command which includes a carriage return

```
Dim cr As String = Chr(13)
    Dim I, J As Integer

    For I = 1 To 2
        For J = 1 To 3
            Debug.Write(I & " " & J & cr)
        Next J
    Next I
```

Any numeric expression can be used with For...Next.

Early exits

If, for some reason, you want to exit the loop before the counter finishes, use the Exit For command, like this:

```
If n > 500 Then Exit For
```

The Exit For command is rarely used, but perhaps you are filling an array that can only hold 500. You don't want to overflow it. So you make a provision for an early exit from the loop if necessary. If the Exit For is carried out, execution moves to the line of code following the Next command. There are Exit Do (for Do...Loops), Exit Function, Exit Do, and Exit Sub commands as well.

Working with Do...Loops

Some loop structures use the Do and Loop commands; they offer some advantages over For...Next in some situations.

Do While

Sometimes, you might prefer the Do...While structure; in fact, some programmers favor it over For...Next. Do...While can be a bit more flexible.

In its most common style, Do...While uses a comparison operator at the start of the loop to test something (is it = or =>, and so on). The first time the comparison fails, the loop is skipped and execution continues on the line of code following the loop structure. The Loop command signals the end of the Do...While structure just as the Next command signals the end of the For...Next loop structure:

```
Dim I As Integer

Do While I < 11
    I += 1
    Debug.Write(I)
Loop
```

Recall that I += 1 means the same as I = I + 1.

Be sure to do something in the code within the loop that *changes the comparison value*. Otherwise, you have created an endless loop that will never stop looping. Also note that if I already holds a value of 11 or more when the program reaches this loop, the loop will never execute. The comparison test will fail the very first time the loop is encountered, and none of the code within the loop will execute at all.

Do Until

A version of Do While is Do Until. It's just another way of expressing the same idea, but you might find it a little clearer. Do While loops as long as the comparison is true, but Do Until loops until the comparison is false:

```
Do Until y = 11
    y = y + 1

Loop
```

Loop While and Loop Until

If you want to put the comparison test at the end of the loop structure, there are two additional ways to construct a Do...Loop:

```
Do
    y = y + 1
Loop While Y < 11
```

This works the same way as the previous Do...While example. The difference is that when you put the test at the end, the loop will always execute at least once — no matter what value is in the variable y when you enter the loop:

```
Do
    y = y + 1
Loop Until Y = 11
```

Which of these four structures should you use? Use Do While or Do Until if you don't want the loop to execute *even once* if the condition test fails at the start. As for the difference between the While and Until styles, it's merely a rhetorical, not a logical, distinction:

It's the difference between "do the dishes while any are still dirty" versus "do the dishes until all are clean."

Use the version that seems to you to be more readable, or that works better with the comparison test.

While . . . End While: A Simple Loop

The `While...End While` structure, though, is little used. It's simple, but relatively inflexible. If you are interested in it, see the Supplementary notes for Chapter 17 on this book's CD.

Done!

REVIEW

Having finished this session, you know how to store groups of values in arrays. You found out the ways you can access those values using an index number (mathematically), rather than accessing each value via a separate variable name. You saw how to associate more values to a given index number by adding a second index number — thereby creating a multidimensional array. Then you learned how to get the computer to do a repetitive job, and how to get it to stop. You worked with `For...Next`, and saw how to nest `For...Next` loops. You saw the distinction between putting your comparison test at the start or end of a loop structure. And you learned the difference between `While` and `Until`.

QUIZ YOURSELF

1. How do arrays differ from ordinary variables? (See "Understanding Arrays.")
2. What are the line-break characters in VB and when is this technique useful? (See "Using line breaks.")
3. If you create a two-dimensional array and the first index is (100), can the second index be (2) or does it have to be (100) or larger? (See "Multidimensional arrays.")
4. What does the `Step` command do? (See "Using the Step command.")
5. What's the reason for sometimes putting a comparison test at the end of a loop structure? (See "Working with Do...Loops.")

Making Decisions (Branching)

Session Checklist

✔ Working with `For...Next`

✔ Using `Else` to branch to a second course of action

✔ Understanding the `Select...Case` structure

✔ Exploring various data types

✔ Grasping variable scope

**30 Min.
To Go**

In this session, you'll first see how to help the computer with the important task of making decisions. Then you'll return to the topic of variables, to deepen your understanding of numeric variables, and to learn about the significant idea of variable *scope*.

Making decisions is central to any intelligent behavior. The `If...Then` structure is one of the most important features in any computer language — indeed, in any kind of language.

`If...Then` is the most common way that decisions are made. After the decision is made, actions are taken that are appropriate to the decision. A program is said to *branch* at this point, as if the path it was following splits into more than one trail. The path the program follows is decided here at the `If...Then` junction. For each of the paths, you write code appropriate to that path.

Many times a day you do your own personal branching using a similar structure: If you're hungry, then you eat some breakfast. If it's nice weather, then you don't wear a jacket. If the car windows are fogged up, then you wipe them off. This constant cycle of testing conditions, and making decisions based on those conditions, is what makes human behavior intelligent and adaptive. This same kind of testing is what makes computer behavior intelligent.

You try to make your programs behave intelligently by giving them decision-making rules in the code. You put `If...Then` structures into a program so it reacts appropriately to various kinds of user input, as well as such additional events as incoming data from a disk file, the passage of time, or other conditions.

Understanding If...Then

In previous sessions, you've experimented a little with If...Then. Here's a simple example:

```
Dim response, M As String


Response = InputBox("How many calories did you take in today?")

If CInt(Response) > 2200 Then
    M = "Keep that up and you'll have to buy new pants."
Else
    M = "Good self-control on your part."
End If

MsgBox(M)
```

Note that this example had to use the CInt command to change the data type of the variable Response from a string into an integer.

The line of code starting with If tests to see if something is true. If it is true, then the code on the line or lines following the If are carried out. If the test fails (the test condition is not true), then your program skips the line or lines of code until it gets to an Else, ElseIf, or End If command. Then the program resumes execution. Put another way, the If test determines whether or not some lines of code will be executed.

Notice that if you are making a simple decision (either-or) with only two branches, you can use the Else command. In the previous example, if the user's response is that he or she ate more than 2,200 calories, the first message is displayed. Or, if the opposite happened, the message following the Else command is displayed.

What if you want to branch into more than only two paths? You can use the ElseIf command, but it's fairly clumsy:

```
If X = "Bob" Then
   MsgBox ("Hello Bob")
ElseIf X = "Billy" Then
    MsgBox ("Hello Billy")
ElseIf X = "Ashley"
   MsgBox ("Hello Ashley")
End If
```

In a way, using ElseIf is like using several If...Thens in a row. But for situations in which you want to test multiple conditions, the better solution is to use the Select Case command, as you'll soon see.

 As with loops, it's traditional to provide a visual cue by indenting all lines of code that will be carried out inside the If...Then **structure.**

There is also a simplified, one-line version of If...Then. If your test is simple enough (true or false) and short enough, you can just put the entire If...Then structure all on a single line. In that case, you do not use End If (the If...Then structure is assumed to be completed by the end of the line of code). The computer knows that this is a single-line If...Then because some *additional* code follows the Then command. In a multiline If...Then structure, the Then command is the last word on the line, and the code to carry out should the test pass is on the following line or lines.

```
Dim PassWord, Reply as String
PassWord = "sue"

Reply = InputBox("What is the password?")

If Reply <> PassWord Then MsgBox ("Access Denied"): End

MsgBox "Password verified as correct. Please continue."
```

Notice the colon that appears at the end of the If...Then line. This is a rarely used technique, but you should be aware of it. It's handy for single-line If...Then code, as this example illustrates. You want to do two things should the user-entered password fail the test:

1. Show a message box.
2. End the program.

Normally, the End command would have to be on a line of its own in the code. When you use the colon, VB reads the code that follows it as a *separate* line of code. Recall that you can use the space/underscore characters to break a single, long, logical line of code into two physical lines. (*Logical* here means *what VB acts on*, and *physical* means *what you see onscreen*.) Using a colon is the opposite of the space/underscore. A colon allows you to place two logical lines on the same physical line. (You can even cram more than two logical lines on one physical line: X=X+1:A=B:N="Hi.", for example.)

Remember that the condition you test with If is an expression, so it can involve variables, literals, constants, and any other valid combination of VB language components that can make up an expression. For instance, you can use a function in an expression:

```
If InputBox("Enter your age, but it's optional") <> "" Then
MsgBox "Thank you for responding"
End If
```

The InputBox function is executed, and its result is tested to see if it does not equal (<>) a blank, empty string (""), which would mean that the user failed to type anything into the InputBox.

Some programmers like to use optional parentheses around the comparison test in an If...Then structure. They feel that it makes the line more readable, isolating the test itself from surrounding code:

```
If (Reply <> PassWord) Then MsgBox ("Access Denied"): End
```

To me, though, it's easy enough to see that the test starts with the If command and ends with the Then command.

**20 Min.
To Go**

Multiple Choice: The Select Case Command

If...Then is great for simple, common testing and branching. But if you have more than two branches, If...Then becomes clumsy. Fortunately, there's an alternative decision-making structure in VB that specializes in multiple-branching. Select Case should be used when there are several possible outcomes, several possible alternative pathways for your program to take.

The main distinction between If...Then and Select Case goes something like this:

If CarStatus = burning, *Then* get out of the car.

But the Select Case structure tests many and various situations:

```
Select Case CarStatus
    Case Steaming
        Let radiator cool down.
    Case Wobbling
        Check tires.
    Case Skidding
        Steer into skid.
    Case Burning
        Leave the car.
End Select
```

Select Case works from a list of possible "answers." Your program can respond to each of these answers differently. There can be one, or many, lines of code within each case:

```
Dim Response As String

Response = InputBox("What's your favorite color?")

Select Case Response.ToLower

Case "blue"
    MsgBox "We have three varieties of blue"
Case "red"
    MsgBox "We have six varieties of red"
Case "green"
    MsgBox "We have one variety of green"
Case Else
    MsgBox "We don't have " & Response & ", sorry."
End Select
```

This example illustrates that you can use any expression (variable, literal, function, compound expression, or other kind of expression) in the Select Case line. The example used the ToLower method to reduce whatever the user typed in to all lowercase letters (you would not want the test to fail, simply because the user typed a capital letter). Then VB goes down the list of cases and executes any lines in which the original expression on the first line matches one of the Case lines. Note that the final case is special: The optional Case Else command means that if there were no matches, execute the following code.

Using the Is command

You can use the special Is command with each case to run comparison tests on that case:

```
Dim Response As String

    Response = InputBox("Your weight, please?")

    Select Case CInt(Response)
        Case Is < 200
            '(put one or more commands here)
            MsgBox("Good for you")
        Case Is < 300
            '(put one or more commands here)
            MsgBox("Watch your weight.")
    End Select
```

In this example, if the number is lower than 200, the first block of code executes, and then execution jumps to the line right after End Select. If the number is lower than 300, the second block of code executes (any code between Case Is < 300 and End Select). Note that as soon as one of the cases triggers a match, no further cases are even checked for a match. The Case structure is merely exited.

Using the To command

If you want to check a *range* of data, use the To command. It can be a numeric range (Case 4 To 12) or an alphabetic range (based on the first letter of the string being tested):

```
Dim Response As String
Response = InputBox("Type in the first letter of your last name.")
Select Case Response.ToLower
    Case "a" To "m"
        MsgBox("Please go to the left line.")
    Case "n" To "z"
        MsgBox("Please go to the right line.")
End Select
```

You can also combine several items in a Case, separating them with commas:

```
Case "a" To "l", "gene", NameOfUser
```

This combination is an Or type. It means *display the following message box if the answer begins with a letter between a and l, or if it's gene, or if it matches the value in the variable NameOfUser.*

Now that you understand branching, let's return to an important topic introduced in Session 14: variables.

Understanding Data Types

Text variables (strings) are pretty simple. The string is the only fundamental text data type. You learned all about strings in Session 14. Now it's time to learn more about numeric variables.

There are several fundamental subvarieties of numeric variables. The reason for these different numeric data types is that you can speed up your applications with some of them, and achieve greater precision with others.

In previous versions of VB, there was a default variable type. By default, unless you specifically defined them as something else with `Dim`, VB made all variables the *variant* type. This was convenient because that meant you didn't have to worry about saying: ThisVariable will hold strings, but ThisOtherVariable will hold only whole numbers (no fractions). Instead, you let VB decide which type to use based on the value you assigned to it, or the context in which it was used. For example, if you assigned what was a numeric variable type to a TextBox, the variable type was automatically changed from numeric to string (because a TextBox can only display a string type).

However, the variant type, efficient though it often was, had two fatal flaws from the VB .NET perspective. First, in some cases, VB had a hard time figuring out which type the variant should change to — resulting in an error. Second, the other languages in the .NET universe do not use variants — and the .NET philosophy requires conformity between its various languages (at least on the fundamental issues, such as variable typing). Therefore, the variant variable is no longer part of the VB language. It has been banished in VB .NET.

Here's an example that shows how variants achieved their chameleon changes:

```
A = 12
B = 12.4
```

When it assigns the 12 to A, VB figures that 12 can be an integer type, but when it assigns 12.4 to B, VB knows that this number has to be the floating-point (decimal) type because it is a fraction. So VB types the variables for you. It can even convert some kinds of data:

```
A = "12"
B = 14
B = B + A
MsgBox (B)
```

You get the correct mathematical answer of 26 because when you assigned 14 to B, it became an integer variable type, and then you assigned a string to it, which converted the string into an integer. However, don't take this too far. It's best not to mix types if you can avoid it.

The interpreting that VB must do when it works with variants was said to slow program execution down some, though I never noticed it. The simplest variable type is Boolean. It can only hold two states: True and False (it defaults to False). Use this when you want a toggle variable (something that switches off and on like a light switch). To create a Boolean variable, use the following code:

```
Dim MyToggle As Boolean
```

Another simple data type is the Integer and its larger sister, the Long type. Before VB .NET, the Integer data type was 16-bits large and the Long data type was 32-bits large. Now these types are twice as big: Integer is 32-bits large and Long is 64-bits large (it's an Integer too, no fraction, no decimal point). If your program needs to use a 16-bit integer, use the new type *Short*.

So if you're translating pre-.NET VB code, you need to change any As Integer or Cint commands to As Short and Cshort, respectively. Similarly, As Long and CLng now must be changed to As Integer and Cint.

You'd be surprised at how often the only thing you need is an integer. In most programming, the Integer is the most common numeric data type. No fractions are allowed. If your non-fractional number is larger or smaller than an integer can hold, make it a long data type.

```
Dim MyLittleNumber As Integer
Dim MyBigNumber As Long
```

The other major numeric type is called *floating point*. It has similar small and large versions called Single and Double, respectively. It's used when a number involves a fraction:

```
Dim MyFraction As Single, MyBiggerNumber As Double
```

Here are some other changes to data types. In VB .NET there is a new Char type, which is an unsigned 16-bit type that is used to store Unicode characters. The new Decimal type is a 96-bit signed integer scaled by a variable power of 10.

Scope: The Range of Influence

**10 Min.
To Go**

So far, we've been using variables inside procedures. When you declare a variable inside a procedure, the variable only works within that procedure. When the program executes the procedure (or event), the variable comes to life, does its thing, but then dies (disappears) as soon as the End Sub line is executed.

Variables that live only within a single procedure are called *local variables*. Local variables have two qualities that you should understand:

- No programming outside their own procedure can interact with them, either to read their value or to change their value. Their "scope" is limited to their own procedure.

- When VB finishes executing the procedure in which they reside, their value evaporates. If that procedure is executed a second time, whatever value the local variable once contained is no longer there. One execution of the procedure is their "lifetime." There are some situations in which you do want a local variable's value to be preserved. Recall that in those cases, you use the Static command rather than the Dim command:

```
Private Sub Form1_Load(ByVal sender As System.Object, ByVal e As
System.EventArgs) Handles MyBase.Load

    Dim n As Integer
    Static x As Integer
End Sub
```

In this example, the variable n loses its value when the End Sub is executed. However, the variable x retains its value until the program is shut down. Another way of putting it is: When you use the Static command with a local variable, the value of that variable is preserved for the lifetime of your application. (*Lifetime* means how long something is in existence in a program.)

What do you think would happen if you clicked Command1, and then clicked Command2, in this next program?

```
    Private Sub Button1_Click(ByVal sender As System.Object, ByVal e As
System.EventArgs) Handles Button1.Click
        Dim X As Integer
        X = 12
        X = X + 5
    End Sub

    Private Sub Button2_Click(ByVal sender As System.Object, ByVal e As
System.EventArgs) Handles Button2.Click
        Dim X As Integer
        MsgBox(X)
    End Sub
```

The message box would display nothing. The variable X in Command1's Click event is a completely different variable from the X in Command2's Click event. They are *local* and simply have no relationship to each other — any more than two strangers named Mike who happen to live in the Bronx and never meet.

But what if you want both of these procedures to be able to access and manipulate the same variable? To do this, move your insertion cursor to near the top of the Public Class code. Insert your Dim in this location:

```
Public Class Form1
    Inherits System.Windows.Forms.Form
    Dim x As Integer
```

That's where you want to put any variables that you want to give *form-wide* scope — in other words, to permit all the procedures in that form (Form1 in this case) to be able to read, and modify, the variable. (The area where you put form-wide variables used to be called the General Declarations area, pre VB .NET.)

Now, with that *X* variable Dimmed up there above (outside) all the Subs and other procedures, when you run the same program, click Command1, and then click Command2, you will see the result you want to see: the number 17. By declaring X to be form-wide in scope, the two Buttons share the *same* variable name. (You'll have to remove the two Dim statements that previously declared *X* within those two Button events.)

When a variable has form-wide scope, it's then available to all of the procedures in that form. It's not available, however, to the procedures in any *other* forms (or *classes* as forms are technically called) in the project.

What if you want to make a variable available to *all* of the procedures in *all* of your forms in a given project? In such a case, you have to use the Public command rather than Dim. What's more, you have to put this Public declaration into a *standard module*.

Variables declared Public in a standard module are visible from anywhere in your project. (Note that variables declared Public in a *class module* can also be accessed anywhere, but you must first declare an object variable in the calling code that references the class.)

A module is similar to a form, but it doesn't have a user interface. It is never made visible to the user. It also contains no events. It's just a code window — a location where you put public declarations (program-wide in scope), or a place to put program-wide scoped procedures. Some programmers put all the subs or functions they write into modules. That way they are available to the entire program.

To add a module to your program, choose Project|Add Module. The Add Module dialog box opens. Double-click the Module icon and a new module (named Module1) appears in your Solution Explorer window. You also see the module's code window.

Both form-wide and program-wide variables are preserved for the lifetime of your application. They never lose their values.

It's considered good programming practice to try to avoid using Public variables. Variables with that much scope make your programming harder to debug. Looking at the status of variables is one of the primary ways to find out where a problem is located in a program. If you use a local variable, any problem involving that variable can be found in its procedure. That really narrows your search for a bug. By contrast, you have more code — probably much more code — to search and analyze if there's a bug involving a form-wide (or worse, project-wide) variable.

You may have noticed that procedures also have scope. By default, VB makes some events Private (`Private Sub Button1_Click`) and others Public. If you don't want to permit code outside your current form to access a procedure, declare it (or leave it defaulting) as `Private`. If you do want to permit outside code access, declare the procedure as `Public`.

Private events can be triggered only from within the form (or module or class) in which they reside. However, you can change the default `Private` to `Public Sub Button1_Click`. When thus made `Public`, you can trigger the procedure from another form (module or class). Here's how to trigger an event or other Public procedure from code in Form1:

```
Private Sub Form1_Load(ByVal sender As System.Object, ByVal e As
System.EventArgs) Handles MyBase.Load

      Dim frm As New Form2()

      frm.Button1_Click(Me, e)

   End Sub
```

It's uncommon to trigger an *event* from within another procedure (generally the user triggers events). I've never heard of anyone wanting to trigger one form's events from another form, but you never know.

Also, remember that you must change the button event in Form2 from the default `Private` to `Public`, otherwise this `Click` event cannot be triggered from code outside Form2:

```
Public Sub Button1_Click(ByVal sender As System.Object, ByVal e As
System.EventArgs) Handles Button1.Click
        MsgBox("Me clicked")
    End Sub
```

There used to be six commands in VB that define scope: Public, Private, Dim, ReDim, Friend, and Static. We've discussed all but the ReDim and Friend commands. ReDim is not often used, and it works only with arrays. So we'll postpone discussing it until Session 17. Friend access is similar to Public, but only code within its project (or application) can access a variable or procedure declared with Friend. This means that another, separate application cannot access a Friend. (Separate applications *can* make use of Public variables or procedures.)

VB .NET adds these nine additional procedure declaration commands related to scope: Overloads, Overrides, Overridable, NotOverridable, MustOverride, Shadows, Shared, Protected and Protected Friend. The majority of these commands involve "inheritance" (see Session 30). If you want to try inheritance, please look up their syntax and behavior in VB help.

Done!

REVIEW

This session is all about how to write code that makes choices during runtime, how to effectively work with numeric variables, and how to understand scope. You saw how to use an If...Then statement to evaluate an expression and to take one of two courses of action based on that evaluation. It's possible to extend If...Then to take more than two branches with a series of ElseIf commands, but that quickly becomes awkward. So it's better, as you saw, to use the Select Case statement for situations in which you want to offer multiple branches.

QUIZ YOURSELF

1. What is the purpose of the Else command? (See "Understanding If...Then.")
2. If you put a colon (:) in a line of code, what does it do? (See "Understanding If...Then.")
3. When using Select Case, is there a command that executes code if no match is found? (See "Multiple Choice: The Select Case Command.")
4. What is the most common numeric variable type in ordinary programming? (See "Understanding Data Types".)
5. Explain the concept of *scope*. (See "Scope: The Range of Influence.")

Using Timers and Object Collections

Session Checklist

✔ Understanding what Timer controls do

✔ Gang-programming with object collections

✔ Changing colors

✔ Reducing redundancy using the With...End With structure

**30 Min.
To Go**

There are three cool features in VB that you'll want to know about: Timers, object collections, and the With...End With structure. In this session, you'll get to experiment with each of them.

The Timer component has several uses: It can make things happen at intervals (for instance, animation), remind people that it's time to do something, measure the passage of time, cause a delay, and several time-related tricks. It's versatile.

The second cool feature discussed in this session is the object collection. Object collections are useful in somewhat the same way that arrays are: A group of components is given the same name, but a different index number. You can therefore manipulate the components using math to access their index numbers. In this session, you'll see how this works, and also how to bring components into existence during runtime.

You use the third cool feature, With...End With, to avoid unnecessary redundancy when changing several properties for the same component.

But let's start with the Timer component; it's one of the standard, classic components that is always on the VB Toolbox.

Getting a Grip on Timers

A Timer component is a sophisticated clock. It is accurate to a millisecond — 1/1,000th of a second. To specify a delay of two seconds, set a Timer's Interval property to 2000, like this:

```
Timer1.Interval = 2000
```

Once started, a Timer works independently and constantly. No matter what else might be happening in your Visual Basic program — or indeed, in Windows itself — your Timer keeps ticking away.

A Timer's `Interval` property specifies a duration. The `Interval` determines how long the Timer waits before it executes any code you've put into the Timer's event. In other words, when a Timer's event is triggered, nothing happens — none of the code in that event is executed — until the `Interval` is finished counting down to zero. This is the same way that a kitchen timer works: You twist it around to define an interval, but nothing happens until the interval passes and only *then* does the bell go off.

How Timers differ from other components

The Timer's `Tick` event (which used to be confusingly called the "timer" event) is quite different from the other events in VB. For one thing, the code within all other events in VB is executed as soon as the event is triggered. The `Button1_Click` event is triggered the very moment the user clicks that Button, for example.

But a Timer's event is different: When its event is triggered, it looks at its `Interval` property, and then it *waits* until that interval of time has passed before it carries out any instructions you've put into its event. After all, that's the purpose of a Timer: to time things. Its whole reason for being is to be able to delay carrying out the code in its event.

I keep saying *its event*, as if the Timer has only one event. And, in fact, it does have only two events! This is another way that Timers are different from other components you're used to. Most components have many events; for example, a VB .NET Button has 58 events. (The Button used to have 36 events in VB version 6. Increased freedom of choice for the programmer, or inflation? You be the judge.)

As useful as they are, Timers are a little confusing when you first start to work with them. They're unlike other components in several ways. Here is a summary of the ways in which a Timer is a unique component:

- Most controls have more than a dozen properties; Timers have only four.
- Most controls have at least ten events they can respond to; Timers have only two.
- Most controls are visible and can be accessed and triggered by the user of the program; Timers work in the background, independent of the user. They are invisible when a program runs.
- Most controls' events are triggered instantly; Timers don't carry out the instructions you've put into their event until their `Interval` (the duration) passes.
- Most controls' events are only triggered once; Timers will *repeatedly* trigger their event until you either set their `Interval` property to 0 or their `Enabled` property to `False`.

Think of a kitchen timer

As I pointed out, it's best to think of a Timer as one of those kitchen timers that you wind to, say, ten minutes, and then it starts ticking. Ten minutes later, it goes BING! The BING is whatever code you have put into the Sub `Timer1_Tick ()` event. The ten minutes is the value in the Timer's `Interval` property, the amount of time that you set the Timer to. For a Timer to be active, its `Enabled` property must be `True`. The `Interval` property defaults to 100, but the `Enabled` property defaults to `False`. Therefore, to get a Timer going, you'll want to change the `Interval` to whatever delay you need, and also change the `Enabled` property to `True`.

There's just one way that this kitchen timer analogy breaks down. Unlike a kitchen timer, a VB Timer resets itself after going BING. Then it starts counting down from ten again (or whatever `Interval` it's set to). After ten more minutes pass — BING! Reset. Count down. BING! And on and on.

This resetting and countdown repetition will continue forever unless the program stops, or somewhere in your code you deliberately turn off the Timer by setting the `Interval` to 0 or the `Enabled` property to `False`. If you need the Timer again, put some number other than 0 in the `Interval` (and if necessary, set `Timer1.Enabled = True`). The recommended practice is to turn timers on and off by adjusting their Enabled property, and adjusting the Interval property only if you need to change it for some other programming reason.

**20 Min.
To Go**

The theory of Timers

What can Timers do for you? When you put a Timer onto one of your forms, you can make it repeatedly interrupt whatever else might be going on in the computer — even if the user is doing something outside your VB program, like working within another application. You can make a Timer do pretty much anything you want that involves duration, timing, clock effects, delay, or repetition by using the `Interval` and `Enabled` properties in various ways.

Once turned on, a Timer becomes an automaton, a relentless robotic agent that's loose in Windows. It has its instructions, and it knows how often you want the job repeated. Try it out:

1. Start a new VB project and double-click the Timer icon on the Toolbox (it looks like a stopwatch, and you'll have to scroll the ToolBox to find it). The Timer will go into the special tray at the bottom of the Design window. The icon — in fact that entire tray — turns invisible at runtime. Also add a Label to your form.

2. Click the Timer icon to select it.

3. Press F4 to display the Properties window.

4. Change the Timer's `Enabled` property to `True` and its `Interval` property to 1000 (1,000 milliseconds, or 1 second).

5. Double-click the Timer to get to the code window, and in the Timer's `Tick` event, type this:

   ```
   Public Sub Timer1_Tick(ByVal sender As Object, ByVal e As
   System.EventArgs) Handles Timer1.Tick

       Label1.Text = CStr(TimeOfDay)


   End Sub
   ```

6. Press F5 and now you see a digital clock that changes every second, as shown in Figure 19-1.

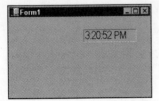

Figure 19-1 *You can create a digital clock with only one little line of code.*

Turning a Timer off

To turn off a Timer, just set its `Enabled` property to `False`.

You cannot use the Tick event to hold the code that turns the Timer on (that sets its `Enabled` property to `True`). For one thing, the Tick event will *never execute* unless the `Enabled` property is set to `True` in the Properties window, or during program execution, such as in a `Button1_Click` event.

Setting longer intervals

A Timer's `Interval` property can range from 0 to 2,147,483,647 milliseconds. (The Interval is an Integer data type, *Int32*, which can hold a number plus or minus 2,147,483,647.)

In practical terms, this means that you can set the `Interval` to anything between 1 millisecond up to 35,791 minutes (which is 596 hours, or almost ten days).

This amount of time should do for most applications. However, there are always exceptions. Perhaps you want to cook Chinese 1,000-year-eggs, a real delicacy if you like unrefrigerated eggs buried in clay. The whites become amber-colored and take on a firm, yet gelatinous texture, but the real treat is the yolks, which turn a lovely army-blanket green and give off a head-spinning cheesy aroma. Surprise your guests with these treats as breakfast *hors d'oeuvres*. It's a good thing!

You can easily extend the amount of time that a Timer will delay beyond ten days if you wish. You can make it wait until next Labor Day if that's what you want. Or even 1,000 years.

One way to measure time in longer intervals than the ten-day limit of a Timer's `Interval` property is to use a `Static` variable within the `Tick` event, and increment it (raise it) by 1 each time the `Tick` event is triggered.

Recall that a Timer keeps going off, repeatedly triggering its `Tick` event, until it's turned off (with `Timer1.Enabled = False`). To illustrate how this technique works, we'll create an interval of two hours: First set a Timer's `Interval` property to 60000 (one minute) in the Properties window, and then enter the following code:

```
Public Sub Timer1_Tick(ByVal sender As Object, ByVal e As
System.EventArgs) Handles Timer1.Tick
Static Counter As Integer
Dim Counter As Integer
Counter = Counter + 1

If Counter >= 120 Then
   MsgBox ("TIME'S UP!")
```

```
        Timer1.Enabled = False
End If

End Sub
```

Of course, because the Timer can hold an interval up to ten days, you could just multiply 60,000 (the number of milliseconds in one minute) by the number of minutes you require (120 for a delay of two hours): 120 x 60,000 = 7,200,000. Then just set the Interval property to 7,200,000 and you need not bother with a Static Counter.

Setting a specific future time

In personal information managers (PIMs) and other reminder programs, the idea is that you specify a specific date or time when you want a message to be displayed. Instead of saying, *delay 10 minutes*, you say, *show the message at 4:00 PM*. Or *next Tuesday*.

The job of the Timer in this example is to take a look at the computer's clock at regular intervals, independently of what the user might be doing or what else is going on in Windows. When the specified time is matched (or exceeded), the Timer will remind us to feed the puppies or whatever.

To make a Timer remind us to do something in the future, just set the Interval to 60000 in the Form_Load event, and also set its Enabled property to True. This way, the Timer "goes off" every minute (60,000 milliseconds = 1 minute). Note that the Enabled property is off by default — so you must set it to True. Here's the code:

```
Private Sub Form1_Load(ByVal sender As System.Object, ByVal e As
System.EventArgs) Handles MyBase.Load

        Timer1.Interval = 60000
        Timer1.Enabled = True


    End Sub
```

Next, you put code into the Tick event that sees if the built-in Time function is equal to or greater than the specified time:

```
    Private Sub Timer1_Tick(ByVal sender As System.Object, ByVal e As
System.EventArgs) Handles Timer1.Tick

    Dim SpecifiedTime As Date

    SpecifiedTime = TimeValue("4:21:00 PM")

    If TimeOfDay >= SpecifiedTime Then
        MsgBox("It's time to feed the pups.")
        Timer1.Enabled = False
    End If


    End Sub
```

This example uses the `TimeValue` function to provide a value that VB can compare to the `TimeOfDay` function. Use the greater-than or equal operator (>=) in these situations rather than equals (=);otherwise, your code might skip right over the comparison value. In other words, the time might be checked at 8:43:33 and again a minute later at 8:44:33 and, therefore, would never equal 8:44:00. Seconds are required in both the `TimeOfDay` and `TimeValue` functions — so they do matter.

**10 Min.
To Go**

Suggested uses for the Timer

As the previous examples have illustrated, a Timer can do various jobs for a programmer. Here is a summary of the main ways in which you can employ a Timer:

- It can act like a traditional kitchen timer — counting down from a preset time and then ringing a bell (or doing whatever you want) after the preset interval has elapsed.

- It can cause a delay so that, for example, your program displays a message in a small window (a form), but the user doesn't have to click any buttons to make the window go away. Instead, the form appears onscreen for maybe four seconds and then disappears automatically.

- It can cause events to repeat at prescribed intervals, like a digital clock changing its readout every second. Or it can save the user's work to a disk file every ten or twenty minutes or whatever backup interval the user selected in an Options menu in your program. Another use for this repetition is to animate something, as discussed at the end of this session.

- It can repeatedly check the computer's built-in battery-powered clock to see if it is time to do something. In this way, you can build reminder programs that display a message or take some other action based on a predefined time or date. The Timer looks at the computer's clock at regular intervals, independent of what the user might be doing or what is going on in Windows.

- It can measure the passage of time, acting like a stopwatch and reporting how long it took for something to finish what it was doing.

Manipulating Object Collections

Control arrays have been removed from the language in VB .NET. If you don't know what a control array is, don't worry — it's gone now anyway.

However, in VB .NET you can still do what control arrays did. You can instantiate controls during runtime, and they can share events. (Even different *types* of controls can share events.)

Here's an example showing how you can add new controls to a form while a program is running. Assume that the user clicked a button asking to search for some information. You then create and display a TextBox for the user to enter the search criteria, and you also put a label above it describing the TextBox's purpose:

```
Public Class Form1

    Inherits System.Windows.Forms.Form
```

```
Dim WithEvents btnSearch As New Button()


Private Sub Button1_Click(ByVal sender As System.Object, ByVal e As
System.EventArgs) Handles Button1.Click

    Dim textBox1 As New TextBox()
    Dim label1 As New Label()



    ' specify some properties:
    label1.Text = "Enter your search term here..."
    label1.Location = New Point(50, 55) 'left/top
    label1.Size = New Size(125, 20) ' width/height
    label1.AutoSize = True
    label1.Name = "lable1"

    textBox1.Text = ""
    textBox1.Location = New Point(50, 70)
    textBox1.Size = New Size(125, 20)
    textBox1.Name = "TextBox1"

    btnSearch.Text = "Start Searching"
    btnSearch.Location = New Point(50, 95)
    btnSearch.Size = New Size(125, 20)
    btnSearch.Name = "btnSearch"


    ' Add them to the form's controls collection.
    Controls.Add(textBox1)
    Controls.Add(label1)
    Controls.Add(btnSearch)


'display all the current controls

    Dim i As Integer, n As Integer
    Dim s As String
    n = Controls.Count


    For i = 0 To n - 1

        s = Controls(i).Name

        Debug.Write(s)

        Debug.WriteLine("")
```

Continued

```
        Next


    End Sub



Private Sub btnSearch_Click(ByVal sender As System.Object, ByVal e As
System.EventArgs) Handles btnSearch.Click

        MsgBox("clicked")

    End Sub


  End Class
```

When adding new controls at design time, you'll want to at least specify their names, sizes, and positions on the form. Then, use the Add method to include these new controls in the form's controls collection. There is also a Remove method, should you need it.

Here's how to go through the current set of controls on a form and change them all at once. In this example, you'll turn them all red:

```
        n = Controls.Count

        For i = 0 To n - 1
            Controls(i).BackColor = Color.Red
        Next
```

Remember that one of the benefits of an array (and a collection is a kind of array) is that you can use a loop to read or write to the entire array.

Of course, a control without any events is often useless. To add events to runtime-created controls, you must add two separate pieces of code. First, up at the top (outside any procedure, because this declaration cannot be *local*), you must define the control as having events by using the WithEvents command, like this:

```
Dim WithEvents btnSearch As New Button()
```

Then, in the location where you want to provide the code that responds to an event, type this in:

```
Private Sub btnSearch_Click(ByVal sender As System.Object, ByVal e As
System.EventArgs) Handles btnSearch.Click

        MsgBox("clicked")

    End Sub
```

This event code is indistinguishable from any other "normal" event in the code.

 VB .NET will create the event in the code window for you, if you wish. The btnSearch doesn't show up in the design window, so you cannot double-click it there to force VB .NET to create a Click event for it. However, you can use the drop-down lists. Once you have declared a control WithEvents (Dim WithEvents btnSearch As New Button()), drop the list in the top left of the code window, and locate btnSearch. Click it to select it. Then drop the list in the top right, and double-click the event you want VB .NET to create for you in the code window.

Typically, all the controls in a control collection use a *single* event. You can make them share an event by using multiple Handles code phrases, like this:

```
Private Sub cmd_Click(ByVal sender As System.Object, ByVal e As
System.EventArgs) Handles cmdOK.Click, cmdApply.Click, cmdCancel.Click

        Select Case sender.Name
```

For additional details on how to use this technique, see Appendix C on this book's CD.

Using With...End With

The With...End With feature can simplify your programming. Use it to avoid having to repeat a component's name over and over if you're adjusting it in several ways at once. With...End With can also be used with other objects (such as forms or objects you create, as is described in Session 30).

Suppose you want to change four properties of a TextBox. You can type the six changes in, like this:

```
TextBox1.Text = ""
TextBox1.Left = 12
TextBox1.Top = 100
TextBox1.Width = TextBox2.Width
```

Or, you can use the With...End With structure, like this, to save some typing:

```
With TextBox1

    .Text = ""
    .Left = 12
    .Top = 100
    .Width = TextBox2.Width

End With
```

Done!

REVIEW

This session exposed you to what I think are two of the more interesting features in VB: the Timer and the object collection. You saw all of the ways that Timers can be used, and how to use them for any length of interval you need. Then you explored object collections—learning to group components or other objects into an array, or to create new members of the array during runtime. Finally, you saw how to simplify code when assigning values to multiple properties of the same component by using the With...End With structure.

QUIZ YOURSELF

1. Name two ways that a Timer is unlike any other component. (See "How Timers differ from other components.")

2. How do you turn off a Timer? (See "Turning a Timer off.")

3. How many minutes can you set the Interval property to? (See "Setting longer intervals.")

4. What programming do you use to create components dynamically during runtime? (See "Manipulating Object Collections.")

5. What shortcut can be used to change several properties of an object all at once? (See "Using With...End With.")

Tracking Down Bugs (and Smashing Them Dead)

Session Checklist

✔ Fixing typos and bad punctuation

✔ Trapping runtime bugs

✔ Locating logic bugs

✔ Using alternative debugging tools

**30 Min.
To Go**

Bugs — errors in a computer program — are inevitable. You can be enormously painstaking, tidy, and thoughtful, but if your program is more than 50 lines long, errors are likely to occur. If it's longer than 100 lines, errors are virtually certain.

Errors in computer programming fall into two primary categories:

- Typos
- Logic errors

This session deals with each in turn, starting with the easiest. Logic errors are the toughest.

Fortunately, Visual Basic provides a powerful suite of tools to help you track down and eliminate bugs — VB programmers have been the envy of programmers using other languages. However, with Visual Studio .NET, all supported languages now share the same editor (*IDE* or *Integrated Design Environment*) and, therefore, the other languages have finally caught up.

The purpose of this chapter is to provide an overview of the various types of errors that occur in computer programming, and how to deal with them. One particular kind of error — runtime bugs — is best delt with using VB .NET's new structured error handling code (`Try...End Try`) which replaces traditional VB's `On Error Resume Next`. However, `Try...End Try` is a bit too complicated to fit into a 30-minute session, so I explain it in depth in Appendix C as well as in the Supplementary Notes (both are on this book's CD).

Wiping Out Typos

Typos are the easiest errors to locate and deal with. Visual Basic knows at once that you've mistakenly typed **Prjnt** instead of **Print**. If it doesn't recognize the word, it can detect that kind of error and will alert you.

When you give VB impossible commands like that, VB realizes that it cannot do anything with that line of code, because some of the words are not in the language's vocabulary.

Or perhaps you didn't mistype; you merely mistakenly thought VB knew a command that it doesn't know. For example, suppose you type in the command **Pass the Salt**, like this:

```
Private Sub Button1_Click(ByVal sender As System.Object, ByVal e As
System.EventArgs) Handles Button1.Click

     Pass the Salt

  End Sub
```

As soon as you press the Enter key after typing **Salt**, that line of code is underlined. In this way, VB immediately alerts you that it cannot understand what you've typed — that something's wrong with the line of code.

Also, VB displays its best guess as to the nature of the problem in the Task List window, as you can see in Figure 20-1.

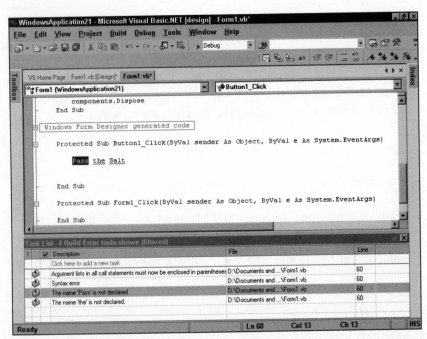

Figure 20-1 *Problem code is underlined, and descriptions of the problems are listed in the Task List window.*

Punctuation counts, too

If you press F5 to run the code, VB displays a message box informing you that there were build errors, and asking if you want to continue trying to run the project.

VB expects to see a command at the start of that line, and `Pass` is not part of the list of commands that VB understands. VB also expects correct punctuation, so `Form1..BackColor = Blue` would trigger a syntax error. There's no double-period punctuation in VB's little book of correct punctuation.

Related to typos are errors you make when you don't provide the right type of information, or enough information, for VB to carry out a command:

```
Button1.Top
```

This information is incomplete; you've given only the name of a control and one of its properties — but you haven't provided information about the location, in this case. That's as incomplete as a "sentence" such as: *Mary's Hair.*

A third variety of easily detected, easily fixed error is an inconsistency of some kind between parts of your program. Suppose you have a procedure that expects three arguments:

```
Sub Transf(ByVal a As String, ByVal b As String, ByVal c As String)

End Sub
```

And you try to call it, but give only two arguments:

```
Dim a, b As String

    Transf(a, b)
```

VB will catch the error right away. It will display this message in the Task List window: `No argument specified for non-optional parameter "c"` etc.

> **If you have the Auto List Members option selected in Tools ➪ Options ➪ Text Editor ➪ All Languages, VB will display the argument list for any procedure you're trying to call. This happens as soon as you type the left parenthesis, (, following the procedure's name.**

Keep your finger near F1

If the explanation that VB provides in the Task List error message isn't sufficient to point you to the problem, press F1. VB's Help feature will pop up and give you the possible reasons for this kind of error in greater detail.

**20 Min.
To Go**

Handling Runtime Errors

Some errors occur only during runtime. Your code is valid code, but something unexpected happens when the program is running. This is often a problem related to contacting a peripheral, such as a hard drive. For example, suppose the user has no diskette in Drive A and your program executes this code:

```
Open(5, "A:\Test.Txt", OpenMode.Input)
```

In this case, the error message shown in Figure 20-2 will be displayed.

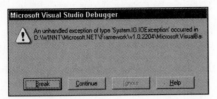

Figure 20-2 *A run-time error message gives you four choices: Break, Continue, Ignore, or Help.*

You need to prevent, or at least gracefully handle, runtime errors. It's no good having a smoothly running program that suddenly halts if the user has, say, forgotten to put a disk into Drive A, or failed to close the drive door.

How runtime errors occur

Runtime errors include those unexpected situations that can come up when the program is running. There are a number of things you cannot know in advance (while you're writing the program) about the user's system. For example, how large is the disk drive? Is it already so full that when your program tries to save a file, there won't be enough room? Are you creating an array so large that it exceeds the computer's available memory? Is the printer turned off, but the user tries to print anyway?

Whenever your program is attempting to interact with an entity outside the program — the user's input, disk drives, Clipboard, RAM — you need to take precautions by using the `Try...End Try` structure. This structure enables your program to deal effectively with the unexpected while it runs.

Unfortunately, your program cannot correct many runtime errors. For instance, you can only let the user know that his or her disk drive is nearly full. The user will have to remedy this kind of problem; you cannot fix it with your code.

Using Try...End Try

The `Try...End Try` runtime error-trapping structure is new in VB .NET. Explaining it is beyond the scope of this session, but it is a valuable and important topic, so I do urge you to take the time to learn how to use it. See Appendix C and the Supplementary Notes to Session 20 on this book's CD.

Tracking Down Logic Errors

The third major category of programming bugs — logic errors — is usually the most difficult of all to find and fix. Some can be so sinister, so well concealed, that you think you will be driven mad trying to find the source of the problem within your code. VB devotes most of its debugging features and resources to assisting you in locating logic errors.

A logic error occurs even though you have followed all of the rules of syntax, made no typos, and otherwise satisfied Visual Basic so that your commands can be carried out. You and VB think everything is shipshape. However, when you run the program, things go wrong: Say, the entire screen turns black, or every time the user enters **$10**, your program changes it into $1,000.

VB .NET's set of debugging tools help you track down the problem. The key to fixing logic errors is finding out *where* in your program the problem is located. Which line of code (or multiple lines interacting) causes the problem?

Some computer languages have an elaborate debugging apparatus, sometimes even including the use of two computer monitors — one shows the program as the user sees it, the other shows the lines of programming that match the running program. Using two computers is a good approach because, when you are debugging logic errors, you often want to see the code that's currently causing the effects in the application.

It's not that you don't notice the symptoms: Every time the user enters a number, the results are way, way off. You know that somewhere your program is mangling the numbers — but until you X-ray the program, you often can't find out where the problem is located.

The watchful voyeur technique

Many logic errors are best tracked down by watching the contents of a variable (or variables). Something is going wrong somewhere, and you want to keep an eye on a variable to find out just where its value changes and goes bad.

Three of VB's best debugging tools help you keep an eye on the status of the variables. You'll take a look at them in the following examples. First, type in a simple program, like this:

```
Private Sub Button1_Click(ByVal sender As System.Object, ByVal e As
System.EventArgs) Handles Button1.Click

        Dim a As Double, b As Double

        a = 112

        b = a / 2

        b = b + 6

End Sub
```

Now press F8 once to take your first step into the program. After (*it must be after*) you've pressed F8 to take that first step, make two of the debugging windows visible: Choose Debug ⇨ Windows, and then select the Locals, Watch, and Immediate windows. (Recall that each time you press F8 to execute the next line of code, the program again goes into Break mode. On the Debug menu, the single-stepping feature is called Step Into.)

The Watch and Locals windows share the same space, and you can switch between them by clicking the tabs on the bottom of their shared window.

For now, press F8 about 20 times until the Form is displayed, and then click the Button control on that form. Then press F8 enough times to get past the lines in your code that assign values to your variables.

Now look at the Locals window. It displays the contents of all variables that have been declared within the currently executing procedure. Watch the variables in the Locals window change as you press F8 to execute each line in this example code, as shown in Figure 20-3.

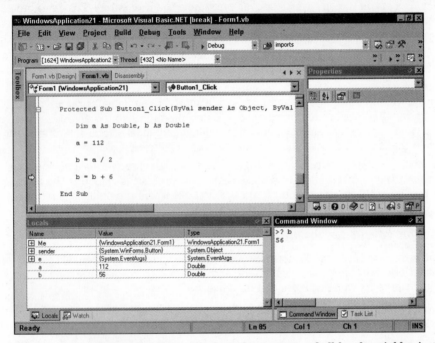

Figure 20-3 *The Locals window displays the contents of all local variables in the currently executing procedure.*

Also take a look at the Immediate window. In this window, you can directly query or modify variables, or expressions. To find out the value in variable b, for instance, just type the following into the Immediate window, and then press Enter:

```
? b
```

The answer — whatever value b currently holds — will be printed in the Immediate window. (The ? command is shorthand for the Print command.)

If you want to experiment and actually change the value in a variable during break mode, delete the number in the *value* column in the Locals or Watch windows, and then type in your new value.

You can also launch and test procedures (events, subs, or functions) by typing their names and pressing the Enter key. VB will execute the procedure and then halt again. This is a good way to feed variables to a suspect procedure and watch it (and it alone) absorb those variables to see if things are going awry within that procedure.

Using Debug.Write

Recall from Session 17 that some programmers like to insert Debug.Print commands at different locations within their code (I don't). This also has the effect of displaying the contents of the variable B in the Output window. But in this case, you're causing the values in the variables that you choose to Debug.Write to be displayed via code within your program. Try inserting some Debug.Write (MyVariableName) lines here and there in a VB program, and then run the program and watch the results appear in the Output window.

Actually, you can type any executable commands that can be expressed on a single line into the Immediate window to watch their effects. This is all done while the VB program is halted during a run — you can test conditions from within the living program while it's in Break (pause) mode. You can get into Break mode several ways: by inserting a Stop command into your code, by setting a breakpoint (discussed later in this session) in the code, by single-stepping (F8), by choosing Break from the Run menu (or the Toolbar), or by pressing Ctrl+Break.

The Add Watch technique

The Locals window is fine for local variables, but what about form-wide, or project-wide variables? They don't show up in the Locals window. To watch one of these other kinds of variables, put your program in break mode, then right-click the variable you're interested in, and choose Add Watch from the context menu. You can alternatively select and then drag a variable from the code window and drop it into the Watch window.

Also, while you're in break mode you can simply pause your mouse pointer on top of a variable to see its contents in a small box.

When you add a watch, VB keeps an eye on whatever expression (or expressions) you have asked it to watch. You can watch a single variable, an expression, a property, or a procedure call. The Watch window shows the current status of any watched expressions.

In previous versions of VB, the Watch window permitted some highly useful debugging techniques: conditionally halting the program (throwing it into break mode so you could examine variable values, see where the break occurred, and examine surrounding conditions). You could break when a condition became true (such as the variable I holding a value, say, larger than 44: I > 44) and other tests. This ability to break conditionally is now, in VB .NET, part of the Breakpoint debugging feature, discussed in the next section.

Setting breakpoints

Sometimes you have a strong suspicion about which form or module contains an error. Or you might even think you know the procedure where the error can be found. So instead of single-stepping through the entire code, you want to press F5 to execute the program at normal speed, but then stop when execution enters the dubious form or procedure. After halting the program in a suspect region, you can slow down and press F8 to single-step.

Breakpoints can be one of the most useful debugging aids. As you know, you can press Ctrl+Break and stop a running program in its tracks. But what if it's moving too fast to stop just where you want to look and check on things? What if it's alphabetizing a large list, for example, and you can't see what's happening? What if you want to specify a condition (n = 1445, for example) that triggers a break?

You can specify one or more breakpoints in your program. While running, the program will stop at a breakpoint just as if you had pressed Ctrl+Break (or if you've made the breakpoint conditional, it will break when that condition occurs).

When the IDE enters break mode, the code window pops up, showing you where the break occurred, so you can see or change the code, or single-step, or look at the Watch window or Command window to see the values in variables. (In the Command window you can type ? i and press Enter to see the current contents of the variable i.)

You set a breakpoint by clicking the gray margin to the left of the line in the code window where you want the break. A red dot appears in the gray margin. The red dot alerts you that a line of code is a breakpoint. Execution will halt on this line (or perhaps not if the breakpoint is conditional), and VB .NET will enter break mode. Click the red dot a second time to turn it off.

You can set as many breakpoints as you wish.

Another use for breakpoints is when you suspect that the program is *not* running some lines of code. Sometimes a logic error is caused because you think a subroutine, function, or event is getting executed, but, in fact, the program never reaches that procedure. Whatever condition is supposed to activate that area of the program never occurs.

To find out if, as you suspect, a particular event is never executing, set a breakpoint on the first line of code within that procedure. Then, when you run your program — and the breakpoint never halts execution — you have proven that this procedure is never called.

Sometimes you set several breakpoints here and there in your code, but then you want to delete all of them. If you've set a lot of breakpoints, the Clear All Breakpoints (Ctrl+Shift+F9) feature allows you to get rid of all of them at once without having to hunt them all down and toggle each one off individually by locating them and then clicking their red dot.

Setting conditional breakpoints

Remember the example earlier in this session when $10 grew to $1,000 for no good reason? You would want to find out where that happened in your code. You could add breakpoints to stop the program when $10 grows larger than, say, $200 (that's your *condition*). Then, while the program is running and $10 is transformed into $1,000 — the logic error — VB will halt the program and show you exactly where this problem is located.

Type in this code:

```
Private Sub Button1_Click(ByVal sender As System.Object, ByVal e As
System.EventArgs) Handles Button1.Click

    Static moneyvariable = 55

    moneyvariable = moneyvariable + 44

  End Sub
```

To set a conditional breakpoint, go to the second line in this procedure where the money-variable is increased by 44. Click in the gray area to the left of that line of code. The red dot appears and the line is changed to a red color as well. Right-click the red part of the line (*not* the red dot) and choose BreakPoint properties from the content menu that pops up.

Click the Condition button in the Breakpoint Properties dialog box. In the BreakPoint Condition dialog box that appears, type the condition that will trigger the break when this variable goes above 200: moneyvariable > 200, as shown in Figure 20-4.

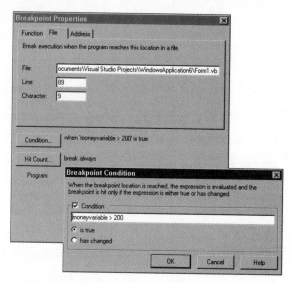

Figure 20-4   *Here's where you can specify a conditional breakpoint.*

Press F5 and keep clicking your button five times — then your variable will have exceeded the conditional value and the editor will enter break mode.

You can specify *any kind of condition* by using the Is True, Has Changed, or Hit Count option in the Breakpoint Properties dialog box.

Alternative Debugging Strategies

You likely noticed several other tools on the Debug menu. They're not as widely useful as breakpoints, single-stepping, or watches — but when you need these lesser tools, you will be glad they're available.

Done!

REVIEW

This session explored the topic of debugging — from fixing the easy culprits like typos to tracking down those tough logic errors. You learned how to use the impressive suite of debugging features built into VB .NET, including watches, breakpoints, and single-stepping.

QUIZ YOURSELF

1. When you press Enter after typing a line of code that contains a syntax error, what does VB do? (See "Wiping Out Typos.")
2. Can you use expressions in the Immediate window? (See "The watchful voyeur technique.")
3. How do you insert a breakpoint on a line of code? (See "Setting breakpoints.")

PART

IV

Saturday Evening
Part Review

1. What is an array?

2. Can you beak a logical line of code into two physical lines of code?

3. How are arrays used? When are they more efficient than ordinary variables?

4. What is the Step command used for?

5. What does the If...Then structure do?

6. Parts of an If...Then structure are traditionally indented. Which parts, and why?

7. When is the Select...Case structure preferable to If...Then?

8. What is the purpose of the Case Else command?

9. Can you use Select Case to test for the condition "any number lower than 200"? If so, what is the code that accomplishes this?

10. Can you use Select Case to test for an alphabetic range, such as a name that begins with any letter between *n* and *z*? If so, what is the code that accomplishes this?

11. Name two jobs that a Timer control can accomplish.

12. Timers are unique components in several ways. Describe one way that a Timer is unlike any other component.

13. How do other applications running in Windows affect a Timer's behavior?

14. What measure of time is represented by the Interval property of a Timer?

15. Do VB .NET components have a default property?

16. Does VB .NET support control arrays?

17. What are the easiest kinds of programming bugs to fix, and why?

18. Is punctuation important in computer programming?

19. What is the most common VB .NET error-trapping code structure?

20. Which debugging feature should you use if you want to skip over a For...Next loop and resume single-stepping just after that loop?

☑ **Friday**

☑ **Saturday**

☑ **Sunday**

PART

V

Sunday Morning

Building a User Interfacee

Session Checklist

✔ Planning an application's user interface

✔ Understanding databases

✔ Learning about records and fields

✔ Building tables

✔ Using indexes

✔ Starting to create an application

**30 Min.
To Go**

One significant job that nearly all programmers must frequently face is creating an efficient and ergonomic user-interface. VB .NET offers you lots of controls you can place on your forms to permit the user to interact with your program. This session explores some techniques and approaches that can assist you in creating a solid user-interface for your applications. (You'll continue working on this in future sessions as well.)

Some programmers prefer to first design the user-interface, and then fill in the programming "underneath" the various controls (in their Click event or other events). This is known as the *top-down* approach. Other programmers like to first use paper and pencil to create an outline of the various functions and features of their program, and then decide which user-interface controls are most appropriate.

No matter which approach you use (top-down or bottom-up), you have to pick and choose user-interface components at some point in the process of building an application.

To illustrate the top-down approach (which I prefer), you'll create a visual interface first, and then write the code that makes the interface controls actually do their jobs.

The goal is to give you experience creating a moderately sophisticated program. However, the application you create will also likely serve you well in the future in other ways. The example program you will build is *useful*, in addition to its value as a teaching tool. Perhaps best of all, because you built this application, you can customize it to your satisfy your needs as time goes on. You can add a report-printing feature, an encryption engine (if your personal secrets are *explosive!*), or whatever other improvements you want. But even as is, this program can be quite useful.

Let's call our program the Personal Data Manager.

The Plan

The plan for this exercise is to design, and then build, a general-purpose collection tracker. It's designed to let you easily add, modify, search, and save information about every item in your collection. What collection? That's why it's called the *Personal Data Manager* (PDM). It works with whatever kind of collection you have.

What do you collect? Books, financial records, videos, stamps, passwords to Internet sites, recipes, *secrets*, photos, buttons? Whatever it is that interests you, the PDM lets you type in a title, and as much additional data as you wish, about each item in your collection.

Sessions 21 through 25 will be devoted to constructing your PDM. In this exercise, you'll make it a freeform database — not a group of rigid little cells to fill in, but instead a single large TextBox where you can type in as much information about each item as you'd like. In the process of building the PDM, you'll see how to sketch, and then organize and build, a VB application of some sophistication.

Making Your Wish List

First you sketch your ideas, just like an architect. What do you want this program to do? The first step in designing an application is to make a list of the jobs it does for the user.

You'll want to let the user create as many different databases as they wish — so you'll need to provide New and Open submenu options under the File menu.

Each of the items in your database will have two elements in a record: the record's title and its description. (The description field can include any information you want.) The elements that make up a record are known as the record's *fields* (or *columns*). Your records will have two fields.

What else? There should be a way of deleting a record, and you want to provide an Undo feature that restores the most recently deleted record, if the user should change his or her mind. Also, the user should be able to see a complete list of all the titles in the data (an *index*). When the index list is displayed, the user can simply click any item and its entire record will be displayed in the main TextBoxes.

There should be a backup feature, to automatically save the data every 10 minutes. Let's also allow the reader to specify the color of the form. Finally, the user should be able to search the data for any word, phrase, or even partial word — and then you'll display a list of all the records that contain that text. The user can then click one of the records within the list to see that entire record displayed.

What Shows, What Doesn't?

Now that you know all the things you want accomplished, they can be divided into three categories:

- Things the user always sees:
  - A TextBox showing the Title field
  - A TextBox showing the Description field
  - A pair of buttons (Previous and Next) to let the user move through the database sequentially
  - A set of buttons for the common tasks: Search, Index, Add New Record, Delete, Undo Delete, and Exit

- Things the user sometimes sees:
  - The ListBox that displays an index (list) of each title so the user can quickly select an item from anywhere in the entire database
  - A second ListBox that displays the results of a search
  - A dialog box (InputBox) into which the user can type the query that begins a search

- Items on menus:
  - A File menu with New, Open, Close, and Save
  - An Edit menu with choices for automatic backup and form background color

Now you know what should be visible on the main form (what the user always sees), and what should be on the form, but usually hidden (such as the ListBoxes).

Understanding Databases

20 Min. To Go

Before taking the decisions made earlier in this session and applying them to building a user interface for your application, let's first spend a little time thinking about the concept of databases. The steps you'll take in building this program will be clearer if you have a good understanding of the fundamentals.

If you have a Rolodex" on your desk, you've got the essentials of a database. To make it a real database, you need to type it into a computer program that stores it as an orderly file. The key word here is *orderly*. The information shouldn't be merely a simple list; it should have an underlying organization.

Records and fields

If you were designing a database to hold the information in your Rolodex, you would recognize that each card in the Rolodex is a single *record* and that each of those records is divided into perhaps eight *fields* (subdivisions or zones): Name, Address, City, State, Zip, Voice Phone, Fax Phone, and E-mail address. (Microsoft has lately been referring to records as *rows* and fields as *columns*, because when you see the contents of a database in a grid- or table-style display, each record is shown as a single horizontal "row" and the vertical "columns" are the fields.)

In this example, you would design the Rolodex database to give each record eight fields. But do you notice a little problem? How is the program going to sort these records? On which field? The Name field is the logical one, but it might be awkward to require that each last name be typed first (alphabetizing on the first names is impractical).

So you change your specs: nine fields now, with the previous Name field now divided into LastName and FirstName fields. Now the alphabetizing can be done on the LastName field. The field (or fields) that you choose to have the records sorted by is called the *index*.

In your PDM database program, there will be only two fields: the Title field (which will serve as the index) and the Description field. Users can type in any information they wish, in whatever fashion they wish.

Separate tables

In a complex database, there may be more than one group of records. If you have a huge Rolodex, you might divide the records into two categories: Personal and Business, for example. This kind of large-scale group of records is called a *table*. A database can have multiple tables, and they can be linked, searched, or otherwise interrelated in various ways. But I propose you don't worry your pretty head about that stuff. Your database will have only a single table (which is all it really needs).

The key to indexes

When you specify that a field is to be indexed, it is maintained in alphabetical (or numeric) order by the database engine (the underlying, low-level support code that does jobs for a database).

If a user asks for a particular record (or set of records, such as *all coins in my collection older than 1890*), and the DateOfCoin field is not indexed, then each record must be searched individually. It's the equivalent of a box of coins — just a pile of them in a box, and you have to pick up each one and look at its date. However, if the DateOfCoin field is indexed, then the computer can very quickly locate a record or set of records (called a *dataset*). Having the DateOfCoin field maintained as an index is the equivalent of having a coin album in which you've put each coin ordered by their dates in plastic pockets.

Searching hundreds of thousands of company records via an index is very efficient. However, indexing isn't all that much of an issue when dealing with the number of records likely to be stored in a personal collection database. A few thousand records can be swiftly searched, if necessary, even if an index isn't used. That many records can also be swiftly alphabetized by a ListBox. But you'll sidestep a ListBox, not use it, and simply make your Title field an index field — so it more quickly displays all the titles alphabetized in the Index ListBox.

Your Goal

The main advantage of a freeform database program, like the one you're going to construct, is that it's up to the user how much, or what kind, of information is saved.

You want to give the user a powerful search engine. How powerful? Suppose that the user includes these lines in the Description field (the Description TextBox) of their recipe collection database:

Fry strips of cooked roast with onions and peppers. Sprinkle with chipotle pepper. Wrap in warmed tortillas.

leftovers Mexican appetizer

That last line, *leftovers Mexican appetizer,* makes it possible to hit this recipe if you search on any of those three words.

You want to give the user a truly flexible search feature. That's your main goal. The user should be able to ask the search feature to find, for example, *Mexican,* and your program should respond by filling the Search ListBox with every recipe in the entire recipe database that includes the word *mexican.* Uppercase or lowercase will not matter (the search feature will be case-insensitive).

That's your goal, and you'll achieve it. You'll employ one of the most interesting new database tools available in Visual Basic .NET: the DataSet.

Now you are ready to create the user interface for your PDM application. You must start with a blank VB .NET form and then add to it the components that the user will interact with to view and modify their PDM database.

Creating a User Interface

10 Min. To Go

You made a list earlier in this session of things the user always sees, so you'll start with that. These components will be on the main form of your application, the form that the user works with most of the time, and therefore sees most of the time.

Start VB .NET running and type in the name for your new project, *PDM* (or whatever name you want to use). Double-click the Windows Application icon in the New Project dialog box. The dialog box closes and you're now seeing the IDE displaying your new form.

Stretch the form so that it's fairly large (see Figure 21-1). Now click the Windows Forms tab in the Toolbox and put two TextBoxes and two Button controls on the form. (You'll later use the Buttons to permit the user to move through the records in your database.)

Stretch the TextBoxes and position the Buttons so they fill about ¾ of the form, as shown in Figure 21-1. Remember, you cannot enlarge the bigger TextBox *vertically* until you first set its MultiLine property to True (so do that in the Properties window).

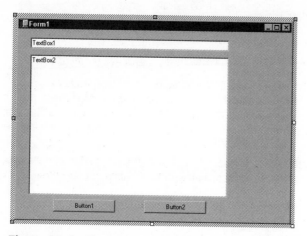

Figure 21-1 *The TextBox on the top is for the title, and the larger one is for the description.*

Change the small TextBox's Name property to *txtTitle*, its MultiLine property to True, and change its Font property to Arial, 12-pt. size (or whatever is readable at your screen resolution). Change the large TextBox's Name property to *txtDesc* (for *description*), and its Font property to 12-pt. Arial. Delete the Text property from both TextBoxes, so the user doesn't see the defaults, *TextBox1* or *TextBox2*.

Now put six Buttons over on the right side of the form. Drag your mouse around all of them to select them as a group. Now you can use the Properties window to adjust some of the properties they have in common. First, fix their width. Choose Format|Make Same Size|Width. Check their Size property in the Properties window to see that it's somewhere around 130 or so (see Figure 21-2).

Change their Font property to 11-pt. Arial (or whatever looks best).

Choose Format ⇨ Align and select Lefts to line the buttons up. Then choose Format ⇨ Make Same Size ⇨ Both so they are all the same size and look good. Finally, deselect them from the group by clicking on the background of the form. Change their individual Name properties to *btnSearch, btnIndex, btnNew, btnDelete, btnUndo,* and *btnExit*. Also change their Text properties to name them as shown in Figure 21-2.

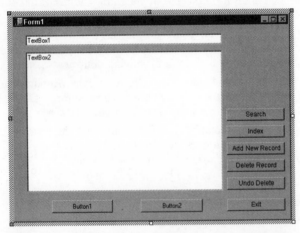

Figure 21-2   *The main window your user will work with is now complete.*

Now change the Name Properties of the two Buttons below the large TextBox to *btnPrevious* (for the Button on the left) and *btnNext*. Similarly, change their Text properties to Previous and Next. And change their Font property to Arial size 11 like the other buttons. Always try to present the user with a neat form where the controls are as consistent as possible, and things are lined up.

At this point, you might as well save this project so that you don't have to redo everything if there's a rolling blackout and the power fails or something. Choose File ⇨ Save.

Adding the Secondary Interface

Recall from earlier in this session that there are a couple of user-interface elements that were not visible by default in this project. When the user clicks the Index button, all of the titles in your database are displayed in a ListBox. When the user clicks the Search button, an InputBox appears where they can type their search criteria; then, if they click its OK button, the subset of titles defined by their query is displayed in a second ListBox.

Both ListBoxes permit users to click any title, and when they do so, the clicked record is immediately displayed (in the two main textboxes — title in the top box, main description in the larger box), after which the ListBox disappears. In addition, these ListBoxes will also display the records in alphabetical order. A DataSet does *not* keep records in any particular order, but users expect to view data in some order — usually alphabetical. You'll see how to alphabetize a DataSet in Session 23.

Two for One?

Using only one ListBox for both the Index and Search features might at first seem more efficient. In some ways, it would be (it saves a little memory usage), but if you want to make anything particular to one of the ListBoxes, you will run into a problem. You'd then have to keep track of *which* mode (Search or Index) the current instance of the ListBox is in.

This kind of programming can get messy fast. So I suggest you simply use two ListBoxes; one dedicated to showing the Index and one dedicated to showing the results of a search query. Then you can customize each ListBox and its behaviors to your heart's content without worrying about which is which when the program runs. Using two ListBoxes won't put any strain on the monitor or the computer — so be generous when faced with this kind of programming decision and employ different controls for each different feature. (You'll break this rule with the Exit Button, but more on that later.)

Getting Underway

Put *four* ListBoxes on the form (it doesn't matter where — you'll position them for the user with programming code). Change their Name properties in the Property window to *lstSearch*, *lstResults*, *lstAlpha*, and *lstIndex*. Change their ListBoxes' Font properties to 12-pt. Arial, or whatever is readable. Change all their Visible properties to False — you want two of them initially hidden when the program runs. And two others will *never* become visible.

Four, you say? Yes, sometimes an invisible control can be useful. For example, you'll use the lstSearch ListBox merely to hold (but never show) the description fields of each record. You could use an array, but what the heck — a ListBox is quite similar to an array, and has some extra features (such as permitting you to view its contents easily during debugging).

Also, the lstAlpha ListBox will always remain invisible. It will be used merely as a way of alphabetizing your DataSet. Dump anything into a ListBox with its Sorted property set to True, and the ListBox obediently alphabetizes those items for you.

So, set the lstAlpha ListBox's Sorted property to True.

Make these ListBoxes small on your form, and move them off to one side or the bottom so they're out of the way. (You'll be putting a bunch of other controls on the form in the next session.)

Done!

REVIEW

In this session, you saw how to sit yourself down and write yourself a list. When you're creating a new application in VB .NET, you want to plan it. You want to see its parts and how they might fit together. I'm not saying that some gifted programmers can't build a program the way that Tennessee Williams wrote great plays: by wrestling them into existence with no preliminary outlining. But most of us have to do at least a little preliminary planning if we want the project to go smoothly and end up logically structured. So, first you list all the things you want your program to do for the user. Then you decide which of those things should be put in menus, which should be visible to the user at all times, and which are usually not seen. You learned about the primary terminology of databases: records, fields, tables, record sets, and indexes. And finally, you began designing the user interface for your PDM database.

QUIZ YOURSELF

1. In what ways is a Rolodex similar to a database? (See "Understanding Databases.")
2. How does a record differ from a field? (See "Records and fields.")
3. What do the terms *column* and *row* mean when used to describe elements of a database? (See "Records and fields.")
4. What is a table? (See "Separate tables.")
5. If you specify that a field should be indexed, what happens to that field? (See "The key to indexes.")

Creating a Primary Form

Session Checklist

✔ Putting primary components on the form

✔ Learning how to size and position components via code

✔ Adding shortcut keys and specifying the TabIndex order

✔ Adding menus

✔ Writing some basic code

This session continues with the application you started in Session 21. You will continue building the visible interface that the user interacts with when your application runs.

*30 Min.
To Go*

General Declarations

Double-click your form to get to the code window. Go to the *very top* of the code window (above the line that says Public Class Form1) and type this into the first available line (above the Public Class Form1 line):

```
Imports System.Data 'put this up top in the code window
```

When you work with a DataSet, you want to have the System.Data namespace referenced. It makes life much easier.

Then, a few lines lower down in the General Declarations section of Form1, type these new lines (shown in boldface):

```
Imports System.Data 'put this up top in the code window

Public Class Form1
```

```
Inherits System.Windows.Forms.Form

Dim ds As New DataSet(), dr As DataRow, dt As DataTable

'holds a deleted record
Dim Titlehold As String, descriptionhold As String

'holds the current filenames
Dim Schemafilepath As String, datafilepath As String

Dim TotalRows As Integer, CurrentRow As Integer
```

Windows Form Designer generated code

These are *global* variables. You want to give these variables global scope so that they can be used *anywhere* in our form's code. (If you've forgotten about this issue, review Session 14 and its discussion of scope.)

The ds, dr, and dt variables will point to elements within your DataSet — ds for the DataSet, dr for the DataRow, and dt for the DataTable.

Using the Dim command to declare all these variables up here (outside of any particular procedure — event, funtion or sub), the variables can then be queried or changed from within *any* procedure in this form.

The Titlehold and Descriptionhold variables will temporarily hold a deleted record (the title field and the description field respectively). They are employed when the user chooses to delete a record. You'll store the record in these variables, and then if the user later clicks the Undo button, you can get the stored information from these two variables and restore the record.

The schemafilepath and datafilepath hold the filenames and paths of the two files necessary to save a DataSet. When the user chooses the Open or New options to retrieve an existing, or start a new, DataSet, it's necessary to remember these two file paths. They are later used when the user chooses the Save or Exit options. Using the same filenames to save the DataSet replaces the existing files with new files.

TotalRows keeps track of how many current records are in the DataSet. You could get the same information by querying the Count property of the DataTable object's Rows collection, like this:

```
Total = dt.rows.count - 1
```

But in some programs, you'll need to keep a running total and this example program shows you how that's done by maintaining the TotalRows variable and keeping it accurate whenever the user adds or deletes a record.

The variable CurrentRow will contain a pointer telling you which row is currently displayed to the user in the TextBoxes. You have to do a little housekeeping when using a raw DataSet instead of a data control (such as the VB .NET DataGrid). Data controls and more advanced database tools contain such features as a *BookMark* property, which keeps track of the current row for you. However, for a relatively simple application like the PDM, it's not much trouble to keep track of a few things like this yourself. Besides, that's how you learn programming.

Don't Despair

At this point, some of you, dear readers, are, if not actually wailing, at least muttering quietly to yourselves: "Wow, I could never predict precisely which, and how many, global variables a program of the size of this PDM would end up needing! I couldn't just sit down and write code like that!"

Well, neither can I. I wrote the program, *and then* I wrote these chapters. I'm taking you through the program and explaining what all its parts do, but don't assume that I wrote the program in some linear fashion. I didn't move from part A to part B and so on. For example, only when I worked on the Delete Button's code did I realize that I would have to use global variables to hold the Title and Description fields so they could later be restored, if necessary, by the actions triggered if the user clicks the Undo Button.

So, although it's instructive to follow my narrative tour through this program's various tricks and methods, don't suppose that I didn't spend days struggling to fix bugs and to figure out precisely how to get various parts to work. (The Open new file option was probably the most complicated, but managing the DataSet was no walk in the park either.)

Sizing and Positioning

Making secondary components the right size and putting them in the right position onscreen is often best done via code. Rather than stretching them and dragging them by eye, just use other, always-visible Buttons or other components' Top, Left, Width, and Height properties (or the Form's same properties) to make them line up and look smart when they become visible during runtime. Remember that secondary components are only *sometimes* (or even never) visible when the program runs. You don't want them sitting on top of your primary components while you're designing your program — that's clumsy.

It's good to put sizing and positioning code into the Form_Load event. That way, the code gets executed before the form is made visible, and it's executed only that one time when the form is first created. Put another way: Use the Form_Load event to do any initialization housekeeping chores that your program needs to finish before it becomes visible to the user.

You want the Index ListBox (*lstIndex*) to cover all of the buttons on the right side of the form except for the Exit button. When displaying a secondary component to the user, it's often important that you disable, hide, or otherwise inactivate alternative input devices, such as Buttons. It's a real mess to write programming that must check, for example, whether the user has clicked the Index button right after clicking the Search button and things like that. So, to simplify your programming, you'll simply display the lstIndex and lstResults ListBoxes right on top of most of the buttons — so the user physically cannot click those buttons. The user will not even be able to *see* those buttons.

You also need a pair of buttons that the user will choose between when adding (or cancelling) a new record to the DataSet. Place two more Buttons from the Toolbox onto the form. (Put them somewhere up above the other buttons; you'll move them into position with code.) Change the Name property of one of them to *btnCancel*, and set its Text property to &Cancel. Name the other one *btnAdd*, and set its Text property to &Add This Record. Adjust both Font properties to make them readable, and set both of their Visible properties to False.

To position and size the ListBoxes, type the following code into the Form_Load event:

```
Private Sub Form1_Load(ByVal sender As System.Object, ByVal e As
System.EventArgs) Handles MyBase.Load
        With lstResults
            .Left = btnSearch.Left
            .Top = txtTitle.Top
            .Width = btnSearch.Width
            .Height = txtTitle.Height + txtDesc.Height + 17
        End With

        With lstIndex
            .Left = btnIndex.Left
            .Top = txtTitle.Top
            .Width = btnIndex.Width
            .Height = txtTitle.Height + txtDesc.Height + 17
        End With

        btnCancel.Top = btnPrevious.Top
        btnCancel.Left = btnPrevious.Left
        btnCancel.Height = btnPrevious.Height
        btnCancel.Width = btnPrevious.Width

        btnAdd.Top = btnNext.Top
        btnAdd.Left = btnNext.Left
        btnAdd.Height = btnNext.Height
        btnAdd.Width = btnNext.Width

End Sub
```

Now to test the positioning of the ListBoxes you must first type this into the btnIndex_Click event:

```
Private Sub btnIndex_Click(ByVal sender As System.Object, ByVal e As
System.EventArgs) Handles btnIndex.Click

        lstIndex.Visible = True

End Sub
```

Recall that you can quickly get to a button's Click event in the code window by switching to the Design window. Click the Form1.vb (Design) tab at the top of the code window, and then double-click the button whose Click event you're interested in writing some programming for. The code window will appear, with the Click event displayed.

Notice the fudge factors (+17) in the code that displays the Index and Search ListBoxes. Adjust those as necessary to make your ListBoxes neatly cover the buttons (except the Exit button). Your fudge factors will depend on how large you've made your form, and the buttons you're trying to cover. Press F5, and then click the Index button to see how the ListBox looks. (Don't worry at this point if some of your Buttons are not covered by the ListBox when you press F5 to run this example. That issue is dealt with later in this session, in the section titled "Understanding Zorder." Also, don't worry about the btnCancel and btnAdd behaviors. That, too, will be covered in due time.)

> **If the ListBoxes you put on your form are covering up other components that you want to work with (while you're in design mode), here's one way to get them out of your way. To make them totally invisible during design time, go to the Properties window and change their Location X properties to something like -8325. This moves them way off to the left of the screen — off into Virtual Land. (Just remember that you did this — so if you need them back for some reason, you can change the X property in the Properties window to something reasonable, such as 400.)**

Making Life Easier for the User

20 Min. To Go

Users expect some shortcuts in their applications, and woe be the programmer who forgets them. He or she will be thought unprofessional. Users expect an Alt+ shortcut key on each button, so they can press, for instance, Alt+S to activate the Search button without having to reach for the mouse.

They also expect to be able to press the Tab key to move among the components on a window (to move the *focus*). The order of the TabIndex properties determines the order in which each component gets the focus. On this form, I would say that each button in turn going down should get the focus, starting with *Search*, followed by the Title TextBox and then the Description TextBox.

Also, you should decide which component should have the focus by default when the program first runs, and you should therefore give it the TabIndex of 0. I think that after the user has spent a few days entering all the data, the first thing they will most often want to do when they fire up the application is search for some information within the data. So you'll give the Search button the default focus. That way, the only thing the user needs to do when the program runs is press Enter to trigger the Search button. (However, if you find yourself using the PDM in a different way, you can easily go ahead and modify the program — after all, you're building it from the ground up so you can customize it to suit yourself.)

Creating shortcut keys

Recall that you use the & symbol just before the letter that you want to make the shortcut character in a control's or menu item's Text property. The Text is then displayed with that letter underlined as a cue to the user. Therefore, use the Properties window to change the Search button's Text property to &Search and do the same for &Index, &Add New Record, &Delete, &Undo Delete, &Exit, &Previous, and &Next.

Arranging the TabIndex properties

In the Properties window, change the TabIndex property of btnSearch to 0, and then go down the list giving each button the next higher TabIndex (1 for the btnIndex button, 2 for the Add New Record button, and so on), ending with 6 for the txtTitle and 7 for the txtDesc. Press F5 and press the Tab key repeatedly to make sure that the focus cycles as you planned. Notice that because it has the 0 TabIndex, the Search button always gets the focus first when this program runs so the user can just press the Enter key to "click" that button.

Adding the Menus

You remember how to add menus from Session 10: Just add a MainMenu control from the Toolbox to your form. You want two main menus: File and Edit. So add the MainMenu control, double-click the Type Here field at the top of your form, and then type **&File** in the first box. Press Tab to get to the second top menu and type **&Edit**.

Move down to the submenu below the File menu and type **&New**. Press the Enter key to move down to the next entry. Repeat these steps until you've added &Open, &Close, and &Save.

Now click the submenu under the Edit menu and add these: &Automatic Backup and &BackColor. Using the Properties menu, change all of these menus' Name properties to mnuFile, mnuNew, mnuOpen, and so on until you've renamed them all. (If you wish, you can right-click the File menu item and choose Edit Names. This is a quick way to change all the Name properties of a set of menus. Then just keep typing the names, and pressing the Enter key each time you finish one name — you'll be moved down to the next menu item where you can keep on typing.)

At this point, you probably want to save your work again. You've done a lot to improve your project, and you don't want to have to repeat your efforts because of yet another rolling blackout.

Adding More Features

Now you can write some programming for the Exit, Search, and Index buttons.

Search and Index

The user will display the Search or Index ListBoxes by clicking the buttons associated with them. You'll also sketch in the basic code to configure the user interface to make it possible for the user to add new records. You'll put additional code into these various events after you add a DataSet to the program. But for now, at least you'll have some things happening when you press F5. You can also test to see if the interface responds visually as it should when the user clicks various buttons.

Type in this next code so that when the user clicks the Search button, several things happen — the caption on the Exit button changes, the ListBox is made visible, and the record-maneuvering Buttons are rendered temporarily disabled:

```
Protected Sub btnSearch_Click(ByVal sender As Object, ByVal e As
System.EventArgs)
```

```
        btnExit.Text = "&Exit"
        lstResults.Visible = True
        btnPrevious.Enabled = False
        btnNext.Enabled = False


End Sub
```

Now type in the following code (quite similar to the code you just entered) for the Index button:

```
    Private Sub btnIndex_Click(ByVal sender As System.Object, ByVal e As
System.EventArgs) Handles btnIndex.Click

        btnExit.Text = "&Close List"
        lstIndex.Visible = True
        btnPrevious.Enabled = False
        btnNext.Enabled = False

    End Sub
```

When either ListBox is displayed, the ListBox covers all buttons except the Exit button.

You also want the caption of the Exit button to change while a list is displayed. The changed caption should read: &Close List. I know this violates the rule I mentioned earlier about not using the same control for two different jobs, but what the heck. In this case, the alternative of using two buttons isn't really superior. You still have to keep track of whether ListBoxes are displayed within the code for the Exit/Close List button — so you'll know which behavior to carry out when the user clicks this dual-purpose button.

Understanding Zorder

When you press F5 to test the Index ListBox, you may find that it does *not* cover the Buttons. This is because VB .NET controls have a *Zorder* — a "third-dimension" or "depth" order. Put simply, they can be arranged so one is "on top of" another. By default, the first controls you place on a form are "on the bottom" and therefore are visibly covered by controls added later that are put in the same location.

If you have a problem with some buttons showing when the ListBoxes are displayed, click the lstIndex ListBox to select it, and then choose Format ⇨ Order ⇨ Bring To Front. Repeat these steps to adjust the Zorder of the lstResults ListBox as well.

Now when you press F5 and click the Index button, your ListBoxes should appear as shown in Figure 22-1.

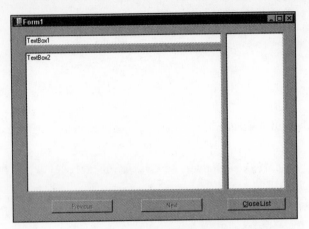

Figure 22-1 *The ListBoxes cover a row of buttons, except for the lowest button that closes the list.*

**10 Min.
To Go**

Coding the Visible Part of the New Record Feature

The final thing you will do in this session is create the visual display necessary when the user wants to add a new record to the database. When the user adds a record, all of the buttons should be made invisible. (You don't want a mishap to occur, such as the user trying to delete a record while the program is in the delicate process of adding a record.)

Also, the two record-navigation buttons (Next and Previous) should be made invisible as well. Two new buttons should replace the navigation buttons while the user is adding a new row (record): *Cancel* and *Add This to the Database*. That is the purpose of the btnCancel and btnNew that we created earlier in this session.

Put the following code into the btnCancel button so that the two buttons disappear, and all the other buttons reappear, if the user clicks this Cancel button:

```
Private Sub btnCancel_Click(ByVal sender As System.Object, ByVal e As
System.EventArgs) Handles btnCancel.Click

        btnPrevious.Visible = True
        btnNext.Visible = True
        btnSearch.Visible = True
        btnIndex.Visible = True
        btnNew.Visible = True
        btnDelete.Visible = True
        btnUndo.Visible = True
        btnExit.Visible = True

        btnCancel.Visible = False
        btnAdd.Visible = False

    End Sub
```

And put this same code into the btnAdd button as well:

```
Private Sub btnAdd_Click(ByVal sender As System.Object, ByVal e As
System.EventArgs) Handles btnAdd.Click


        btnPrevious.Visible = True
        btnNext.Visible = True
        btnSearch.Visible = True
        btnIndex.Visible = True
        btnNew.Visible = True
        btnDelete.Visible = True
        btnUndo.Visible = True
        btnExit.Visible = True

        btnCancel.Visible = False
        btnAdd.Visible = False

    End Sub
```

Finally, type this into the Add New Record Button's (btnNew) Click event:

```
    Private Sub btnNew_Click(ByVal sender As System.Object, ByVal e As
System.EventArgs) Handles btnNew.Click

        btnPrevious.Visible = False
        btnNext.Visible = False
        btnSearch.Visible = False
        btnIndex.Visible = False
        btnNew.Visible = False
        btnDelete.Visible = False
        btnUndo.Visible = False
        btnExit.Visible = False

        btnCancel.Visible = True
        btnAdd.Visible = True

    End Sub
```

Now press F5 to see what happens when you click the Add New Record and Cancel buttons.

That's it. You've built a nice user interface, and made various appropriate things happen when the various buttons are clicked. In the next session, you'll create a new DataSet, and also connect your PDM program to that DataSet.

Done!

REVIEW

This session launched you into the brave task of building a sophisticated program. You learned how to add the major visible components, and then added the secondary components that are only sometimes visible. You created the shortcut keys and massaged the TabIndex property for each major component. Finally, you added the basic code to make several of the buttons respond to clicks — at least to respond with the correct visual reactions (they don't yet have all of the code they'll have when the project is finished).

QUIZ YOURSELF

1. What's usually the best way to size and position secondary components? (See "Sizing and Positioning.")

2. What symbol is used to display an underlined character to the user as a cue that pressing Alt plus that character will trigger a response? (See "Creating shortcut keys.")

3. What is special about setting a component's TabIndex to 0? (See "Arranging the TabIndex properties.")

SESSION

23

Creating DataSets

Session Checklist

✔ Understanding the DataSet object

✔ Creating a new DataSet programmatically

✔ Saving the two DataSet XML files

✔ Learning more about collections

✔ Opening an existing DataSet

**30 Min.
To Go**

The *DataSet* is a brand new .NET item, similar to the traditional RecordSet used for years by database programmers.

A DataSet is a copy of some data (containing as many data tables as you wish) that is held in memory or stored as two XML files on a hard drive. (It's stored in two files because one holds a description of its structure, and the other holds the actual data itself.)

A DataSet does not require any active connection to a database. A DataSet object is fairly self-sufficient — it contains a variety of commands (methods) and properties you can employ to manage its data.

Typically, you connect to a large database and then extract a DataSet from that database. This way, you need not maintain a constant connection between your machine and the database (which might be on the Internet somewhere else in the world). Instead, you can work all you want with the DataSet in your computer, and then after you've made your changes, return the DataSet for merging with the big database.

DataSets are stored in XML files, so they are especially useful for transmitting data over networks, such as the Internet. However, in this session and the next you'll learn how to create an independent DataSet that isn't extracted from some larger database. And you're going to work within a Windows Form, not a Web Form (and Internet Web page document).

Some Barbells for You

The fundamental programming techniques for using a DataSet to manage its data are the same in any environment. Also, I want to demonstrate several programming techniques useful within Windows. Sure, some of the jobs you'll do in the next two sessions can be done for you by data-bound controls. But you won't really learn programming that way — and there are times you'll want to know how to do these things for yourself. (You could go to a health club and just watch other people working out, andthere are easier ways to move barbells than lifting them yourself — but you don't get any stronger just watching.)

You're going to learn some very useful programming techniques — sorting; searching; using pointers; moving forward and back through a set of data, managing a moderately large project; employing hidden controls; and loading and saving DataSet .XML files. Plus, when the dust settles, you'll have a really quite useful program that can manage your collections of coins, secret Internet passwords, books, important dates, financial data, or whatever. You'll be able to search the entire set of data in a flash, looking for any word, phrase, or even partial word within all your descriptions. And because you built this application from the ground up, you'll be able to revise and customize it to your heart's content. I wrote a program like this PDM (Personal Database Manager) years ago and have used it at least once a week since. You might find uses for it, too.

Although a programmer can create a DataSet using the database controls in VB .NET, there are times when you want to let the *user* create his or her own DataSet files from scratch. This is one of those times.

The PDM you've created offers the user this capability in the File ➪ New menu option. You'll now see how to get user input to create and define the structure of a DataSet. That way, whenever the user wants to build a new DataSet . . . well, they can. If the user wants to use one DataSet in the PDM to manage their collection of recipes, and a second DataSet to manage their personal contacts, they can. You'll let your PDM users create as many different DataSets as they wish, just as a word processor user can create as many different documents as they wish.

In many ways, a DataSet is indistinguishable from what has traditionally been called a *database*. For the purposes of storing and managing the information in your PDM, you need not even bother dealing with a full-blown database. A DataSet will be quite sufficient for your needs.

You'll probably notice that in this session (and Session 24) I never say: *Press F5 to test this code*. The reason is that the PDM project you are building contains many interdependent parts. Many features, for example, will not work until you've added the Alphabetizer routine which you'll create at the end of Session 24. So be patient. If you want to get some quick gratification, try the exercise titled "Creating a DataSet Using Code" found in the Supplemental Notes file on this book's CD. As a side-benefit, that exercise will help you understand some of the programming in this session and Session 24.

Creating a New DataSet

If it's not currently loaded in the VS .NET editor, choose File ➪ Open ➪ Project, and load your PDM project (it's the *.SLN*, for *solution*, file in the PDM folder you created).

Now you'll write the programming in the mnuNew_Click event so the user can create a new DataSet any time.

The following code only works if you define the necessary DataSet object variables, and include the necessary Imports statement at the top of the code window. You did this in the Session 21, but double-check it now. The very first line in the code window (above the Public Class), should look like this:

```
Imports System.Data 'put this up top in the code window
```

Then in a line following the Inherets statement, you should see your DataSet object variable declarations, as shown here:

```
Public Class Form1
    Inherits System.Windows.Forms.Form
    Dim ds As New DataSet(), dr As DataRow, dt As DataTable
```

Now, back to our regular programming. You'll need to add a SaveFileDialog control from the Toolbox to your form. And, while you're at it, go ahead and add an OpenFileDialog and a ColorDialog as well (you'll use them later). Remember that to see these dialog controls, you must scroll the Toolbox by clicking its down-arrow button on the bottom.

Type this into the mnuNew_Click event:

```
Private Sub mnuNew_Click(ByVal sender As System.Object, ByVal e As
System.EventArgs) Handles mnuNew.Click

    'Create a new DataSet with a table named Recipes that includes a
title and a desc column.

        'first get user's name for the new DataSet
        Dim userFilePath As String

        SaveFileDialog1.FileName = "MyData"
        SaveFileDialog1.InitialDirectory = "C:\"
        SaveFileDialog1.RestoreDirectory = True
        SaveFileDialog1.Title = "Create a New PDM DataSet"
        SaveFileDialog1.Filter = "PDM|*.PDM"
        SaveFileDialog1.ShowDialog()
        userFilePath = SaveFileDialog1.FileName

        Dim l As Integer = Len(userFilePath)

        If Mid(userFilePath, l - 3, 1) = "." Then
            'they've added an extension, so remove it
            userFilePath = Microsoft.VisualBasic.Left(userFilePath, l - 4)
        End If


        dt = New DataTable("Recipes")
        dt.Columns.Add("title", GetType(String))
        dt.Columns.Add("desc", GetType(String))
        ds.Tables.Add(dt)
```

```
Try
        'save the structure (schema) of this dataset
        ds.WriteXmlSchema(userFilePath & "schm.xml")
        'save data that's currently in this dataset
        ds.WriteXml(userFilePath & "data.xml")

    'store these filenames in global variables for saving later
        schemafilepath = userFilePath & "schm.xml"
        datafilepath = userFilePath & "data.xml"

        'save a file to display their filename:
        ds.WriteXml(userFilePath & ".PDM")

    Catch er As Exception 'if there was a problem opening this file
        MessageBox.Show(er.ToString)

    Finally

    End Try

    dt = ds.Tables!Recipes ' set dt to point to this table

End Sub
```

All you want to do here is establish a new (empty) DataSet. You just want to save its structure (one table, two columns) to the hard drive. You're using the names Recipes, title, and desc for our structure, but that's OK — the user will never see these internal labels any more than they will see the variable names.

All you need to get from the user is their choice of filename, to which you'll append *schm.xml* for the schema file, and any data in a file of the same name, but to which you'll append *data.xml*. Finally, to make things less confusing for the user (when they go to open one of their PDM databases), you'll create a third file with the extension .PDM. This last file has no other purpose than to provide the user with an easily recognizable filename when they use the Open menu option.

You use the SaveFile dialog (see Session 12 for details) to get the user's choice of directory and filename. It's a straightforward request, but you always need to anticipate ways that users might foul things up. In this case, they might get excited and add a file extension like .TXT to their filename. You don't want that — you're actually creating three files and want to add special extensions to them. So, if the user flipped out and added an extension, you remove it in code, like this:

```
If userFilePath.IndexOf(".") Then
        'they've added an extension, so remove it
        userFilePath = userFilePath.Substring(0, 1 - 4)
End If
```

The string-manipulation methods are discussed in Session 15. Here's a reminder, however, of the old (pre-VB .NET) technique:

```
If Mid(userFilePath, 1 - 3, 1) = "." Then
    'they've added an extension, so remove it
    userFilePath = Microsoft.VisualBasic.Left(userFilePath, 1 - 4)
End If
```

Note that you have to add the "compatibility library" Microsoft.VisualBasic reference to use the Left command in this code. The Left command, when used without the compatibility qualifier, refers to the position of an object in VB .NET. (See Appendix C on this book's CD for details.)

In any case, once the user has given you a valid filename and filepath, you create their new DataSet using the WriteXmlSchema method and save a separate .XML file that will hold the data.

Now that you've created the new DataSet and saved its structure to the hard drive, you need to make the global dt (datatable) variable refer to your actual DataSet's table:

```
dt = ds.Tables!Recipes
```

Understanding Collections

20 Min. To Go

Many objects contain *collections*. Collections are similar to arrays. There is a *tables* collection within a DataSet, and, in turn, each table has a *columns* collection (which tells you how that table is subdivided) and a *rows* collection (containing the actual items of data within the collection).

You can usually query or edit individual elements of a collection two ways. You can refer to them by index number (starting with zero):

```
dt = ds.Tables(0) 'same, but here we use the table's index number rather
than its name.
```

Or you can refer to them by name, like this:

```
dt = ds.Tables!Recipes 'by name
dt = ds.Tables("Recipes") 'same, but an alternative punctuation
```

Opening an Existing DataSet

When the user runs your PDM program, they'll usually want to open an existing PDM DataSet located on the hard drive. Put this code into the mnuOpen_Click event:

```
Private Sub mnuOpen_Click(ByVal sender As System.Object, ByVal e As
System.EventArgs) Handles mnuOpen.Click

    Dim userFilePath As String
    Dim userfilenameonly As String, userpathonly As String

    OpenFileDialog1.FileName = "PDM"
    OpenFileDialog1.Filter = "PDM Files|*.PDM|All files (*.*)|*.*"
    OpenFileDialog1.InitialDirectory = "C:\"
```

```
OpenFileDialog1.RestoreDirectory = True
OpenFileDialog1.Title = "Open a PDM DataSet"

If OpenFileDialog1.ShowDialog() = DialogResult.OK Then
    userFilePath = OpenFileDialog1.FileName

    'extract path and filename
    Dim l As Integer, m As Integer

    Dim position As Integer


    Do
        position = m
        m = userFilePath.IndexOf("\", m + 1)
    Loop Until m = -1



    l = userFilePath.Length

    position += 1  'adjust for zero start index

    userfilenameonly = userFilePath.Substring(position, l -
position)
    userpathonly = userFilePath.Substring(0, position)



    'strip any extension from filename:


If userfilenameonly.IndexOf(".") <> -1 Then
    userfilenameonly = userfilenameonly.Substring(0,
userfilenameonly.Length - 4)
End If



    End If

Try
    'get the structure file
    ds.ReadXmlSchema(userpathonly & userfilenameonly & "schm.xml")
    'get the data file
    ds.ReadXml(userpathonly & userfilenameonly & "data.xml")

    schemafilepath = userpathonly & userfilenameonly & "schm.xml"
    datafilepath = userpathonly & userfilenameonly & "data.xml"

Catch er As Exception 'if there was a problem opening this file
```

```
        MessageBox.Show(er.ToString)

    Finally

        dt = ds.Tables!Recipes ' set dt to point to this table

    End Try


    TotalRows = dt.Rows.Count
    CurrentRow = 0

    alphabetizer()

    txtTitle.Text = dt.Rows(CurrentRow).Item(0)
    txtDesc.Text = dt.Rows(CurrentRow).Item(1)

End Sub
```

**10 Min.
To Go**

Don't press F5 and try to test this code yet; we have to create the Alphabetizer function before the menu items become functional. However, let's briefly explore how this code opens files and loads in a DataSet. You show the user an OpenFile dialog window and allow them to double-click a filename (ending in .PDM). You get their choice of database: It might be COOKBOOK.PDM, ADDRESSBOOK.PDM, COINCOLLECTION.PDM, or whatever database they've previously created. Their choice is returned to your program as the FileName property of the FileOpen dialog:

```
userFilePath = OpenFileDialog1.FileName
```

Once you've got the filename (which includes the path, such as: C:\MyCoins.PDM), you have to separate the actual path from the filename (C:\ from MyCoins.PDM). You need these separate strings because you must open two XML files: the schema (structure definition) file (in this example it would be MyCoinsSchm.XML) and the data file (MyCoinsData.XML).

This code finds where the path ends and the filename begins, by searching for the \ symbol within C:\MyCoins.PDM:

```
'extract path and filename
        Dim l As Integer, m As Integer

        Dim position As Integer

        Do
            position = m
            m = userFilePath.IndexOf("\", m + 1)
        Loop Until m = -1
```

Once this loop is finished, the variable *position* contains the location of the rightmost \. Why look for more than one \? Because if the user stored their database in a subdirectory, there will be more than one \ in the filepath, like this: C:\MyData\PDM\MyCoins.PDM.

When you exit this loop, you can then extract the filepath and put it into a variable named userpathonly, like this:

```
userpathonly = userFilePath.Substring(0, position)
```

This will return `C:\MyData\PDM`, for example.

And you can extract the filename, and get `MyCoins.PDM`.

Now you're ready to open your schema and data files, by appending your special extensions to the filename, like this:

```
'get the structure file
ds.ReadXmlSchema(userpathonly & userfilenameonly & "schm.xml")
'get the data file
ds.ReadXml(userpathonly & userfilenameonly & "data.xml")
```

As you did in the mnuNew code, you must save the filenames in global variables so you can later save the data back to these files when the user chooses the Save option in the File menu, or clicks the Exit button:

```
schemafilepath = userpathonly & userfilenameonly & "schm.xml"
datafilepath = userpathonly & userfilenameonly & "data.xml"
```

Technically, you need to keep on saving the structure (scmn.xml) file. The PDM doesn't contain any features for adjusting the structure by adding new tables or columns. However, it doesn't hurt anything — and the capability is in place if you ever decide to expand the PDM and let users add tables.

Next you point the datatable variable to your newly opened DataSet:

```
dt = ds.Tables!Recipes ' set dt to point to this table
```

Then you put the total number of records into the global variable TotalRows, setting the CurrentRow pointer to 0 (the first record):

```
TotalRows = dt.Rows.Count
CurrentRow = 0
```

Next, you run the alphabetizing routine (described in Session 24):

```
alphabetizer()
```

And finally, you display the current record in your two TextBoxes:

```
txtTitle.Text = dt.Rows(CurrentRow).Item(0)
txtDesc.Text = dt.Rows(CurrentRow).Item(1)
```

Done!

REVIEW

This session focused on the DataSet. You learned how to define its structure, add data to it, and save the structure and data XML files to disk. Then you saw how to deal with a DataSet's collections. Finally, you learned to open an existing DataSet and restore it within a program.

QUIZ YOURSELF

1. What does the following code do: ds.WriteXmlSchema(userFilePath & "schm.xml") (See "Creating a New DataSet.")

2. What other programming structure is similar to collections? (See "Understanding Collections.")

3. What information is returned to you in the OpenFileDialog1.FileName property, *in addition to* the filename? (See "Opening an Existing DataSet.")

4. When using the Left function, you must employ a "compatibility library." What is its name? (See "Creating a New DataSet.")

Continuing Your DataSet Project

Session Checklist

✔ Adding data to a DataSet

✔ Canceling an action

✔ Committing rows

✔ Maneuvering through a DataSet

✔ Displaying all rows

✔ Searching data

✔ Removing rows

✔ Learning an undo technique

✔ Alphabetizing data

**30 Min.
To Go**

I n this session, you'll continue fleshing out the fabulous PDM program. You'll start off by providing a feature that permits the user to add new records (rows) to the DataSet.

Adding Data to a DataSet

In the previous session, you got your Open and New menu items written. (Don't try to run the PDM yet.) Now you'll create the programming for three of the buttons: Add New, Cancel, Add This Record. You'll'll write the code necessary to make them do what their captions promise.

Adding a New Record

Double-click the Add New Record button to see its Click event in the code window. Recall that you already put some code into that event. The existing code hides all of the buttons, and then displays two new buttons captioned Cancel and Add This to the Database. However, you must first add a couple of simple lines to the Add New Record button's code.

Add the lines in boldface:

```
Private Sub btnNew_Click(ByVal sender As System.Object, ByVal e As
System.EventArgs) Handles btnNew.Click


        'if they have no active DataSet, refuse to allow a new record:

        If dt Is Nothing Then 'no table exists yet

            MsgBox("Please use File|Open or File|New so there is a
DataSet--before attempting to add a new record.")

            Exit Sub

        End If


        txtTitle.Text = "" : txtDesc.Text = ""


        btnPrevious.Visible = False
        btnNext.Visible = False
        btnSearch.Visible = False
        btnIndex.Visible = False
        btnNew.Visible = False
        btnDelete.Visible = False
        btnUndo.Visible = False
        btnExit.Visible = False

        btnCancel.Visible = True
        btnAdd.Visible = True


    End Sub
```

The first line tests whether or not the user has a currently active DataSet. If not, you post a message and exit this Sub without executing any additional code. If they haven't yet created or opened a DataSet, they obviously shouldn't be trying to add a record to this non-existent data.

All the "New record" button is supposed to do is display an empty canvas — blank TextBoxes — to the user, so they can type in a new title and a new description.

Canceling

The Cancel button needs only to restore the previously visible record to the TextBoxes, and to change the buttons that are visible to the user. You coded the buttons' visibility activity earlier, so all you have to add now is the code to redisplay the text that was in the TextBoxes before the user clicked the New Record button. So add these lines (in boldface) to the btnCancel_Click event:

```
Private Sub btnCancel_Click(ByVal sender As System.Object, ByVal e As
System.EventArgs) Handles btnCancel.Click

        txtTitle.Text = dt.Rows(CurrentRow).Item(0)
        txtDesc.Text = dt.Rows(CurrentRow).Item(1)

    btnPrevious.Visible = True
    btnNext.Visible = True
    btnSearch.Visible = True
    btnIndex.Visible = True
    btnNew.Visible = True
    btnDelete.Visible = True
    btnUndo.Visible = True
    btnExit.Visible = True

    btnCancel.Visible = False
    btnAdd.Visible = False

End Sub
```

This code simply restores the text to the two TextBoxes, grabbing it from the current row in the DataSet.

Committing a new record

However, if the user does type in a new record that they want to save into the DataSet (*committing it* to the database, as the saying is), they'll click the Add This Record button, so you do need to put some new code in that button's Click event to save the record to the DataSet.

Add the lines in boldface to the btnAdd_Click event:

```
Private Sub btnAdd_Click(ByVal sender As System.Object, ByVal e As
System.EventArgs) Handles btnAdd.Click

        ' stick the new data into the first row's two columns
        dr = dt.NewRow()
        dr!title = txtTitle.Text
        dr!desc = txtDesc.Text
        dt.Rows.Add(dr)
        TotalRows = TotalRows + 1
        CurrentRow = CurrentRow + 1
```

```
            btnPrevious.Visible = True
            btnNext.Visible = True
            btnSearch.Visible = True
            btnIndex.Visible = True
            btnNew.Visible = True
            btnDelete.Visible = True
            btnUndo.Visible = True
            btnExit.Visible = True

            btnCancel.Visible = False
            btnAdd.Visible = False

            alphabetizer()
            Me.Text = "Record Added..."

            btnCancel_Click(sender, e)
    End Sub
```

In this new code, you first use the NewRow method to notify your DataSet that a new row of data is coming. Then you fill the new row's two columns (title and desc) with the actual data from your TextBoxes. Then the Add method actually commits the data to the DataSet. You increment your total records counter and your current row pointer. And you add the data to your arrays so they are kept current.

Then, down near the end of the sub, you invoke the alphabetizer so the new record is correctly placed in sorted order within our other records. And, because users don't like to click a button and see nothing happening, you place a reassuring message in the Form's title bar. You might want to add similar code placing other Me.Text messages in some of the other Click events in the PDM. I'll leave that decision up to you. Finally, you close the record-adding mode down by invoking the code in btnCancel's Click event. Sometimes it's useful to simply pretend to "click" or otherwise trigger the code in an event (rather than duplicating all that event's source code by repeating it in another location in your program). This is one of those situations.

Moving Through the DataSet

20 Min. To Go

The btnNext and btnPrevious buttons allow the user to move forward or backward through the currently loaded DataSet. Recall that the records in a DataSet are not maintained in any particular order, so there is no MoveNext or MovePrevious method in a DataSet object. You have to create the code yourself that sorts the records, and also keeps track of where you currently "are" within that sorted list.

Type this into the btnPrevious Click event:

```
Private Sub btnPrevious_Click(ByVal sender As System.Object, ByVal e As
System.EventArgs) Handles btnPrevious.Click

        If CurrentRow = 0 Then Exit Sub

        CurrentRow = CurrentRow - 1
```

```
txtTitle.Text = dt.Rows(CurrentRow).Item(0)
txtDesc.Text = dt.Rows(CurrentRow).Item(1)

Me.Text = CurrentRow + 1.ToString


    End Sub
```

You first must check to see if the user is viewing the lowest record (alphabetically). If CurrentRow = 0, that means there are no additional records to be viewed "below" the currently displayed one. So, if that's the case, you merely Exit Sub. If there *is* a record to display, you adjust the currentrow variable, and then grab the text from the DataSet and assign it to the two TextBoxes. Again, you display something to the user up in the form's title bar. In this case, you show them the record number. How would you show them the record number *and* the total number of records? Here's how:

```
Me.Text = CurrentRow + 1.ToString & " of " & TotalRows.ToString
```

Moving forward (or up, if you prefer) through the records is accomplished in the btnNext procedure:

```
Private Sub btnNext_Click(ByVal sender As System.Object, ByVal e As
System.EventArgs) Handles btnNext.Click

        If CurrentRow = TotalRows - 1 Then Exit Sub

        CurrentRow = CurrentRow + 1

        txtTitle.Text = dt.Rows(CurrentRow).Item(0)
        txtDesc.Text = dt.Rows(CurrentRow).Item(1)

        Me.Text = CurrentRow + 1.ToString

    End Sub
```

Just as in the btnPrevious code, you must first find out if the user is asking to see a record that doesn't exist. If the CurrentRow isn't the highest row, you then proceed to adjust CurrentRow up by one and then display that record. The rest of the code is identical to the btnPrevious code.

Recall that you must use −1 when getting information the TotalRows **global variable in the PDM's code. That's because of a grevious fault in computer programming languages that I've mentioned previously:** *some* **arrays and collections start with an index of 1, and others start with an index of 0. As the PDM program illustrates, you've got both of these ways of counting to deal with when using a DataSet. The Count property of a DataSet's Rows collection begins with 1. However, the DataRecords collection of a DataSet begins with 0. So, to keep things working correctly — to keep the** TotalRows **and** CurrentRow **variables in sync with each other — you must subtract 1 from** TotalRows **each time you use it.**

Responding to a Click within a ListBox

After the user displays the Index ListBox (by clicking btnIndex), they can click any item within the list to cause that record to appear in the TextBoxes. Type this code into the lstIndex Click event:

```
Private Sub lstIndex_Click(ByVal sender As Object, ByVal e As
System.EventArgs) Handles lstIndex.Click

        txtTitle.Text = lstIndex.Items(lstIndex.SelectedIndex)
        txtDesc.Text = lstSearch.Items(lstIndex.SelectedIndex)
        CurrentRow = lstIndex.SelectedIndex

    End Sub
```

All you do here is use the SelectedIndex property of the ListBox to define which item in the lstIndex ListBox to display as the title, as well as which item from within the lstSearch ListBox to display in the larger, "description" TextBox. Note that the description field (column) is kept in the lstSearch ListBox — but that ListBox is never made visible. It's just used as a convenient repository for holding these records.

Finally, the CurrentRow variable is updated to reflect the record number of the currently displayed record.

Searching

Any good database program permits users to search through the entire group of records and return those that match the user's criterion. The PDM has this feature, too. The user can type in a string (text) of any length. A ListBox then displays all records that contain that text anywhere in their description (desc) field. Then the user can click on the title of the record they want to have displayed in the TextBoxes.

Type this into the btnSearch Click event (in addition to the code you typed into this event in Session 23):

```
Private Sub btnSearch_Click(ByVal sender As System.Object, ByVal e As
System.EventArgs) Handles btnSearch.Click

        'if they have no active DataSet, refuse:

        If dr Is Nothing Then MsgBox("Please use the File menu to Open a
DataSet, or create a New one first.") : Exit Sub

        Dim s As String
        Dim i As Integer, x As Integer
        Dim hits(TotalRows) As String 'hold the hits


        s = InputBox("Enter Your Search Term", "Search")

        If s = "" Then Exit Sub
```

```
        s = s.ToLower 'make it case-insensitive


        For i = 0 To TotalRows - 1
            If InStr(LCase(lstSearch.Items(i)), s) Then
                hits(x) = lstIndex.Items(i)
                x = x + 1
            End If

        Next

        If x = 0 Then MsgBox("We found no matches for " & s) : Exit Sub


        lstResults.Items.Clear()

        For i = 0 To x - 1
            lstResults.Items.Add(hits(i))
        Next


        lstResults.Visible = True
btnExit.Text = "&Exit"
        lstResults.Visible = True
        btnPrevious.Enabled = False
        btnNext.Enabled = False



    End Sub
```

In this code, you first see if the current DataRow (dr) contains nothing. If so, there are no records, nothing to search. So you let the user know they cannot search until they've created or opened a DataSet.

Next you create an array named Hits to hold any records that match the user's search string. Then you use an InputBox to get the user's string, and if the variable s is empty (""), it means the user clicked the Cancel button and provided no string, so you exit the procedure.

Then you want to make the search ignore captitalization (either in the user's search string or in the records being searched). So you use the LCase method to reduce both the user's string and the records to all-lowercase characters. This means that "ROMAN" will match "Roman," "roman," "RoMaN," or whatever. The characters themselves, not their capitalization, will trigger hits.

A loop is then used to search from zero to TotalRows -1 (the entire set of records). The InStr (*within the string*) command is often useful when working with text. In this example, if the user's string (s) is found inside any of the records held in the lstSearch ListBox, then you've found a match, so you store the Title field of that record in the Hits array.

A variable, x, keeps track of your loop through all the records and counts any hits. If x is zero when you finish with the loop, you display a message to the user that no matches were found, and you exit the subroutine at that point.

Otherwise, you empty any contents in the lstResults ListBox with the Clear command (in case there was a previous search and some records are still listed). Then you go through the Hits array and put the hits into the lstResults ListBox. Last, the lstResults ListBox is displayed to the user so they can choose any record they want to see (by clicking its title in the ListBox).

Selecting a Search Hit

Now type this code into the lstResults Click event, to permit the user to click a title and view the entire record in the TextBoxes:

```
Private Sub lstResults_Click(ByVal sender As Object, ByVal e As
System.EventArgs) Handles lstResults.Click

    lstResults.Visible = False

    Dim i As Integer
    Dim s As String
    s = lstResults.SelectedItem.ToString

    'find their choice

    For Each dr In dt.Rows
        i = i + 1
        If dr(0).ToString = s Then
            txtTitle.Text = dr(0).ToString
            txtDesc.Text = dr(1).ToString
            CurrentRow = i
            Exit For
        End If
    Next

End Sub
```

In this code, you first close (make invisible) the ListBox. You can, if you wish, permit the user to click multiple hits within the ListBox (see the lstIndex code earlier in this session). Then you put the user's choice (the title field the user selected) into the variable s. Then you go through all the records until you find a match in the title field (dr(0)). When the match is found, you put the text from that record into the two TextBoxes. You also update the CurrentRow variable.

Removing Rows

**10 Min.
To Go**

The user must be able to delete, as well as add new, records from our DataSet. Type this into the btnDelete Click event:

```
Private Sub btnDelete_Click(ByVal sender As System.Object, ByVal e As
System.EventArgs) Handles btnDelete.Click
```

```
'save the current record in case the user wants to Undo this deletion:
      titlehold = dt.Rows(CurrentRow).Item(0)
      descriptionhold = dt.Rows(CurrentRow).Item(1)

      dt.Rows.Remove(dt.Rows(CurrentRow))
      Me.Text = "Record Deleted..."

      TotalRows = TotalRows - 1
      If CurrentRow = 0 Then
          btnNext_Click(Me, e)
      Else
          btnPrevious_Click(Me, e)
      End If

  End Sub
```

Before removing this record, you save its contents into `titlehold` and `descriptionhold` — two global variables whose only *raison d'etre* is to keep a deleted record's contents safe in case the user changes their mind and clicks the Undo button.

Then you use the Remove method, reduce the `TotalRows` variable by one, and use the code already written in the Button Next or Previous Click event to display an adjacent record in the TextBoxes. You don't want to show the user an empty set of TextBoxes, nor do you want to show them a random record. It should be adjacent to the one that was removed.

Notice the code `btnNext_Click(Me, e)`**. You'll sometimes find yourself wanting to do something that has already been programmed in another event. To "trigger" an event, just type its name, and provide the** Me **and** e **variables — required by VB .NET, but in this case unused variables.**

You might wonder if you look in VB .NET's Help that there are actually *two* methods that sound as if they could delete a row in a DataSet: Delete and Remove. However, the Delete method doesn't actually get rid of a row; it simply "marks" the row for later deletion when (or if) the programmer employs the AcceptChanges method. Marking a row is useful for such jobs as later permitting an Undo option, restoring the row. (However, given that you're going to handle the Undo issue with your own programming, you'll just employ the Remove method, which gets rid of the row completely.)

Undoing a Removal

Whoa! I goofed up and deleted a record I wish I'd left alone. Because you thoughtfully saved any deleted record in the btnDelete procedure, you can restore it if the user clicks the Undo button:

```
Private Sub btnUndo_Click(ByVal sender As System.Object, ByVal e As
System.EventArgs) Handles btnUndo.Click

        'restore the text
        txtTitle.Text = titlehold
        txtDesc.Text = descriptionhold
```

```
' click the Add button to enter this row back into the DataSet
btnAdd_Click(Me, e)

End Sub
```

Here, as in the `btnDelete` procedure, you're using code that already exists within another procedure. In this case, after restoring the previously deleted text, you trigger the `btnAdd Click` event. It behaves as if the user had just added a new record to the DataSet: adding it into the DataSet, and then re-alphabetizing the DataSet.

Alphabetizing

I first thought I could put the Title column into one ListBox and the Description column into a second ListBox, and then set both the ListBox's Sorted property to True. Setting a ListBox's Sorted property to True automatically causes those listbox's contents to be alphabetized.

There is also a `Select` method available to the DataSet table object, which can provide you with sorted columns. But we have a more difficult alphabetizing problem to solve here in the PDM.

You do see the problem. If you put the Title column into one ListBox and the Description column into another ListBox, both columns would be correctly alphabetized, but *they would not remain in sync*. The ListBox holding titles might list *Anchovy Surprise* as the first recipe, but the associated description for that recipe might have been alphabetized differently in the ListBox holding the descriptions. (If the description starts off *Mash the anchovies...* it would appear somewhere in the middle of the description ListBox.)

So, I had to come up with another approach. There are, of course, VB routines that you could look up on the Internet to alphabetize data, but you already have the ListBox Sorted feature. You *could* use ListBoxes, as long as you made a provision to keep the columns in sync. Sometimes you have to, so here's what I came up with.

This is not an event; it's a sub that you write. So you must type the lines Sub alphabetizer and End sub, along with all the code in between those lines. Move down to the bottom of the code window, and just above the line End Class, type this sub in:

```
Sub alphabetizer()

        lstAlpha.Items.Clear()

        'alphabetize by sending titles into "sorted" listbox
        For Each dr In dt.Rows
            lstAlpha.Items.Add(dr(0).ToString)
        Next

        Dim i As Integer


        lstIndex.Items.Clear()
        'put titles alphabetically into Index listbox
        For i = 0 To TotalRows - 1
```

```
                lstIndex.Items.Add(lstAlpha.Items(i))
        Next i

        Dim x As Integer

        'arrange descriptions alphabetically in Search ListBox
        lstSearch.Items.Clear()
        For i = 0 To TotalRows - 1
            For Each dr In dt.Rows
                If dr(0).ToString = lstIndex.Items(i) Then
                    lstSearch.Items.Add(dr(1).ToString)
                    Exit For
                End If
            Next
        Next i

        'based on the lstIndex and lstSearch, revise the dataset:
        For i = 0 To TotalRows - 1
            dt.Rows(i).Item(0) = lstIndex.Items(i)
            dt.Rows(i).Item(1) = lstSearch.Items(i)
        Next

    End Sub
```

This is the most complex code in the PDM, but if you want to see how it works, read on. There's a ListBox named lstAlpha that has only one job: to alphabetize. It's the only ListBox in this program that has its Sorted property set to True. So you first fill this ListBox with the all the Titles in your DataSet:

```
        For Each dr In dt.Rows
            lstAlpha.Items.Add(dr(0).ToString)
        Next
```

Then you prepare the lstIndex ListBox to hold the now-sorted Titles column by using the Clear method to first empty that ListBox. Then a loop transfers the now-alphabetized Titles from the lstAlpha ListBox to the lstIndex ListBox. *They remain alphabetized* — adding items to an unsorted ListBox adds them to the list in the order they are entered.

Now, here's the hardest code to understand:

```
        'arrange descriptions alphabetically in Search ListBox
        lstSearch.Items.Clear()
        For i = 0 To TotalRows - 1
            For Each dr In dt.Rows
                If dr(0).ToString = lstIndex.Items(i) Then
                    lstSearch.Items.Add(dr(1).ToString)
                    Exit For
                End If
            Next
        Next i
```

This loop arranges the other (Description) field in alphabetic order. It's one of those (always confusing) nested loops. One loop within another.

Nested loops are fairly rare in the real world. The Mad Hatter ride at Disneyland is one example: people sit in revolving teacups which are, themselves, also circling around in a larger loop on their rotating base. You get the idea.

In this code, for the total number of records (rows), you go through the entire DataSet and locate the match between dr(0) — the Title field — and the alphabetized title field now held in the lstIndex ListBox. This tells you which *record number* in the DataSet matches the alphabetized Title. When you find the match, you put the corresponding Description field, dr(1), into the ListBox that holds your Descriptions column (lstSearch). This process synchronizes the two ListBoxes, ensuring that the Descriptions are in the same order as their Titles.

Then, having synchronized the contents of your two ListBoxes, you alphabetize the actual DataSet itself by pouring the contents of the ListBoxes into the DataSet:

```
For i = 0 To TotalRows - 1
    dt.Rows(i).Item(0) = lstIndex.Items(i)
    dt.Rows(i).Item(1) = lstSearch.Items(i)
Next
```

Job done.

Done!

REVIEW

This was a busy session, and you were the beaver! You learned a variety of programming techniques and some problem-solving strategies. You saw how to add rows to a DataSet, and how to cancel and undo in a typical application. You learned to move up and down through a DataSet's rows and how to search and remove rows. Finally, you used the VB .NET ListBox control to quickly alphabetize a DataSet — indexing on one column (the titles) and then synchronizing a second column to the now-sorted titles.

QUIZ YOURSELF

1. What does it mean to "commit" a row of data? (See "Committing a new record.")

2. Why doesn't a DataSet have MoveNext and MovePrevious methods you can use to go through its records in order? (See "Moving Through the DataSet.")

3. What does the SelectedIndex property tell you about a ListBox? (See "Responding to a Click within a ListBox.")

4. What is one use for the LCase function? (See "Searching.")

5. Do the Delete and Remove methods both eliminate a row from a DataSet? (See "Removing Rows.")

Completing the Personal Database Manager

Session Checklist

✔ Saving a DataSet

✔ Creating an automatic backup feature

✔ Keeping the DataSet's records updated

✔ Fixing a problem unique to VB .NET

✔ Understanding side effects

✔ Searching through multiple records

**30 Min.
To Go**

In this session, you are going to put the finishing touches on your PDM application. You'll begin by creating a Save feature that lets the user store all the data in the PDM on the hard drive. In the process, you'll learn several techniques common to many computer applications, including providing automatic backup, maintaining an updated set of records, and searching through multiple records.

Save

The Save feature is used when the user gets frightened and decides that it would be prudent to save their work. It's similar to the Exit feature, without the actual exiting:

```
Private Sub mnuSave_Click(ByVal sender As System.Object, ByVal e As
System.EventArgs) Handles mnuSave.Click

        If dr Is Nothing Then Exit Sub 'nothing to save

        'otherwise, save the dataset
        ds.WriteXmlSchema(schemafilepath)
```

```
    ds.WriteXml(datafilepath)

End Sub
```

If the DataRecord object variable points to nothing, the user hasn't yet got any data to save, so you'll just quit this sub. However, if there's something to save, you use the two WriteXml methods to save the DataSet's structure and its data.

Exit

Recall that the Exit button serves two purposes: it quits the program or simply shuts the lstIndex, depending on the caption (text) displayed on the button. To see which task the user wants to accomplish when this button's clicked, you can simply look at the button's Text property. If it does not say "Exit," you make the ListBox's Visible properties False and adjust some buttons. If it does say "Exit," the user is clicking the Exit button to quit. When the user wants to quit the program, you save the DataSet to the hard drive, and then the End command quits the program. Here's the code:

```
Private Sub btnExit_Click(ByVal sender As System.Object, ByVal e As
System.EventArgs) Handles btnExit.Click


If dt Is Nothing Then End 'nothing to save

        If btnExit.Text = "&Close List" Then   'they're closing a listbox"
            btnExit.Text = "&Exit"
            lstIndex.Visible = False
            lstSearch.Visible = False
            btnPrevious.Enabled = True
            btnNext.Enabled = True
        Else 'they want to quit the program
            'save the dataset
            FixData()

            ds.WriteXmlSchema(schemafilepath)
            ds.WriteXml(datafilepath)

            End
        End If

End Sub
```

Close

The Close option in the File menu is identical to the user clicking the Exit button, so you merely use that same code:

```
Private Sub mnuClose_Click(ByVal sender As System.Object, ByVal e As
System.EventArgs) Handles mnuClose.Click
```

```
        ds.WriteXmlSchema(schemafilepath)
        ds.WriteXml(datafilepath)

    End
End Sub
```

Finishing the Edit Menu

Adding Backup and BackColor features to your Edit menu is fairly straightforward. If you want to add these features to your PDM, see the Supplementary Notes file on this book's CD. We've got some more important topics to cover in this session, and we don't want to run out of time.

Refinements to the Project

Well, you've done what you set out to do — the PDM works as advertised. But when you create a utility or application yourself, doubtless you'll continue to refine it. If you use it often, you'll notice things — even years later — that you would like to improve. (It's just like getting married.)

You'll want to archive your project (the entire directory that holds all the forms, code, dependency files, and so on). In VB .NET, all files are plain text files, so you can archive by simply copying the entire directory to a safe place. However, I like to keep an extra copy of my source code — all the actual programming code that I typed in. To do this, just drag your mouse down the entire code window to select the whole thing, all the procedures and everything. Then press Ctrl+C to copy it and Ctrl+V in Windows Notepad to paste it. Save the Notepad file. That way, even if the VB language changes significantly in the future, you'll still be able to quickly recreate your project and modify it. You've got the source code safely stashed away in a .TXT file.

Updating Records

**20 Min.
To Go**

The first and most glaring "improvement" you need to make is to permit the user to actually change the data in the TextBoxes, and be sure that those edits are actually saved to the DataSet's data file on the hard drive. This is more of a necessity, truth be told, than an "improvement."

This particular problem — handling updates — is one of the major jobs of a database-management program. And it's time to address this issue in the PDM.

Sometimes the DataSet is updated in the PDM, namely at the end of the Alphabetizer routine:

```
For i = 0 To TotalRows - 1
        dt.Rows(i).Item(0) = lstIndex.Items(i)
        dt.Rows(i).Item(1) = lstSearch.Items(i)
    Next
```

The Alphabetizer is called from the Form_Load, btnAdd, and mnuOpen events. But the real problem here is that when the user changes the description or title textboxes, those changes are simply ignored by the PDM when the user clicks such buttons as Next, Previous, and so on.

As you might imagine, there are several solutions to this problem. You could use the TextBoxes' Change event to save the contents of that TextBox, but the Change event is hyper — it triggers when you load the text from a disk file, when you click Next or Previous, and even for *every letter the user types into it*! Seems like overkill.

Or you could keep copies of the contents of each Textbox each time you display the TextBox with new contents (such as clicking Next), and then compare the saved version to the current version when changing again (such as clicking Next again). But this too seems a bit much.

There are other techniques. But for now, you'll just take a simple approach: you won't check to see if the user has changed either of the textboxes. You'll ignore that. You'll just *always save* the TextBoxes' contents into the DataSet every time the user clicks a button or chooses a menu item that will change the contents of the TextBoxes.

The DataSet is held in RAM memory in the computer, as are the contents of the TextBoxes, so there's no meaningful degradation of your program's speed by using this tactic. RAM memory is fast.

Click the Form1.vb(Design) tab to see all your buttons and menu items. Now think. Make a list of all the buttons and menu items that can change the TextBoxes' contents (thereby causing any user-edits to be lost). Also include events that don't change the TextBoxes, but are supposed to save the DataSet to the hard drive. Here's the list:

- New
- Open
- Close (This menu item calls the Exit event, so you can leave mnuClose out of the list.)
- Save
- Exit
- Previous
- Next
- Search
- Index

 Automatic Backup triggers the Save event, so you can leave mnuBackup **out of the list. Also, the** Add This Record, Delete, **and** Undo Delete **events already adjust the DataSet by using the** Add **and** Remove **methods.**

OK. At the top of the code for each of these events, you'll add a reference to a subroutine that will replace the current row in the DataSet with the current contents of the two TextBoxes.

First, create a new subroutine down at the bottom of the code window, just above the line:

```
End Class
```

Type in this:

```
Sub FixData()

    If dt Is Nothing Then Exit Sub 'no record

    dt.Rows(CurrentRow).Item(0) = txtTitle.Text
    dt.Rows(CurrentRow).Item(1) = txtDesc.Text

End Sub
```

You want to call the FixData **procedure from several of the procedures, but there's now a fair amount of source code in the code in the code window to look through. It's not that easy to locate particular events. Scrolling the code is hard on the eyes and, at least for me, hard on the brain after a while. The best way to quickly locate events is to take advantage of a unique character used in the declaration of every event: the underscore character. When looking for the** btnNew **event, for instance, press Ctrl+F to bring up the Find dialog, and then type new_ into the *Find what* TextBox and press Enter. There it is: the** btnNew_Click **event, ready for you to modify it.**

Now you need to enter the code that calls the FixData subroutine from all the necessary procedures in the source code.

Near the top of the mnuNew_Click event, type this (in boldface):

```
Private Sub btnNew_Click(ByVal sender As System.Object, ByVal e As
System.EventArgs) Handles btnNew.Click


'if they have no active DataSet, refuse to allow a new record:
        If dt Is Nothing Then 'no table exists yet
            MsgBox("Please use File|Open or File|New so there is a
DataSet--before attempting to add a new record.")
            Exit Sub
        End If

FixData()

        txtTitle.Text = "" : txtDesc.Text = ""

        btnPrevious.Visible = False
```

And near the top of the btnNext procedure:

```
    Private Sub btnNext_Click(ByVal sender As System.Object, ByVal e As
System.EventArgs) Handles btnNext.Click

        If CurrentRow = TotalRows - 1 Then Exit Sub
        FixData()
        CurrentRow = CurrentRow + 1
```

In btnPrevious:

```
    Private Sub btnPrevious_Click(ByVal sender As System.Object, ByVal e
As System.EventArgs) Handles btnPrevious.Click

        If CurrentRow = 0 Then Exit Sub
        FixData()
        CurrentRow = CurrentRow - 1
```

In mnuOpen:

```
    Private Sub mnuOpen_Click(ByVal sender As System.Object, ByVal e As
System.EventArgs) Handles mnuOpen.Click

        FixData()
```

```
Dim userFilePath As String
```

In mnuSave:

```
Private Sub mnuSave_Click(ByVal sender As System.Object, ByVal e As
System.EventArgs) Handles mnuSave.Click
        FixData()
```

Low down in btnExit:

```
Private Sub btnExit_Click(ByVal sender As System.Object, ByVal e As
System.EventArgs) Handles btnExit.Click

        If dt Is Nothing Then End 'nothing to save

        If lstIndex.Visible Then  'they're closing a listbox
            btnExit.Text = "&Exit"
            lstIndex.Visible = False
            btnPrevious.Enabled = True
            btnNext.Enabled = True
        Else 'they want to quit the program
            'save the dataset

        FixData()

            ds.WriteXmlSchema(schemafilepath)
            ds.WriteXml(datafilepath)

            End
        End If

    End Sub
```

In the Search routine:

```
Private Sub btnSearch_Click(ByVal sender As System.Object, ByVal e As
System.EventArgs) Handles btnSearch.Click
```

```
'if they have no active DataSet, refuse:

    If dt Is Nothing Then

 MsgBox("Please use the File menu to Open a DataSet, or create a New one
first.")
Exit Sub

End if

    FixData()
```

And in the Index routine:

```
    Private Sub lstIndex_Click(ByVal sender As Object, ByVal e As
System.EventArgs) Handles lstIndex.Click

    FixData()

    txtTitle.Text = lstIndex.Items(lstIndex.SelectedIndex)
```

That's it. Now when the user edits the data, the data is saved to the DataSet.

About this time in my work with the PDM, I came across a problem unique to VB .NET. Even experienced VB programmers, like me, would not think to look for this kink. In fact, it took me about a half hour to track it down, so you might want to memorize this, and watch for it in your own programming. The problem was that the lstResults_Click **event stopped triggering. In other words, I was testing the program, and when I used the Search button, everything worked fine — the results of a search were displayed in the lstResults window. But when I clicked one of those results, *nothing happened*. A day earlier when I had written the Search routine, everything worked as advertised, but now, mysteriously the** lstResults_Click **event was dead. I tried single-stepping, but never got a response — no code in** lstReslts_Click **was executed when I clicked that ListBox. Then I set a breakpoint in the event — same problem. Finally, I had an inspiration and checked the code (which doesn't entirely fit on the screen — the right side of the code isn't visible in the code window unless you make a point to scroll horizontally over to see it). Here's what I saw:**

```
Private Sub lstResults_Click(ByVal sender As System.Object, ByVal e As
System.EventArgs)
```

To a traditional VB programmer, this looks fine (though those two arguments, sender **and** e, **are new — you usually just ignore them). Can you see the problem? VB .NET requires that each event end with a** Handles **reference:** Handles lstResults.Click. **Otherwise, the event will simply not work *as an event* — it will not trigger as an event should. Without the** Handles reference, this Sub is no longer an event handler; it merely becomes a regular subroutine. (It will still work as a subroutine if somewhere in your source code you called it — but that's not your intention at all. You want this to be an event that automatically triggers when the user clicks the Results ListBox.)

Changing the code to this solved the problem and clicks were now responded to:

```
Private Sub lstResults_Click(ByVal sender As System.Object, ByVal e As
System.EventArgs) Handles lstResults.Click
```

Apparently, I had pressed the Enter key on that line by accident deleting the Handles part of the line. Whatever. Just remember that if an event suddenly goes mysterious dead, check to see if that Handles phrase is tacked onto the end of the event's declaration line. (Technically, the actual *event* itself isn't actually dead. It's still available. You're just not correctly referencing it in your source code without that Handles code. In earlier versions of VB, a line that began with Sub lstResults_Click *defined,* in effect, the click event for that ListBox. Not so in VB .NET. It's the Handles code that makes the connection to the event now (that's why you're now allowed to add multiple Handles references to a single Sub, as described in Session 19).

Side Effects

**10 Min.
To Go**

Making a change in one location in a fairly large application like the PDM, often causes a side effect, a problem elsewhere in the project. When you added the FixData routine, it caused a side effect, a bug, in your existing Delete routine.

As originally written, the Delete procedure called upon the code in btnNext or btnPrevious to display something to the user when a record was deleted. However, both btnNext and btnPrevious used FixData, whichcauses a difficulty — forcing a display of a non-existent record. To solve this problem, change the code in the btnDelete event to the following (change shown in boldface):

```
'save the current record in case the user wants to Undo this
deletion:
titlehold = dt.Rows(CurrentRow).Item(0)
descriptionhold = dt.Rows(CurrentRow).Item(1)

dt.Rows.Remove(dt.Rows(CurrentRow))
Me.Text = "Record Deleted..."

TotalRows = TotalRows - 1

If CurrentRow = 0 Then
    CurrentRow = CurrentRow + 1
Else
    CurrentRow = CurrentRow - 1
End If
```

```
txtTitle.Text = dt.Rows(CurrentRow).Item(0)
txtDesc.Text = dt.Rows(CurrentRow).Item(1)
```

This imitates the behavior of the btnNext or btnPrevious events, but leaves out the call to FixData.

> **Remember my previous warning: the longer your program, the more unpredictable the interaction between its parts. Some schemes (structured programming, strict data typing, explicit data declaration, object oriented programming) can reduce the number of side effects, but I doubt that any program of any complexity will ever be built without requiring a considerable, and probably ongoing, debugging process. After all, we've had eons of experience with human language, yet misunderstandings show no sign of lessening. So expect to find additional things about the PDM that you'll want to improve as you use it. Fortunately, you are your own beta tester, and you can fix the source code any time you find a problem. Try, for example, to use the Open feature, with a DataSet already opened in the PDM.**

Improved Searching

In the original PDM design, the search feature only looks through the description field, not the title field. However, it's probably best to search both fields. So, locate this line in the btnSearch event:

```
If InStr(LCase(lstSearch.Items(i)), s) Then
```

And replace it with this line that includes the title column (recall that titles are held in the lstIndex ListBox):

```
If InStr(LCase(lstSearch.Items(i)), s) Or InStr(LCase(lstIndex.Items(i)),
s) Then
```

More Custom Graphics

You might want to offer the user the ability to display a picture as the form's background. The right wallpaper graphic can make the PDM look indescribably cool. To find out how to do this, see the Supplementary Notes file on this book's CD.

Now you've got the PDM. I hope it proves useful to you. Press F5, choose File|New and create a new DataSet. Add some records to it, then test the searching, indexing and other features the PDM offers.

As I mentioned, I've used this program for many years as an electronic cookbook — and have made many improvements to it over the years. I've also learned a good deal about programming by upgrading it and adding new features that are important to me.

PDM includes many of the features common to any computer application. It started out as a DAO program. Then it moved on to the ADO database style, and now employs VB .NET's ADO.NET. I expect it will survive several more generations of database programming technologies.

REVIEW

This session covered the topics of saving a DataSet, creating an automatic backup feature, and how to update a DataSet's records if the user edits them. Then you looked at a couple of bug problems, including one unique to VB .NET. Finally, you saw how to search multiple records and provide graphics on the background of a form.

Done!

QUIZ YOURSELF

1. What is the Checked property and how do you manipulate it? (See "Finishing the Edit Menu.")

2. Why would you want to save the source code of your project for archival purposes? (See "Refinements to the Project.")

3. Describe one technique that can be used to update a DataSet when the user edits its records. (See "Updating Records.")

4. What are side effects? (See "Side Effects.")

5. What use is the Or operator when searching multiple rows in a DataSet? (See "Improved Searching.")

Working with Database Wizards

Session Checklist

✔ Connecting to a database

✔ Installing SQL Server

✔ Using an OleDbCommand control

✔ Previewing your DataSet

✔ Creating a new SQL query

✔ Building a new DataSet

✔ Binding controls

✔ Viewing a DataSet's properties

✔ Working with the Data Form Wizard

30 Min.
To Go

In this session, you'll generate DataSets and *bind* them to data stores (sources). (I'm using the term *data store* here rather than *database* because the ADO.NET database technology in VB .NET is designed to work with sources of data other than the traditional database — namely arrays, email files, and so on.)

As is usual with VB .NET, there are many paths to reach a given goal. In the past several sessions, you've worked with the PDM to create a working database management program, using only a detached DataSet.

There is, however, more to database programming in VB .NET than you've looked at so far. Now you'll explore several paths to data binding in this session. Because Windows Forms can be tested and explored more efficiently in the .NET IDE, this session introduces some database-connection techniques using Windows Forms (traditional Windows) examples.

The differences, however, between Windows Forms and WebForms (server-side controls and server-side VB .NET) are generally trivial. (You'll see just how trivial in the examples in Session 27, beginning with the example titled "Programming a DataSet in a WebForm.")

In any event, this session focuses on several ways to get information from a data store.

As you'll soon see, there is a method of the DataGrid control called DataBind(), and there are Wizards and Connection objects and several other ways to reach your objectives (although again, you'll have to wait until Session 27 to get the full picture).

VB .NET provides a variety of options when you want to connect a data store to your application. Who knows? You might need to use one of these options in your future programming. It's worth knowing about these alternative techniques.

Connecting to a Database

First, you want to connect a Visual Basic form to a database. The following examples illustrate the various steps you take to give a user access to a database, using VB .NET, ASP.NET, and ADO.NET.

Start a new project in VB .NET (File ⇨ New ⇨ Project). When the New Project dialog box opens, name this project **Connecting**. Make this project the one that runs when you press F5 by right-clicking the project's name in the Solution Explorer, and then choosing Set As Startup Project.

Now double-click the Windows Application icon. But hold your horses. Before you can work with a database, you've got to do some preliminary hookup housekeeping.

Installing SQL Server

If you haven't installed SQL Server 2000, install it from your .NET CD now, or download it from:

www.microsoft.com/sql/evaluation/trial/2000/default.asp

After it's installed, you must then connect SQL Server to IIS. Choose Start ⇨ Programs ⇨ Microsoft SQL Server ⇨ Configure SQL XML Support in IIS (Microsoft's Internet Information Services). The IIS Virtual Directory Management for SQL Server dialog box opens. Right-click the Default Web Site in the left pane. (Menus are useless in this situation: To reveal *Default Web Site*, you'll probably have to click the small + next to your computer's name.)

From the context menu, choose New, then Virtual Directory. You'll see the New Virtual Directory Properties dialog box.

In the General tab, type the name **Pub** (in place of the default name *New Virtual Directory*). You can later access this new virtual directory by using this URL in your browser's Address field: http://Dell/Pub. But instead of *Dell*, which is my computer's name, substitute *your* computer's name. You'll find your computer's name displayed next to a computer icon in the IIS Virtual Directory Management for SQL Server dialog box you used just a minute ago when you right-clicked in it, as shown in Figure 26-1.

For the Local Path field in the General tab of the New Virtual Directory Properties dialog box, click the Browse button and locate C:\Inetpub\Wwwroot, or if you're using a different drive, replace C: in this example with the correct drive name. Click OK to specify this path.

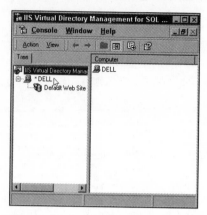

Figure 26-1   *Here's where to find your computer's name.*

If you are connecting to a physical directory on a separate computer, the Browse option isn't available. You must type in the remote computer's `virtualRoot` path.

Click the Security tab in the New Virtual Directory Properties dialog box, and click Use Windows Integrated Authentication. Click the Data Source tab. Click the arrow icon to drop down the list of available databases. Locate *Pubs* in the list of databases, as shown in Figure 26-2.

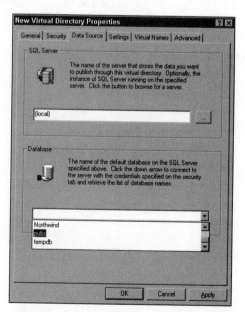

Figure 26-2   *Here's where you specify which database you want to connect to.*

Click the OK button to close the dialog box. Then close the IIS Virtual Directory Manager.

Adding an OleDbDataAdapter

Now click the Data tab on the VB .NET Toolbox, and double-click the OleDbDataAdapter control, as shown in Figure 26-3.

Figure 26-3 *You can begin creating a connection between your VB .NET application and a database using this control.*

The Data Adapter Configuration Wizard window opens. Click Next. On the second page of the Wizard, click the button labeled New Connection. The DataLink Properties dialog box opens. Click the Provider tab and select Microsoft OLE DB Provider for SQL Server (if it's not already selected).

Click the Connection tab and in Step 2 on this page, choose Use Windows NT (or 2000) Integrated Security. (If SQL Server is on a different computer on your network, you will also have to specify the Server Name on the Connection tab.)

In Step 3 on this same Wizard page, drop the ListBox by clicking the down-arrow icon, and then choose Pubs as the database. Click the Test Connection button to reassure yourself that you're now connected to the sample SQL database named Pubs.

Click OK to close the dialog window.

Click Next in the Data Adapter Configuration Wizard. Select the Use SQL Statements option button. Click Next. Click the Query Builder button.

This opens the useful Query Builder utility, as shown in Figure 26-4.

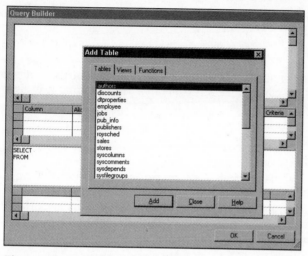

Figure 26-4 *Use this Query Builder to construct SQL queries the easy way.*

In the Add Table dialog box, double-click Authors to add that table to the Query Builder. Click Close to shut the Add Table dialog box.

Click the All Columns button in the Authors table. This generates the following SQL query for you, as you can see in Figure 26-5:

```
SELECT      authors.*
FROM        authors
```

This means "Select all (*) columns (fields or *categories*) in the Authors table.

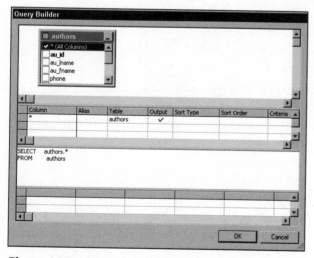

Figure 26-5 *Here's a query that's been written for you, based on your choices.*

Click OK, Next, and Finish to close the Wizard at this point. (You'll come back and work with this Wizard later.)

Now you'll see two icons displayed under your main Design window: OleDbDataAdapter1 and OleDbConnection1. These controls are not directly displayed on your form (they are placed on a *tray* below the Design window). Note that the name of each of these objects ends in *1* — just as when you add a control like a TextBox to a VB .NET form, it is given the default name TextBox1.

Seeing Your DataSet

**20 Min.
To Go**

Each data control has properties (actually, some of the properties are Wizards that pop up) that you might want to experiment with. Right-click the OleDbDataAdapter1 icon, and then choose the Preview Data option. The Data Adapter Preview window pops up. Click the Fill DataSet button on this window and you'll see the data in your DataSet (in this case, it's the SQL statement you created, illustrated in Figure 26-5). You can see the results in Figure 26-6.

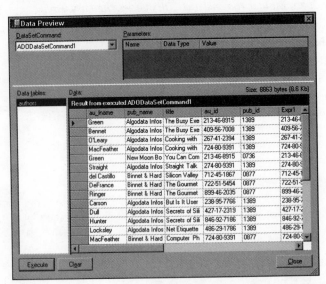

Figure 26-6 *Each OleDbDataAdapter control has this preview utility, so you can quickly see the contents of its DataSet.*

Click Close to shut the Data Preview window.

Creating a Different SQL Query

Right-click the OleDbDataAdaper1 icon again and select Configure DataAdapter. Click Next twice, choose Use SQL Statement in the Choose a Query Type page of the Wizard, and then click Next. Press the Del key to get rid of the query you created earlier. Click the Query Builder button.

Double-click the Authors table to add it. Repeat that process to add the Titles, TitleAuthor, and Publishers tables. Click the Close button.

In the ListBox displaying the Authors table, click *au_Lname* to select it. Also select *pub_name* in the Publishers table and *title* in the Titles table. The SQL Query Builder will create this SQL statement for you:

```
SELECT      authors.au_lname, publishers.pub_name, titles.title
FROM        authors
INNER JOIN
    titleauthor ON authors.au_id = titleauthor.au_id

INNER JOIN
    titles ON titleauthor.title_id = titles.title_id

INNER JOIN
    publishers ON titles.pub_id = publishers.pub_id
```

Click OK to close the SQL Query Builder. Click Next (don't worry about the two methods the Wizard is unable to create), and then Finish, to close the Wizard. Click the Preview Data link in the Properties window. (This group of links in the Properties window can be used instead of the context menu, which displays the same options if you right-click the OleDataAdapter1 icon in the tray.) The Data Preview window pops up. Click the Fill DataSet button on this window to see the list generated by your new SQL statement. Notice that the three columns you selected are displayed, along with other columns for each _id field. These are *joins* connecting these tables with each other. The id fields are also the index fields of their respective tables. (More on this later.) Click Close when you've finished looking at this DataSet.

Creating a DataSet

Now it's time to actually generate a usable DataSet and put it into your source code. Right-click the OleDbDataAdapter1 icon, and in the context menu, select Generate DataSet. Type **dsAuthors** as the name for your new DataSet class in the New TextBox, and click the "Add this DataSet to the designer" checkbox. Click the OK button.

VB .NET grinds away inside the computer (you cannot hear its screams) as it generates the DataSet you have requested. When the new DataSet is added, you'll see a new icon appear in the tray named DsAuthors1. Click the Form1.VB tab at the top of the designer window to view the source code. (If you don't see this tab, right-click Form1.vb in the Solution Explorer, then choose View Code.) Click the + next to Windows Form Designer generated code to reveal what VB .NET was doing while it was screaming behind the scenes.

You'll see that quite a bit of source code has been added to your application.

Binding Controls to a DataSet

Binding causes a property to change, automatically, when the user moves to a different record in the database. Binding keeps the data (or other property in a control) in sync with the currently selected record(s) in the data store. For example, if a TextBox is bound to a particular column, and the user clicks a button named *Next* to move to the next row (record) in the DataSet, they will see the next row displayed in that TextBox. To bind controls to a particular column (field) in a DataSet, you use the DataBindings collection (or you can think of it as a property if you wish).

It's good to know how to modify SQL queries and also create new DataSets. Before binding a TextBox to a DataSet, you'll first create a new DataSet by following the steps described earlier in this Session. Here's a quick reminder of how to create a new DataSet:

Right-click OledbDataAdapter1in the tray, choose Configure Data Adapter, use the Pubs database, in the Query Builder add the Authors table and click au_Lname in that table. Click OK, Next and Finish. Right-click OledbDataAdapter1 in the tray, choose Generate DataSet, click the New option button in the Generate DataSet dialog, name the new DataSet **dsLname**, click OK.

Now you will bind a TextBox to your new DataSet. If necessary, click the Form1.VB (Design) tab on the top of the main window to display the visual elements of the form. Click the Windows Forms tab in the ToolBox. Add a TextBox to the form by double-clicking that icon in the Toolbox. Click TextBox1 to select it, and then press F4 to display the Properties window. Click the + symbol next to the DataBindings property. (Interestingly, if you click the Advanced button, you'll see that you can bind virtually *all* properties — and multiple properties — but you'll use the Text property in this example.)

Click Text under the Bindings property, and then click the Text down-arrow icon to drop down the list for the Text binding. Locate the *dsLname1* DataSet. Then click the + symbols below dsLname1 until you locate the Authors table, and the *au_Lname* field. Double-click *au_Lname* to put it into the Properties window as the field that binds to this TextBox. (You must click the word *au_Lname*, not the icon to its left.) You'll see DsLname1 - authors. au_lname listed in the Properties window.

When you adjust the Bindings property, VB .NET inserts code like the following into the InitializeControl section of your Form's source code: (You can find the Bindings property definition right in the source code with other properties such as Location and Size.)

```
Me.TextBox1.DataBindings.Add(New System.Windows.Forms.Binding("Text",
Me.DsLname1, "authors.au_lname"))
```

Now, you're itching to see an actual connection during runtime between this database and your TextBox, right? OK. Let's do it. You must write one line of code to fill your DataSet with actual data from the Pubs database. Double-click the title bar of Form1 to get to the Form_Load event in the code window. Type this into the Form_Load event:

```
Private Sub Form1_Load(ByVal sender As System.Object, ByVal e As
System.EventArgs) Handles MyBase.Load

    OleDbDataAdapter1.Fill(DsLname1)

End Sub
```

Now press F5 and you will see your TextBox display the last name of an author in this DataBase. You've made the connection.

Viewing a DataSet's Properties

To see, or modify, the properties of a particular DataSet, click that DataSet's icon to select it in the tray in the Design window. Click dsAuthors1 icon. Press F4 to see its Properties window. You'll immediately see some of its properties. Note the difference between the name you use in code to identify the DataSet object (in this example, *dsAuthors1*) versus the DataSetName property (the name of the cache — in this example, *dsAuthors*). This is the same distinction as there is between a TextBox class and a TextBox1 instance (object) created from that class. (More on this in Session 30.)

**10 Min.
To Go**

The TableMappings Editor

Now click the OleDbDataAdapter1 icon in the tray to select it. Look in the Properties window and locate the TableMappings collection. Click that property, and then click the icon with . . . (ellipsis) to bring up the Table Mappings dialog box, as shown in Figure 26-7.

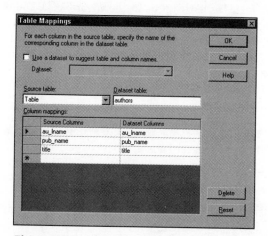

Figure 26-7 *Use this dialog box to view or modify the tables' mappings in a DataSet.*

A *mapping* shows which table in the data source is attached to which table in the DataSet.

Click the OK button to close the Table Mappings dialog box. Now locate the CommandText property (click the + next to the SelectCommand property) and click its ellipsis. This is a quick way to bring up the Query Builder utility without having to run the full Data Adapter Configuration Wizard. (The ConnectionString property, located under the Connection property, is another shortcut, should you ever want to use it.)

Click Cancel to close the Query Builder.

Using the DataForm Wizard

As usual in VB, there are many ways to accomplish a given task. A grid offers the user an excellent, efficient way to interact with a dataset. You can employ the DataForm Wizard to add a grid, and a second, alternative view, of a DataSet. This next example assumes that you've already followed the instructions earlier in this session to create an SQLServer connection to the Pubs sample database. Such a connection lives outside your VB .NET projects, so the connection still exists and can be used in future projects.

You'll now see how to use the DataForm Wizard. Create a new Windows Application style project in VB .NET (File ⇨ New ⇨ Project) and name it **WinDataWiz**.

Choose Project|Add Windows Form. Double-click the Data Form Wizard icon in the New Project dialog. The DataForm Wizard starts running. Click Next. Type in **dsAuthors** as the name of your new DataSet. Click Next. Choose *YourComputersName.*Pubs.dbo as the connection to the Pubs database. Click Next and double-click Authors in the Available tables list to move it to the Selected items list. Click Next.

All the columns in the Authors table are checked in the Columns list. That's fine — there's plenty of room for them in the Grid. Click Next. Leave this page in the Wizard as is. You want the Grid style. Click Finish. Great! There's your Grid, with the appropriate column names already filled it, plus some buttons that load, update, or cancel data.

If you press F5 now, you'll be the goose. Form1 is still the Startup Form for this project, not this DataForm1. Right-click the name of this project (WinDataWiz) in the Solution Explorer and choose Properties. In the Startup Object list choose DataForm1. Click OK. *Now* press F5.

When the DataForm appears, click the Load button. Impressive, isn't it, what you can do with a few minutes alone with a VB .NET Wizard? You can even modify any of this data and click the Update button to change the data in the actual Pubs database.

Figure 26-8 shows what your Grid should look like.

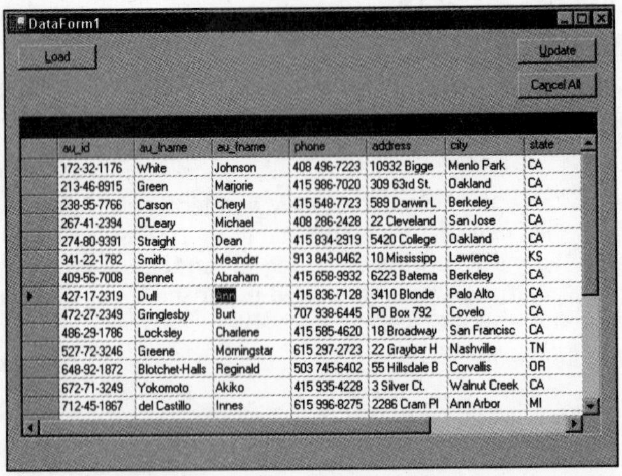

Figure 26-8 *After a little time spent with the VB .NET Data Form Wizard, you can construct full-featured database displays like this.*

Note the *dsAuthors.XSD* file in the Solution Explorer. There's an additional file (currently hidden) that also supports your DataSet. To see it, click the icon at the top of the Solution Explorer to "Show all files." Then click the + symbol next to *dsAuthors.XSD* and there it is, *dsAuthors.VB*. Right-click *dsAuthors.VB* and choose Open. Then click the "Click here to switch to code view" link in the Design window.

You'll see a hair-raising chunk of somewhere between 300 and 500 lines (give or take a few dozen) of code — code *you* didn't write — classes within classes, imported namespaces, overridden functions, and members without end. Best close this and not tamper with it. That's my advice. Just stop trembling, and thank goodness *you* didn't have to write this stuff.

Done!

REVIEW

This session is full of examples showing you how to use DataSets in various contexts, how to bind to ASP.NET controls, and how (in general) to manage the disconnected ADO.NET architecture. You should now have a good foundation, a good understanding of the basics of disconnected database programming. Now it's time to turn our attention to databases attached to Internet Web pages.

QUIZ YOURSELF

1. What does the Query Builder do? (See "Adding an OleDbDataAdapater.")
2. Which property of a control can be bound to a DataSet? (See "Binding Controls to a DataSet.")
3. What happens when a control is bound to a data source? (See "Binding Controls to a DataSet.")
4. How do you see a DataSet's properties? (See "Viewing a DataSet's Properties.")
5. What does "mapping" mean? (See "The TableMappings Editor.")

PART

V

Sunday Morning
Part Review

1. What does *top-down* programming mean?
2. Describe *bottom-up* programming.
3. Define the terms *record* (row) and *field* (column) when used with database programming.
4. Define the term *table* when used with database programming.
5. What is an index in a database?
6. If you plan to size and position components during runtime, what is an advantage of putting the code that does this into the Form_Load event?
7. How do you define shortcut keys for your components, so the user can press Alt + Shortcut Key to activate that component?
8. What is the purpose of the TabIndex property?
9. What does pressing F5 do?
10. What does the end command do?
11. Can you use the same control for two different purposes? Are there any drawbacks to this technique?
12. What's ZOrder?
13. What is a DataSet?
14. Is a DataSet a database?
15. What does the file extension .SLN mean?

16. What does this code do for you:

```
Dim ds as dataset
s = ds.Tables(0).Columns.Count.ToString
```

17. When adding a new record to a DataSet, what is the difference between the NewRow and Add methods?

18. Describe the distinction between using the Remove and Delete methods, when removing a record from a DataSet?

19. What does the WriteXMLSchema command do?

20. In programming, what is a *side-effect*?

PART

VI

*Sunday
Afternoon*

Attaching a Database to a Web Page

Session Checklist

✔ Working with the DataForm Wizard

✔ Data binding

✔ Binding properties

✔ Getting data from a control

**30 Min.
To Go**

S ession 28 goes into some of the basics of ASP.NET, and Session 29 provides you with some programming experience. This session focuses on some preliminary Web-related VB .NET database programming.

As you doubtless know by now, sometimes the best way to learn how to accomplish a job in VB .NET is to use a Wizard. It generates code (often *lots* of code) that you can then modify, or cut and paste, to do tasks that you want to get done. Or, perhaps you just want to learn more about VB .NET programming. In either case, Wizards can be very valuable.

You'll start off this session by presenting a Web site visitor with a display of data from your local database. It's quite common for a Web programmer to need to display the latest offerings from a company's inventory database, or to show a list of upcoming events, current prices, or whatever. The value of fetching the data directly from a database — *whenever a user requests it by visiting a Web page* — is that the data the user sees is up-to-the-minute accurate.

You'll use the trusty Pubs sample database. You will construct a Web page that displays a DataSet extracted in real time from the database.

Off to See the Wizard

It's time to fire up the DataForm Wizard. It will add a Button, a Grid, and the underlying source code that loads the data and displays it to the user.

Start a new project: File|New|Project. In the New Project dialog box, name it **WebApplicationx.** (If you are working on a network and IIS is installed on a different machine, you must also type in the server machine's name in the textbox, for example `http://development`)

Double-click the ASP.NET Web Application icon.

Choose File ⇨ Add New Item. Double-click DataForm Wizard in the Add New Item dialog box. The Wizard begins running. Click Next.

Select the "Create a new dataset named" radio button. (The other button is disabled anyway, because you've not yet created any DataSets in this project.) Type **MySet** as the DataSet name, as you can see in Figure 27-1.

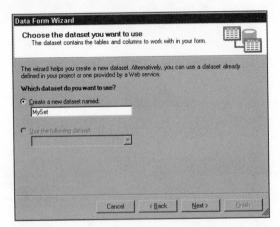

Figure 27-1 *Name your new DataSet in this dialog box.*

Click Next. Choose the *pubs.dbo* database you've used in previous examples in this book, as shown in Figure 27-2. (Your connection will not be displayed exactly as shown in the figure. Instead of beginning with *Dell* (which is the name of my computer), you'll see the name of your computer.)

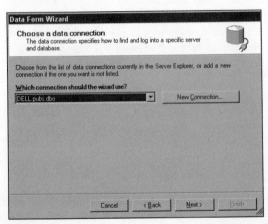

Figure 27-2 *Specify the pubs.dbo database as your data source.*

Click Next. Double-click Authors to add it to the Selected Items list. Click Next. Deselect the Address, City, State and Zip columns (fields) so they will not be part of the displayed results, as shown in Figure 27-3.

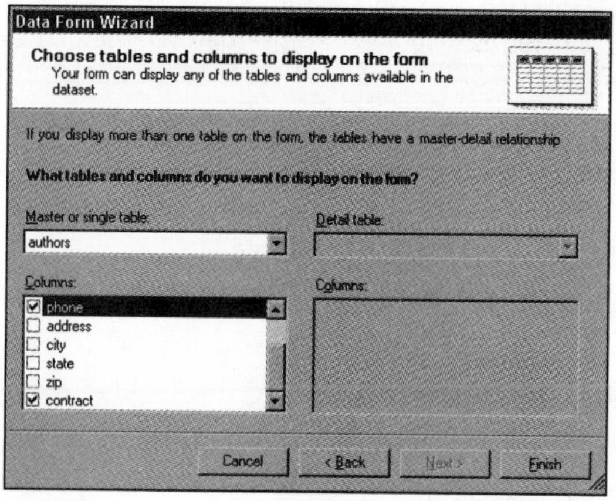

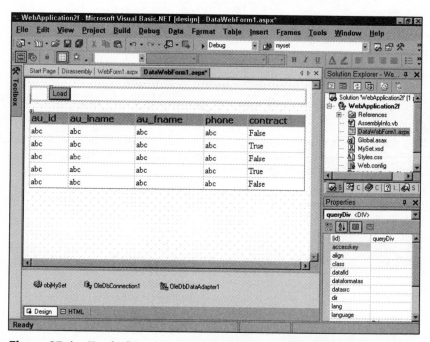

Figure 27-3 *Define which columns you want displayed in this dialog box.*

Click Finish. You now see the structure of your read-only data display, as shown in Figure 27-4.

Figure 27-4 *Here's the grid and the button that loads the DataSet into the grid.*

The Load Button at the top is can be clicked by the user to fill this grid with the DataSet's data. But don't press F5 just yet, cowpoke. As usual, there's something you must do first before running this application (Wizards, good as they are, almost always leave just *one little thing* for you to do before the dang thing actually works. Can't say I know why.)

In Solution Explorer, right-click DataWebForm1.aspx and choose Set as Start Page. *Now* go ahead and press F5. Then when the Load button is displayed in Internet Explorer, click that button. You'll see the results shown in Figure 27-5.

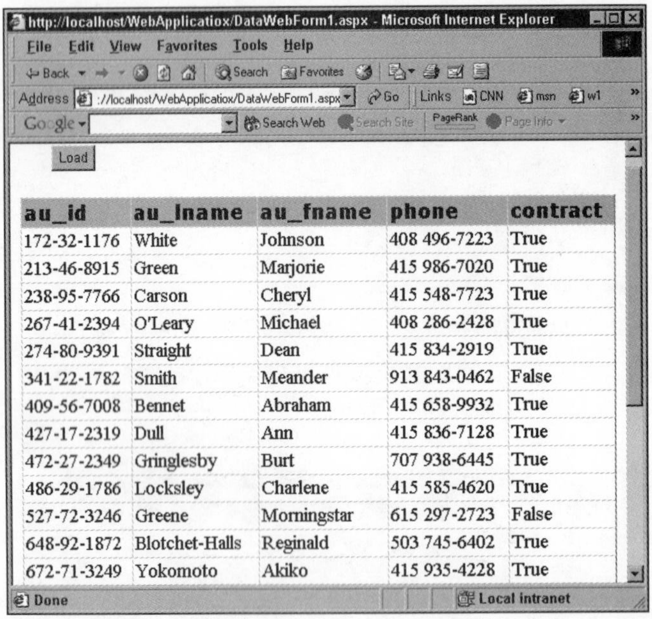

Figure 27-5 *Here's your grid, filled with data, and then displayed to users when they visit your Web page.*

To see the code that fills this grid when the user clicks the Load button (code generated by the Wizard), click the Design tab at the bottom of the Design window, and then double-click the button labeled Load in the Design window.

This takes you down into the VB-style code window (not the HTML). This is the "code-behind" file, and you can see how busy this Wizard has been. The following objects have been declared:

```
    Protected WithEvents OleDbSelectCommand1 As
System.Data.OleDb.OleDbCommand
    Protected WithEvents OleDbInsertCommand1 As
System.Data.OleDb.OleDbCommand
    Protected WithEvents OleDbUpdateCommand1 As
System.Data.OleDb.OleDbCommand
    Protected WithEvents OleDbDeleteCommand1 As
System.Data.OleDb.OleDbCommand
    Protected WithEvents objMySet As WebApplicationx.MySet
```

```
    Protected WithEvents OleDbConnection1 As
System.Data.OleDb.OleDbConnection
    Protected WithEvents OleDbDataAdapter1 As
System.Data.OleDb.OleDbDataAdapter
    Protected WithEvents ButtonLoad As System.Web.UI.WebControls.Button
        Protected WithEvents masterDataGrid As
System.Web.UI.WebControls.DataGrid
```

Nothing happens in the `Page_Load` event, but in the Button's `Click` event, the DataSet is stuffed into the grid:

```
Private Sub buttonLoad_Click(ByVal sender As System.Object, ByVal e As
System.EventArgs)

        Me.LoadDataSet()
        Me.masterDataGrid.SelectedIndex = -1
        Me.masterDataGrid.DataBind()

End Sub
```

Most WebForm controls have a DataBind method that allows you to bind many kinds of data to them (including arrays, the results of functions, and more traditional data stores). You'll look more closely at data binding techniques later in this session.

The `LoadDataSet` function is one that the Wizard wrote. Take a look at it for a moment:

```
Public Sub LoadDataSet()
        Dim objDataSetTemp As WebApplicationx.MySet
        objDataSetTemp = New WebApplicationx.MySet()
        Try
            'Execute the SelectCommand on the DatasetCommmand and fill the
dataset
            Me.FillDataSet(objDataSetTemp)
        Catch eFillDataSet As System.Exception
            'Add exception handling code here.
            Throw eFillDataSet
        End Try
        Try
            'Merge the records that were just pulled from the data store
into the main dataset
            objMySet.Merge(objDataSetTemp)
        Catch eLoadMerge As System.Exception
            'Add exception handling code here
            Throw eLoadMerge
        End Try

    End Sub
```

And, in turn, the `FillDataSet` function was also written for you by the Wizard:

```
Public Sub FillDataSet(ByVal dataSet As WebApplicationx.MySet)
        Me.OleDbConnection1.Open()
```

```
dataSet.EnforceConstraints = False
Try
    Me.OleDbDataAdapter1.Fill(dataSet)
Catch fillException As System.Exception
    Throw fillException
Finally
    dataSet.EnforceConstraints = True
    Me.OleDbConnection1.Close()
End Try


End Sub
```

Both of these functions employ the new VB .NET Try...Catch...Throw...End Try error-handling structure. You can find out more about this technique in the section titled "Using Try...End Try" in Session 20 if you've grown hazy about it.

What the Wizard Did to the HTML

20 Min.
To Go

Now right-click DataWebForm1.aspx in the Solution Explorer to glance at the code the Wizard entered into the HTML (it's abridged here to save space). This shows you the DataGrid and the columns you requested, complete with the correct column header text:

```
<asp:datagrid id="masterDataGrid" runat="server" DataSource="<%# objMySet
%>" CellPadding="2" DataMember="authors" Width="100%" Height="50px"
AutoGenerateColumns="False" PageSize="5" DataKeyField="au_id">
<Columns>
                                        <asp:BoundColumn DataField="au_id"
HeaderText="au_id"></asp:BoundColumn>
                                        <asp:BoundColumn DataField="au_lname"
HeaderText="au_lname"></asp:BoundColumn>
                                        <asp:BoundColumn DataField="au_fname"
HeaderText="au_fname"></asp:BoundColumn>
                                        <asp:BoundColumn DataField="phone"
HeaderText="phone"></asp:BoundColumn>
                                        <asp:BoundColumn DataField="contract"
HeaderText="contract"></asp:BoundColumn>
                        </Columns>

<HeaderStyle Font-Names="Verdana" Font-Bold="True" Height="10px"
ForeColor="Black" BackColor="Silver"></HeaderStyle></asp:datagrid>

<asp:button id="ButtonLoad" style="Z-INDEX: 101; LEFT: 8px; POSITION:
absolute; TOP: 8px" runat="server" Text="LOAD"></asp:button>
```

You also see the Button with its ID attribute named "ButtonLoad". This is the equivalent of the ordinary VB .NET Name property, and it's how any events for this control are defined:

```
Sub buttonLoad_Click
```

Binding Properties to Controls

ASP.NET — the technology that permits you to write VB .NET code in a server that communicates with visitors to your Web site — permits a great freedom and variety of ways to connect to data, and to send an HTML page displaying that data back to the visitor.

ASP.NET is as important a technology as VB .NET in some ways. ASP.NET *uses* VB .NET to write programming that works on the Internet. (And we all know how important *that* kind of programming is becoming.) So, as the Nova Scotians say, "Put on your gum boots and let's go explorin'."

First you're going to write server code that you can run and test in the Internet Explorer browser. This behavior will imitate a Web page on the Internet (the server) responding to a user visiting that page (the browser). By going back and forth between these two entities, you can successfully reproduce the intercourse between a Web server and people contacting that server over the Internet. In many cases, you'll be adding data to a Web page (server-side), and then displaying that data to the visitor (browser-side).

You'll see how easy it is to test an ASP.NET application written to deal with Internet traffic. You get to test it in the good, old VB way: Just press F5, and the page the visitor to your Web site sees is automatically displayed in all its glory in Internet Explorer (IE).

If you test a Web Form page in the VB .NET IDE — click a button on the Web page displayed when you've pressed F5, for example — the results are automatically sent from IE to the "server" (the virtual directory that you created when you installed the IIS server in Session 26).

Click a button in the browser, and the results arrive at the virtual "server" inside your machine. Then an HTML response is composed by your ASP.NET code, and sent back to IE for you to see (you, posing as the visitor to your virtual Web site).

It's all very smooth and very easy to do. It mimics the communication between a guy in Oregon surfing the Web and visiting a Web site server located in England. This little VB .NET virtual "server" is also known as the *local host*.

Anyway, if you've got your gum boots on by now, start VB .NET, choose File ⇨ New ⇨ Project, and double-click the ASP.NET Web Application icon.

As in the first example in this session, you see VB .NET say that it's creating a new Web, as shown in Figure 27-6.

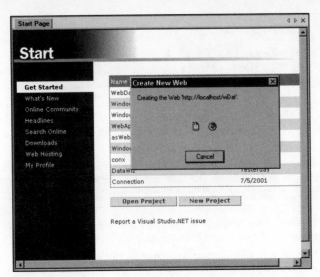

Figure 27-6 *A virtual (imitation) "Web" is being created for your experimental purposes.*

> After VS .NET creates the WebForm and its support files, you'll see a message in the Design window informing you that you are currently in *grid layout mode*. In other words, any controls you add to this page will be located exactly where you put them (like on a traditional Windows form). You can drag them around anywhere on the page. You are told that you can choose to use "flow" layout, if you wish. It's the rather lame way that traditional HTML positions everything against the left side of the page. To switch to that mode (although I don't know why you would want to do this), change the PageLayout property to FlowLayout.

For now, you'll just stick with the default grid layout mode, which gives you the freedom to put anything anywhere on the page. You should now be in the Design mode. Get to the HTML code window by clicking the HTML button on the bottom of the main document window. A WebForm (a Web application's equivalent to the traditional VB form) uses *two kinds of code* in two separate code windows. There is the HTML code (which you're looking at now), and there is also a VB-like code window that you'll explore later.

Erase all the default code that VB .NET put into the HTML code window. Why? Because we're experimenting now with hand-coded programming, so you'll build the entire HTML code yourself. It's sometimes good to get in there and see precisely how to do things for yourself.

Type this into the (now-blank) HTML code window:

```
<html>
    <script language="VB" runat="server">
        Sub Page_Load(sender As Object, e As EventArgs)
            Page.DataBind
        End Sub
```

```
          ReadOnly Property CountryName() As String
                Get
                     Return "Canada"
                End Get
          End Property

          ReadOnly Property Population() As Integer
                Get
                     Return 12000000
                End Get
          End Property

ReadOnly Property Languages() As Integer
                Get
                     Return 3
                End Get
          End Property

     </script>
     <body>

     <form runat="server" ID="Form1">
                Country: <b>
                     <%# CountryName %>
                </b>
                <br>
                Pop.: <b>
                     <%# Population %>
                     <br>
                </b>Number of Spoken Languages:
  <b>
                     <%# languages %>
                </b>
     </form>

     </body>
</html>
```

This example illustrates that you can create properties within your HTML code, and then later use the `<%# PropertyName %>` code to read and display the data in a property. The `runat="server"` command announces that this code will be executed at the server in the Web site's computer, not in the computer (the browser) of the visitor to this Web site.

If you've created classes in VB .NET, you'll recognize the classic syntax for creating a property:

```
          ReadOnly Property Population() As Integer
                Get
                     Return 12000000
                End Get
          End Property
```

Notice that the property names are not case sensitive (you used Languages and later languages, to refer to the same property). Finally, note what happens when this page first loads:

```
Page.DataBind
```

You can use the DataBind method to bind not only to traditional data sources (like a database), but also to simple properties (as illustrated in this example), controls' properties, expressions, collections, or the results of methods.

The data will not be evaluated (<%# CountryName %> replaced with Canada) until the Page's DataBind method is executed. In this case, it is done within the Page_Load event. Many ASP.NET server controls also have their own DataBind property. As is illustrated next, however, the binding need not take place immediately upon the page load.

Notice that ASP.NET data being bound must use the <%# %> punctuation to indicate where the data will appear.

Getting Data from a Control

10 Min.
To Go

This example illustrates how you can use the DataBind method in locations other than the Page_Load event. You'll also see how data can be extracted from a control. Delete everything in the HTML code window, and then type this in:

```
<html>
    <script language="VB" runat="server">

        Sub Button1_Click(sender As Object, e As EventArgs)
                Page.DataBind
        End Sub

    </script>
    <body>
        <form runat="server">
            <asp:DropDownList id="TheirChoice" runat="server">
                <asp:ListItem>Bach</asp:ListItem>
                <asp:ListItem>Beethoven</asp:ListItem>
                <asp:ListItem>Sam Johnson</asp:ListItem>
            </asp:DropDownList>
            <asp:button Text="Click Me" OnClick="Button1_Click"
runat="server" />
            You chose
            <asp:label text='<%# TheirChoice.SelectedItem.Text %>'
runat="server" />
        </form>
    </body>
</html>
```

The primary line of code to notice here is this one:

```
<asp:label text='<%# TheirChoice.SelectedItem.Text %>' runat="server" />
```

This data is bound from the selection the user makes within the ListBox. But the actual binding doesn't take place until the user clicks the *Click Me* button. Press F5 to try it. You'll see results like those shown in Figure 27-7.

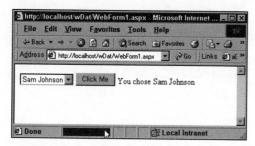

Figure 27-7   *Notice the black rectangle at the bottom of the browser window. This is your clue that information has been sent on a round trip from the browser to the server and back to the browser.*

When you click the button, the information about the currently selected item in the ListBox is sent back to the server. The server binds the data, evaluating which is the SelectedItem in the ListBox, and then displaying that item in the Label. All this is then translated into an HTML page, which is sent back to the visitor's browser.

You might want to know how to manage a couple of additional WebForm data-binding techniques: how to bind to an array and an expression (function). Also, you might want to see how to accomplish this same binding behavior within a traditional Windows form as well. Alas, there's no time left in this session for these topics, but they aren't that long or that complicated. I suggest that when you have a few free minutes, you take a look at the Supplementary Notes file for Chapter 27 on this book's CD. There you'll find these extra-credit topics covered in a couple of easy-to-do exercises.

Done!

REVIEW

This session explored various facets of Internet database-related programming. You used the DataForm Wizard to display up-to-date information to a visitor in a Web page grid control. You then saw how some of the code-behind worked to actually display this data (see the text just below Figure 27-5 for an explanation of code-behind). You experimented with the DataBind method to insert data into a Web page server-side from a property.

QUIZ YOURSELF

1. Which two WebForm controls does the DataForm Wizard employ? (See "Off to See the Wizard.")
2. What attribute in HTML code is used to identify a control, such as a button, so that events can be written for it? (See "What the Wizard Did to the HTML.")
3. What role does the IIS server play in testing WebForm ASP.NET programming? (See "Binding Properties to Controls.")
4. Can the DataBind method be used outside the Page_Load event? (See "Getting Data from a Control.")

All About ASP.NET: Internet Conversion

Session Checklist

✔ An overview of ASP.NET

✔ What ASP does

✔ ASP.NET improvements

✔ Using segregated source files

✔ Automated browser independence

✔ Moving to strong typing

✔ Sharing a common IDE

✔ Beefed-up security

✔ Deployment improvements

✔ Cross-language debugging

30 Min. To Go

In the previous session you jumped right into the deep end of the pool and got some hands-on experience with ASP.NET. In this session you'll learn the fundamentals of this important new technology. Sometimes it's fun to reverse the usual order of things and get your feet wet before going into theory.

If you plan to do any programming for the Internet, you'll need to understand the ideas in this session. ASP.NET offers significant benefits to programmers and developers. The ASP technology — Active Server Pages — has been used the world over since early 1997. However useful and widespread it has become in the past four years, ASP nonetheless has some serious drawbacks.

Now, as part of your VB .NET bag of tricks, ASP.NET avoids those drawbacks and offers a variety of valuable new tools. ASP.NET is not merely the next version of ASP. Microsoft threw out their code for ASP and wrote ASP.NET from the ground up — it's a brand new, object-oriented technology.

One Microsoft spokesman compared ASP.NET's significance to the impact that Visual Basic Version 1 had back in 1990. That may be stretching things a bit — but I suspect that you'll want to learn ASP.NET. It's clearly a superior approach to Web application programming.

The Essentials of ASP.NET

In a whitepaper explaining the ASP.NET technology, Microsoft's Anthony Moore points out that ASP.NET and its WebForms feature represent an important advance in programmer-friendly tools. He even compares these new tools to the vast improvement in traditional Windows programming efficiency that occurred when Visual Basic version 1 was introduced over ten years ago.

Before VB came along, Windows applications were very difficult to build: time-consuming, complex, and disagreeable. The C language, with all its syntactic convolutions and complicated references, was all that was available to Windows programmers until VB 1 made its welcome appearance.

Similarly, programming Web sites before ASP.NET came along had been a pretty nasty business. Now, though, ASP.NET, VB .NET and improvements to the Visual Studio IDE promise to bring VB-like efficiencies to what has previously been tedious and cumbersome CGI and ASP programming. Mr. Moore puts it this way:

> As with creating Windows applications, creating a reliable and scalable Web application is extremely complicated. Our hope for ASP.NET is that it hides most of this complexity from you just as Visual Basic 1.0 did for Windows development. We also want to make the two experiences as similar to each other as possible so that you can "use the skills you already have."

We'll get to the advantages offered by ASP.NET shortly. But first, a brief overview of the previous technology, ASP.

The Purpose of ASP

The core idea of Active Server Pages is that somebody (or many people at once) is surfing around the Internet (or a local intranet) and arrives at a page in your Web site. When they arrive, their browser sends a request to your server to send the page. But instead of merely sending them a canned, previously written, static, page, you can dynamically generate the page on your server right then and there — as a response to their visit — and send the resulting *fresh* HTML page to the visitor. Your page can display the current time and date, the current status of an order they placed with you, your latest catalog, and so on. This is how to make your Web site attractive, up-to-date, varying and *interesting* to the visitor.

Also remember that your Web page might be requested by thousands of people *simultaneously*. This possibility requires some adjustments in how you program, particularly how you handle persistent global (`Public`) variables. (You'll create Web applications in Session 29 that demonstrate techniques you can use to address this issue, which is called the problem of *preserving state*.) For this, and other, reasons, Web programming is simply not the same as writing a traditional Windows program where only one person at a time will be using your application.

HTML Cannot Compute

HTML merely describes how text and graphics should *look* — size, location, color, things like that. You can do no significant *computing* with HTML. You cannot add 2+2. HTML merely specifies that the headline is relatively large, that the body text is colored blue, and so on. HTML also includes a few, simple objects such as tables, buttons, and list boxes.

The *active* server idea permits you to compute on your server, and then, as the result of the computation, compose a page of HTML right then and there — and send it off to the visitor's computer for viewing in their browser.

ASP uses a script language (JavaScript or VBScript) to do its computing. Script languages are a subset of their parent language (Java or Visual Basic). However, the visitor need have none of these script or language features built into their computer — they get the *results* of your server-side computing, which is sent as an ordinary HTML page. One reason that the result is sent as a *display* (HTML) rather than as executable (runnable) programming is that many people and companies use a firewall to prevent any executables from getting into their computers. Why? There's no safe way to distinguish between a benign executable and a virus.

ASP permits you to do lots of useful things on your server: access a database, insert pre-written components, revise your Web pages (include the latest news about your company, today's date, and so on) so visitors don't get bored seeing the same content each time they visit, and many other valuable techniques.

And because standard HTML is sent out to the visitor, you also overcome the browser-compatibility problem. It doesn't matter if they're using Netscape, Internet Explorer (IE), or AOL — they'll be able to view your standard HTML pages.

You *can* insert scripting into an HTML page and therefore let the visitor's computer do some computing. This is called *client-side* scripting. It works fine if you're sure that all your visitors have the necessary language components installed on their machines, that they are all using the same browser (and that browser supports scripting), and that your scripting will slip past firewalls.

Intranets (in house networks) are somewhat different. If you're merely creating a site that is intended for use in-house, and everybody in your company uses IE, and you're sure they all have the right components on their hard drives, go ahead and try some client-side computing. However, there are many reasons to prefer server-side scripting.

ASP, during its brief few years of life before it was eclipsed by ASP.NET, served programmers fairly well. It offers easy access to tools such as Excel or databases; improved security; targeted data transmission (send only what a particular visitor requests) to speed up getting a page to the visitor; browser- and component-independence; and so on. However, ASP had its weaknesses (including clumsy validation, state management, and caching). It is now passing into history as an important first step. Its successor, ASP.NET, offers advantages over ASP. ASP.NET cures most of the weaknesses found in ASP.

Marching Toward ASP.NET

**20 Min.
To Go**

Programmers wanted more than ASP offered, and now you can expect to start seeing file and Web page extensions named ASPX. That extension tells you that ASP.NET is being used. In fact, much ASP source code can run just fine without any serious modifications using the

ASP.NET engine. So, to force an ASP source code file to run under ASP.NET, just change its filename extension from .ASP to .ASPX. Then insert this line of code:

```
<%@Page aspcompat=true Language = VB%>
```

 ASP.NET doesn't require that you jettison any existing ASP code you've written. In fact, ASP pages can run side-by-side simultaneously with ASP.NET pages. You can keep your current ASP Web applications running on the same server as new ASP.NET web applications you create.

Now for an overview of the strengths and features you'll find when you begin using ASP.NET and Visual Basic .NET.

ASP.NET code is easier to write, debug and maintain than ASP, particularly for larger projects. You can leverage your existing programming knowledge, transferring your experience from the Windows OS platform to the intranet or Internet platform.

The Visual Studio .NET integrated-development environment (IDE) offers you all the support you've always enjoyed with mature, RAD (rapid application development) languages such as Visual Basic. In fact, often you don't need to write code at all. ASP.NET gives you a toolbox full of smart, rich server-side components you can just drop right into your ASP.NET projects (you'll find that many programming tasks — validate, cache, get user input — are now handled for you by components). It also provides powerful debugging tools; WYSIWYG design and editing; and lots of Wizards to step you through tedious or complex tasks. Likewise, legacy ActiveX components you've written can be used with .NET languages.

Script languages offer most, but not all, of the commands and features of full languages. Programmers wanted full languages. ASP.NET allows you to program with languages such as Visual Basic .NET, C#, and other .NET languages, instead of VBScript or JScript.

Segregated source files

With ASP, you have to mix your programming (script source code) in with the HTML source code. These ASP-HTML files can grow large and unwieldy (including the mess that programmers have for decades called *spaghetti code* because the execution path — what happens when — is difficult to trace by merely reading through the code). Another quality of ASP source code is that it's a patchwork quilt of HTML and scripting (code). Usually the person who is talented at designing the *look* of a Web site is not the best person to write scripting, and vice versa.

Here's the scenario: A designer comes up with a nice-looking page. He hands this (purely HTML code) to a programmer who inserts her ASP scripting into the file. Next the artist decides to make some changes to the page's appearance, so the .HTM file is passed back to the artist for some touching up. Pretty soon the artist and the programmer are stepping on each other's toes and the source code is a mish-mash. ASP.NET solves this problem by permitting you to separate programming source code from visual design (HTML) source code into two different files. (You *can* segregate files in traditional ASP with Include files and style sheets — but this isn't as effective a solution as ASP.NET now offers.) With ASP.NET, programming code can be stored in a class module file, separate from the HTML file that the designer works with.

The object-oriented foundation of ASP.NET programming also makes it easier to read, reuse, maintain, and share among groups of programmers.

Browser independence

The old bugaboo — are they using IE or Netscape's Navigator/Communicator? — is now easier for a programmer to handle. These browsers have different capabilities and some incompatibilities.

ASP.NET includes *components* (prewritten controls you just drop into your ASP.NET source code) that can detect the user's browser version. The component is smart enough to generate HTML best suited to the visitor's browser. So, you, the programmer, no longer have to write various If ... Then structures to accommodate the 30% or so of people who've chosen not to use the latest version of IE. For example, if they're using an older, less-capable version such as IE version 3, the ASP.NET component will "gracefully degrade" the Web page (make it look as good as IE 3's limited resources can manage).

Also, these new client-container-sensitive ASP.NET components can even work with the new specialized devices, such as those little handheld PDA computers. You really have to be "graceful" when you degrade a Web page from the typical 15" desktop monitor to a little 3" screen.

Speed

ASP.NET runs faster than scripted (interpreted) code. ASP.NET is compiled so it can offer various efficiencies, such as *just-in-time* (JIT) compilation, optimization, early binding, and caching. You, the developer, can specify when compilation takes place. Source code is translated into an *intermediate language* (IL). Then, if you wish, the IL can be translated (compiled) into native code right away. Or, if you prefer, you can choose just-in-time compilation that occurs when the project is executed. The older ASP interpreted code means that every time a page was requested, the source code had to be reread (or at least reinterpreted). Obviously this can be a serious performance hit. Also, scalability suffers (interpreted pages will not run, as-is, in a Web farm). ASP.NET's scalability makes it possible to permit many incoming requests to be handled at the same time, without slugging the servers into catatonia.

Understanding Strong Typing

VB programmers might not be familiar with the concept of a strongly typed language. Until VB .NET, Visual Basic has not been strongly typed. In VB, you've always been able to use *implicit* declaration of your variables. This means that you can just use a variable and bring it into existence, like this:

```
Sub Form1_Click
X = 1

End Sub
```

A strongly typed programming language (which VB .NET by default is) asks that all variables must first be declared before they can be used, like this:

Continued

Understanding Strong Typing   *Continued*

```
Sub Form1_Click
Dim X As Integer
X = 1

End Sub
```

Or, you can use the new VB .NET shorter form of declaration that, at the same time, assigns a value:

```
Dim X As Integer = 1
```

In a strongly typed programming language, each type of data (integer, string, long, double, and so on) defines which operations can be carried out on that data. The compiler knows about its list of data types (you are not allowed to invent your own types). Strongly typed languages generally run faster, though for most applications, speed differences are not noticeable.

VB's controversial *variant* data type (which is in fact the *only* data type supported by VBScript) can shift itself into any other data type, depending on the context. For example, if you write X = 1, VB would consider X to be an integer type, but if later in the program you write Print X, then X would be treated as a string type. In VB .NET, undeclared variables default to object types. But try to avoid them.

One final point: Recall that you can put an Option line at the top of your code window if you prefer to use the traditional (weakly typed) VB variables. If you want to use implicit declaration (not have to declare each variable before using it), type this at the top:

```
Option Explicit Off
```

10 Min.
To Go

Multiple New Advantages

The ASP.NET runtime has been built to take advantage of multiprocessor or clustered server structures. Also, the runtime ensures robust, continuous performance by keeping track of all running processes. If any process freezes or begins to leak, the runtime kills the process that is behaving badly and spawns a new process to take its place.

ASP.NET sits on top of the .NET runtime library. .NET is designed from the ground up as an Internet-based platform.NET will offer such interesting "services" as natural language processing, rich application development, a new user interface, and even a new file system. Unlike previous versions of computer languages, all the languages that can be used with ASP.NET share the same runtime (the .NET runtime is also called CLR, Common Language Runtime). This means that you can write some code in VB, and someone else can write in C++ or C#, and these pieces can be combined in the *same* ASP.NET project. Languages can also now share each other's objects and libraries.

Deployment is made easier because of the common language runtime (the library of functions that actually carry out the commands you write in the source code) and also because you, the programmer, may no longer need to worry about ensuring that the runtime is available — it is expected to be embedded into future versions of Windows. The .NET runtime also manages some aspects of your code for you, including garbage collection.

A shared IDE

There is now a *single* language runtime (the collection of functions, such as the ability to add two numbers, to change a string of text into all uppercase, and all the other necessary services a computer language provides). The CLR, used by each different language, represents that single library.

There is a grand unification going on here in the .NET programming model. Prior to .NET, you would choose your language based on what kind of work you were doing: ASP and script languages for Web page programming; VB for fast, efficient programming and RAD features like forms; or the C-like languages when you wanted optimization, sub-classing and other tricks.

The programming you were working on sometimes forced you to choose a particular language. And your choice of language also determined which of the various API's you would be using. Now, with the single .NET API, and all languages sharing the same IDE for designing your programs, there is no longer such a tower of programmer babble. What's available to one language is simultaneously available to all. No more learning various IDE's and various API's if you need to switch between languages to accomplish your goals. All the new languages — ASP.NET, ADO.NET (database programming), C#, VB .NET, VC++.NET, and so on — sit on top of the .NET CLR.

For example, the ASP.NET Page Framework handles *events* in a straightforward way that will be familiar to any Visual Basic programmer who has worked with VB forms.

Improved security

Security is simplified. You'll want to control access to your server and any secrets on it or connected to it. *Authentication* means that a user must prove their identity (usually by typing in a login name and password). If they pass that test, you then *authorize* them to access certain areas of your data. ASP.NET offers both authentication and authorization features, including Windows-based and forms-based authentication. You can even create your own custom security system, because ASP.NET is designed to be easily extended or personalized. You can modify, or completely replace, most of the components in ASP.NET, including the security elements.

Easier deployment

Deployment is simplified. You add an ASP.NET application to your server *merely by copying the ASP.NET application's files to the server's hard drive*. No need to go through an elaborate setup and registration process. You can even upgrade an ASP.NET application on the fly while it's running, without needing to reboot the server.

ASP prior to .NET wasn't this easy. If you deployed a small ASP application, there wasn't too much of a hassle. But larger, more complex ASP n-tier apps that used components created problems of registration, versioning, and others (sometimes called "DLL Hell"), making life difficult for programmers and administrators alike.

ASP.NET completely abolishes DLL locking, XML configuration files, and component registration (applause! applause!). To deploy your ASP.NET Web application, just copy directories.

Controls located in your application's BIN subfolder are simply available to your application — you need not worry about registering them, or that they are "locked." They're not locked and they're not registered — but they *work* just fine. That's the new model.

Upgrading your work is simple. Did you write a newer, better version of a control you used previously? Just copy the new one into the folder on the server (use the same name as the one you're replacing). It runs right away.

Also, adjusting settings in an ASP.NET application is as simple as changing a text file. ASP.NET applications avoid Registry complexity by maintaining their customization and other configuration data in simple text files (discussed in Session 4). No need to use special administrator utilities such as the MMC, or hand-editing the Registry itself.

Cross-language debugging

The rich Visual Studio .NET suite of debugging tools can debug *across languages*. This means that if you do use more than one language for a project, you can nonetheless seamlessly analyze and test the code. You can even use error-handling exceptions across different languages. What's more, it's expected that by the time Visual Studio .NET is officially released, it will be able to debug *across machines* (permitting distributed code debugging).

If you've been writing ASP code, you're probably quite tired of having to base your debugging technique on the lame, retro `Response.Write` command. It's as crude an approach as trying to watch variables or insert breakpoints in VB with no other tool than the `MsgBox` command, or `Debug.Print`.

ASP.NET is free. It's embedded in the latest operating system (Windows 2000). ASP.NET is part of Microsoft Internet Information Services (IIS) 5.5, which is part of Windows 2000.

After the .NET beta, an update will be provided for the older operating systems, and that update (likely a "service pack") will support .EXE files built on the .NET CLR. There will be an ASP.NET version for Windows NT 4.0, and "personal versions" for Windows 95/98 users. Ultimately, you'll be able to create and run a .NET .EXE application (a traditional Windows executable program) on Windows 95, 98, or NT computers, as well as in Internet applications.

Done!

REVIEW

As you've seen in this session, ASP.NET isn't simply an incremental, modest upgrade of ASP. Instead, it's been completely rewritten to take full advantage of the .NET environment. Segregated source files, browser independence, a common IDE, language-independence, improved security and deployment, cross-language debugging, and other features should make ASP.NET your language of choice for Web programming.

QUIZ YOURSELF

1. Why has ASP.NET been compared to Visual Basic? (See "The Essentials of ASP.NET.")
2. What is the difference between ASP and HTML? (See "The Purpose of ASP.")
3. Name three advantages of ASP.NET over ASP. (See "Marching Toward ASP.NET.")
4. What does *strong typing* mean? (See "Understanding Strong Typing.")
5. Can you use more than one language in a single .NET application? (See "A shared IDE.")

WebForms: Writing VB .NET Applications that Run on the Internet

Session Checklist

✔ The advantages of WebForms

✔ Rapid Application Development (RAD)

✔ Understanding the DISCO file

✔ The default style sheet

✔ WebForm controls

✔ Using the WebForm code model

✔ Steps in WebForm processing

✔ Thinking about statelessness

✔ WebForm events

✔ Application and session events

WebForms are like traditional VB forms, but WebForms are designed to be displayed as Internet pages rather than as windows in the Windows operating system.

**30 Min.
To Go**

Advantages of WebForms

WebForms offer a new way of programming based on the time-tested Rapid Application Development (RAD) model. WebForms will not be new to VB programmers. If you're familiar with the classic Visual Basic form, you'll immediately understand WebForms. They're the same idea, just applied to Internet programming.

Here are some of the advantages that WebForms offer the programmer:

- You can write better, clearer code because some features are hidden away in server controls (controls that run on your Web site rather than in the browser of visitors to your site), and other code goes inside events.

- Tasks that required you to write code in Active Server Pages (ASP), such as validation, are now handled for you by prewritten controls.

- You can segregate your VB source code from the HTML used by page designers — so neither of you step on each other's feet. This separation of source code into separate files is sometimes called the *code-behind* technique. *Code-behind* means that you can now more easily separate the job of programming from the job of design. The programming code is in its own file. The HTML is in its own, different file. Therefore, artists can freely fiddle with the look of a Web page, without messing up the programmer's code for that same page.

- You can now use VB .NET rather than VBScript, with all the advantages VB .NET offers.

- Visual Studio .NET now gives you a simplified, more efficient way of sizing, positioning, and otherwise *visually* manipulating the various user-interface controls on a Web page. (This, too, is quite similar to the familiar VB *form* that you've used to design traditional Windows applications.) When you first start a Web application in VB .NET, you're asked if you want to switch to GridLayout (by changing the PageLayout property of the Document object). If you choose GridLayout, you can drag and resize controls on the Web page, just as if you were working within a traditional Windows-style VB form.

- You get direct, easy access to the members (events, properties, and methods) of the Web controls. For example, there is the Properties window that VB programmers have grown to love.

- You get a whole slew of new controls, specialized for Web pages.

WebForm RAD

Choose File ➪ New ➪ Project in Visual Studio .NET. Click Visual Basic Projects in the New Project dialog box, and then name it whatever name you want to use. Double-click the ASP.NET Web Application icon. After VB scurries around a bit, the project is created and the set of default files are added to what VS calls your *solution* (you *hope* it's going to be a solution to something, don't you?).

Now open the Solution Explorer to see (some of) the files that have been automatically created for your new project, as you can see in Figure 29-1.

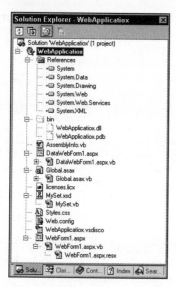

Figure 29-1 *All the support files in the Solution Explorer window are created for you automatically.*

Take a look at the default files. You'll see some global settings files: Config.Web., Global.asax, and Global.vb.

The WebForm1.aspx file is where the designer can create the look of the page — it's the WYSIWYG form on which controls and other elements can be placed (its source code is HTML).

The WebForm1.aspx.vb file is where you can write your source code for the page (its source code is written in, you guessed it, VB .NET). By default, the Solution Explorer hides this file. To see it, click the name of your project (the line in boldface in the Solution Explorer) to reveal the icons in the Solution Explorer toolbar. Then click the Show All Files icon. Now click the + symbol next to WebForm1.aspx. There's your WebForm1.aspx.vb file. It's referred to as the *code-behind* file because the VB .NET code works behind the scenes to assist the ASP.NET and HTML code.

Notice that the code-behind technique — segregating the programmer's source code from the designer's (HTML) work into two files — is automatically created for you when you start a new Web application. These two files can be used by two different people, but when the Web application is finally finished and deployed, the two files' different elements will be merged.

Double-click the WebForm1.aspx file (in the Solution Explorer), and then click the HTML tab at the bottom of the main Design window. Take a glance at the default HTML code.

Then double-click the WebForm1.ASPX.VB filename in Solution Explorer and glance at the programmer code. Notice that some of the code is hidden from you (it has a little + next to it). You'll find hidden files in the Solution Explorer, too. VB .NET attempts to display what it thinks you might want to work with, and hides things you normally don't need to work with.

The DISCO file

20 Min. To Go

There is also a .VSDISCO file. The *disco* extension is short for *discovery*. A remote application can browse the root of a Web server looking for a discovery file, and then examine the file to find out what services are offered. (This is similar to objects exposing their members, as described in Session 30.)

The default style sheet

Yet another default file is the style sheet (.css). It contains settings describing how the Web page will look. You are free to change these settings — just double-click the Styles.css file in the Solution Explorer window. Here are some of the default style definitions:

```
/* Default CSS Stylesheet for a new Web Application project */

BODY
{
    BACKGROUND-COLOR: white;
    FONT-FAMILY: Verdana, Helvetica, sans-serif;
    FONT-SIZE: .8em;
    FONT-WEIGHT: normal;
    LETTER-SPACING: normal;
    TEXT-TRANSFORM: none;
    WORD-SPACING: normal
}

H1, H2, H3, H4, H5, TH, THEAD, TFOOT
{
    COLOR: #003366;
}
```

WebForm Controls

Recall that traditional VB separates source code into two primary categories: the visible user interface (the *form*) and the underlying programming logic (the *code*). These elements work together to produce the final application.

For instance, if you put a button on a form, its size can be specified by stretching it on the form with the mouse. What happens when the user clicks on that button is specified in programming code, in the button's Click event in the code window.

WebForms work in a similar way, but they have *three* primary categories — three places where you can adjust properties or write programming. To review:

- The .aspx file contains the HTML code that describes the Web page.
- The .vb file contains the Visual Basic code where you specify how objects behave by programming their events. This is also known as the *code-behind* file. (It can be written in languages other than VB, such as C#.)
- The Design page is the same as a VB form, except that it represents the user interface of a Web page rather than a traditional Windows application. (Note that anything you place or modify in the Design window becomes part of the .aspx file. To see the Design page for a WebForm, click the .aspx tab at the top of the code window, and then click the Design tab at the bottom of the window.)

You switch between the three primary WebForm editing windows by clicking tabs. Notice the two tabs at the bottom of the editing window: Design and HTML. Use these to switch between the user-interface form and the underlying HTML. Now notice the .aspx and .vb tabs at the top of the editing window. Use these to switch between the HTML editor (.aspx) and the Visual Basic editor (.vb). When you click the .vb tab, the tabs on the bottom, Design and HTML, disappear.

WebForm Events

In traditional Windows applications, a user clicks a button and immediately the code in that button's Click event is executed. Things happens a bit differently when a button is displayed on a Web site visitor's browser. For one thing, the server that will react to this click is perhaps thousands of miles away. And perhaps it's busy with some other visitor's click. Dealing with this fractured, unconnected, multiple-location computing is called *distributed programming*. That means that some things happen in the user's browser (the click, for example) in one place, like Oregon, but the code that responds to that click is located in another place, like England. And, worse, maybe the database that's needed by the code in England is itself located in Austria, in a castle, high in the Alps.

Most VB .NET Webform controls' events are triggered from the visitor's browser, and then processed on a server perhaps thousands of miles away. (Some page events and a few controls' events — notably the calendar and ad rotator controls — are actually triggered on the server.) However, it does not matter to you (the server-side code programmer) precisely *where* the event is triggered. You can simply write your code to respond to that event, and not bother yourself with where the event triggers. Your programming that responds to events in VB is coded within the familiar Sub...End Sub structure, like this:

```
Private Sub Button1_Click(ByVal sender As System.Object, ByVal e As
System.EventArgs) Handles Button1.Click

        Response.Write("HI")
End Sub
```

Notice that each Webform event requires two arguments: the object that triggered the event and an *event object* that provides information about the event, if there is any. The event object's argument is usually an EventArgs type, but it can be different for a few controls. As always, you have to use the Help system, or an object browser utility, to learn the syntax and uses of the arguments for a particular control.

Almost always you simply *ignore* a control's event arguments when you're programming, just as you ignore that `Handles Button1.Click` tagged onto the end of each event. Nonetheless, this `Handles` clause and those two arguments are required. In other words, if you type in an event sub, you must include the argument list in parentheses, and tack on `Handles`.

That's one good argument for double-clicking. When you double-click a control in the design view, VB .NET automatically types in that control's most frequently used event (usually `Click`). Alternatively, when you're in the code window, you can have any event typed in for any control currently on your form. Just click the drop-down list at the top left of the code window to select a control, then drop the list on the top right of the code window, and click to select the event you want typed in.

In a WebForm, you'll usually work with `Click` events, but a few controls have `Changed` events — indicating that the user adjusted the value of the control. For example, a TextBox control has a `Changed` event:

```
Private Sub TextBox1_TextChanged(ByVal sender As System.Object, ByVal e As
System.EventArgs) Handles TextBox1.TextChanged

End Sub
```

Unlike `Click` events, a `Changed` event does not immediately result in a postback to the server. All `Changed` events are, of course, remembered (cached) and later triggered when a postback does eventually occur. (*Postbacks* usually take place when the visitor *clicks* a Submit button; it means that something is sent from the visitor's browser to the server — the server where your ASP.NET code resides, and can respond to the postback.)

This makes sense — you don't want a `Changed` event sending a postback every time the user types each new character into a TextBox, for instance. This would really slow things down on the server and is very inefficient. Your server code will probably need to go through and process every modified textbox; so you do need to know which textboxes were changed. But you need not get that information to the server until the visitor finishes filling in all the forms, and then clicks the Submit button.

It's useful to remember that neither the set of `Click` events nor the set of `Changed` events are processed on the server in any predictable order. That is, one `Click` event has just as much chance of being the first `Click` event processed as any other `Click` event. However, a given set of `Changed` events is always processed before the `Click` event that posted them, and then that `Click` event is processed. So there is *some* order of precedence to event processing on a server.

If your application actually requires that a `Changed` event force a postback, you can do it. All controls that have a `Changed` event also have an `AutoPostBack` property that forces an immediate postback wherever in your code you set that property to `True`.

HTML Controls

There are two types of controls you can use on your WebForms: traditional HTML controls and the newer Web controls. These two sets are contained within two different tabs on the ToolBox: the Web Forms and HTML tabs respectively.

The HTML controls offer you the option of using a variety of events that permit you to choose whether to write script that executes on the client-side (to run in the visitor's browser) or in the Click or Changed events that run on the server.

Web controls are designed specifically to run within ASP.NET pages (WebForms). Therefore, Web controls have different features than traditional Windows controls, such as the classic Visual Basic Textbox or Button. You can freely mix HTML controls and Web controls in your WebForms.

Application and Session Events

**10 Min.
To Go**

As you've seen in this session, there are Webform page events and Webform control events. There are two additional types of events used in WebForms: session events and application events.

Session refers to an individual instance of a Webform: a visitor surfs to your Web page, thereby triggering a request to the server that the Web page be transmitted. The OnSessionStart event is then triggered. When the session times out or your source code forces the application to close, the OnSessionEnd event triggers.

Similarly, an Application object has two events: OnApplicationStart and OnApplicationEnd. These trigger when your Web application first executes, and when it ends (versus the session, which represents only a single visitor's interaction with your application). You can use these events to initialize and or discard objects or variables that are application-wide in scope. This is known as *preserving state* and it's a technique that a Web site programmer will eventually want to know about. If you are interested in this, take a look at the Supplemental Notes file on this book's CD in the section titled "Managing State."

Creating a WebForm

Let's jump right in and design a simple WebForm, then run it and test it. You'll see how easy it is. You get to test it in the good, old VB way: Just press F5 and the page is automatically displayed in all its glory in Internet Explorer (IE).

If you test the page in the VB .NET IDE — press a button on the Web page displayed when you've pressed F5, for example, the results are automatically sent from IE to the "server" (the virtual directory that you created in Session 26 using the IIS Virtual Directory Management for SQL Server). The results arrive at the virtual "server" inside your machine, and then an HTML response is composed by your ASP.NET code, and sent back to IE for you to see. It's all very smooth and very easy to do. (It mimics the communication between the guy in Oregon surfing the Web and a server located in England.) This little virtual "server" is also known as the *local host*.

Double-click WebForm1.aspx in Solution Explorer. You should now be in the Design mode, but if you're in the HTML mode (you can see HTML code in the main window), click the Design tab on the bottom of the main document window.

Open the Toolbox and double-click the ImageButton control (on the WebForms tab in the ToolBox). That control will be placed on your Web page. Click somewhere in the Web page (the document window) to close the Toolbox. If the Toolbox doesn't close, right-click the Toolbox title bar, and then choose Auto Hide.

Drag the ImageButton anywhere you think it will look nice, and stretch it to enlarge it.

Look at the WebForm1.VB source code (double-click the ImageButton control to get down to the code window). You'll see that the following line of code has been automatically inserted for you. This line instantiates (brings into existence) the ImageButton control. It's lucky all this is automatically written for you because it *has to be exactly right*.

```
Protected WithEvents ImageButton1 As System.Web.UI.WebControls.ImageButton
```

These events are also generated automatically:

```
Private Sub Page_Load(ByVal sender As System.Object, ByVal e As
System.EventArgs) Handles MyBase.Load
        'Put user code to initialize the page here
    End Sub

    Private Sub ImageButton1_Click(ByVal sender As System.Object, ByVal e
As System.Web.UI.ImageClickEventArgs) Handles ImageButton1.Click

    End Sub
```

Now go back to the WebForm design view by clicking the WebForm1.ASPX tab on the top of the Design window. Click the Design tab on the bottom of the document window if it's not selected.

Notice the Properties window (if it's not visible, press F4). It contains properties for the document (the WebForm). The Properties window also contains all the properties for controls, the ImageButton in this case. It also contains the single Name property for WebForm1. (Why have a separate view in the Properties window for the WebForm when you've already got the document? Beats me.)

What you want to know, though, is how to change most of the properties of a Web page, such as its BackColor. Here's one way to change the backcolor of the WebPage: Right-click the WebForm, and then choose Properties. You'll see the Document Property Pages dialog box, where you can click the Color and Margins tab, and then click the . . . button next to the Background field and choose a light blue. Click OK to close the dialog box and apply the color.

Now it's time to work with the ImageButton. Click it to select it. In the Properties window, click the ... button on the ImageUrl property. Click the Browse button and locate a graphic file on your hard drive. Click OK to close the property window. Stretch the ImageButton so it looks good.

The special feature of the ImageButton is that it can report the precise *X,Y* coordinates where the user clicked on your graphic. This means that you can display several icons, or a map, on an ImageButton, and then respond in various ways, based on which area of the ImageButton picture the user clicks.

Double-click the ImageButton in the document window to get to its Click event. Type this into the Click event to display the *X,Y* coordinates when the button is clicked:

```
    Private Sub ImageButton1_Click(ByVal sender As System.Object, ByVal e
As System.Web.UI.ImageClickEventArgs) Handles ImageButton1.Click

        Response.Write("You clicked X/Y " & e.X.ToString() & ", " &
e.Y.ToString())

    End Sub
```

Press F5 to test this and you should see results like those shown in Figure 29-2.

Figure 29-2 *Click the ImageButton control, and you can see the coordinates where the mouse pointer clicked the image.*

Look on the CD

To find some additional information about positioning controls when designing a Web page, look at the Supplemental Notes file on this book's CD in the section titled "Positioning Controls."

Done!

REVIEW

As you've seen in this session, WebForms grow out of the familiar RAD VB forms model, but Internet programming does require some special techniques. To name two of these techniques, you must learn new ways to preserve state and to position controls. Not to despair, though. VB .NET, as always, is ready to assist you with Wizards, designers, Help tutorials and many other features that make VB the language of choice for the majority of the world's programmers.

QUIZ YOURSELF

1. Name three reasons to use WebForms rather than traditional HTML Web page construction. (See "Advantages of WebForms.")
2. What is the purpose of an .aspx file? (See "WebForm RAD.")
3. What's the difference between a session event and an application event? (See "Application and Session Events.")

Understanding Classes and Objects

Session Checklist

✔ Understanding the main components of an object

✔ Using encapsulation to avoid bugs and facilitate reusability

✔ Validating data sent to properties

✔ Working with the Class Builder to create properties more easily

✔ Creating, and then accessing, an object

**30 Min.
To Go**

What, you might well ask, is an *object*? The items on the VB Toolbox are objects. Put a Button on a form, and you have a Button object. And lots of other things are called objects, too, as you'll soon see. Truth be told, *everything in VB .NET is an object* — even a lowly integer.

If everything is an object, is there any meaning to the concept object, you might be asking? Does the term *object* have any value in categorizing things? Good points, friend. But we're getting ahead of ourselves.

Understanding Objects, If Possible

To try to get a sense of what an object is, let's ask this question first: How does an object differ from a traditional variable? An object is more powerful and sophisticated — some objects are like self-contained mini-programs (quite *mini*). A *variable* contains a value, a single piece of data. An *object*, on the other hand, usually contains several pieces of data. An object's data are known as its properties, such as the Button's Forecolor property, which describes the color of its text (caption). Another piece of data, its Image property, specifies a graphic that is displayed within the button.

In addition to its data, an object also usually includes programming — things it knows how to do with its data (or data passed to it), such as the Button's DataBind method, which connects the button to a database. An object's programming is known as its *methods*.

Finally, objects can (but don't necessarily) have *events* — a place for a programmer to define how the object behaves if some outside action (such as a mouse click) happens to that object.

To summarize: an object can have properties (qualities), methods (abilities), and events (responses). Together, this entire group of features is known as the object's *members*.

Also note that an object can (but doesn't necessarily) include a visible user interface. A Button component does have a visible user interface, but a Timer component does not. Some objects just do math, for example, or search for a particular name in a database. Other objects display the results of the math or the search to the user, or invite the user to modify the objects data.

However, don't get the idea that objects are limited to components (controls) on your Toolbox. True, all components are objects, but not all objects are components.

As you'll learn in this session, you can create objects that are intended to be used only within a single program. This kind of object isn't compiled into a component (such as an ActiveX Document object) to make it possible to add that control to the Toolbox and drop it into other programs. Instead, using objects can merely be a useful way of organizing your programming.

Object-Oriented Programming

Some programmers believe that all Visual Basic programs should be written using OOP (Object-Oriented Programming). I'm not one of them. I feel that objects are most useful with large, complex programs, or when you're writing a program with other programmers, as a group effort. Some people also advocate OOP because they claim that you can easily re-use objects in future programs.

Programming with objects forces you to follow some strict rules that can help avoid problems commonly encountered when group-programming, working with complex applications, or reusing code. Smaller, simpler applications may not benefit from OOP techniques. But if you've never been exposed to OOP, you might find this session helpful. I will show you some of what OOP can do for you, should you need to use it.

Encapsulation

A primary benefit of OOP is known as *encapsulation*. This means that an object doesn't permit outside programming to directly manipulate its data. (None of an object's variables should be declared `Public` — they're all `Private` or `Dim` or `Friend` or declared with some other self-application-only scope.)

Any properties that you want to permit outsiders (source code that *uses* the object) to read (query) or set (change) can be "exposed" to the outside code (another program) in a special way, using property procedures. The outside code must contact these procedures, and then the procedures in turn deal directly with the object's data. The outside code doesn't get to manipulate an object's actual data directly.

**20 Min.
To Go**

Classes Give Birth to Objects

The line End Class ends the code that describes the form object named
Form1. Between the Class...End Class commands is the definition, the
code that creates an object. Recall the distinction between design time and
runtime? Design time is when you are typing in code or arranging controls.
Runtime is when you press F5 to actually execute your code (or when the
user runs your final .EXE application).

The word *class* refers to the design-time work: code that defines your object
(all the code between Class and End Class). Later, when the program runs,
a class becomes an actual object. An object is said to be *instantiated* (an
"instance" of it comes into existence) during runtime. This distinction between
class and object is the same as the distinction between a TextBox icon dropped
from the Toolbox into a form during program design, and the actual TextBox
that is created when the program runs. The icon is equivalent to the class,
and the TextBox that the user sees is an object. You can instantiate multiple
objects from a single class, just as you can add multiple TextBoxes to a form.

To illustrate the idea of encapsulation, let's create an object. It holds five strings (pieces
of text) and its job is to provide whichever string an outside application requests.

Start a new project in VB .NET (make it a traditional Windows style project by clicking
the Windows Application icon in the New Project dialog) and scroll down to the very bottom
of the code window. You'll see a line of code like this:

```
End Class
```

Now, back to our example. Go to the very bottom of the code window and type in this
new class:

```
Namespace MySpecialLibrary

    Public Class StringArray

        Private StringArray(5) As String

        Public Sub New()
            MyBase.New()

            StringArray(0) = "First String in Class"
            StringArray(1) = "Second String in Class"
            StringArray(2) = "Third String in Class"
            StringArray(3) = "Fourth String in Class"
            StringArray(4) = "Fifth String in Class"
        End Sub

        Public Function GetString(ByVal index As Integer) As String
            If ((index < 0) Or (index >= Count)) Then
```

```
            Throw New IndexOutOfRangeException()
        End If
        GetString = StringArray(index)
    End Function

    ReadOnly Property Count() As Long
        Get
            Count = StringArray.Length
        End Get
    End Property



    End Class

End Namespace
```

Take a look at the various elements of this class. There are several *scoping* commands: Public, Private, and ReadOnly. Public Class means that this class can be instantiated (brought into existence and used) by *any source code* located anywhere in this or any outside application. Public Function and Public Sub mean that these two procedures can be used by code located anywhere.

Private means that this StringArray can only be accessed from within this particular class. The ReadOnly command means what it says: the Count property (how many strings are available) can be *read* (queried), but not *written to* (changed), by any code.

The Public Sub New....End Sub code is required in VB .NET when you are creating a class. This is called a *class constructor*. You must use the line of MyBase.New as well. This *calls the constructor*. Don't worry about an explanation of *why* these lines of code are required. Just remember that you need to type them in when creating a new class. (You'll find the same lines up higher in the code window where the Form1 class is defined.)

Within the Public Sub New, you write any initialization code. In this case, you assign the data (the actual text) to the five cells in your string array. Public Function GetString is the *method* that this class exposes to the outside world.

Outside code provides an integer to the GetString function (to tell it the *index* number of the string in the array that is wanted). Then the function returns the correct string to the outside caller.

The index number provided by outside code is tested (*validated*) to see if it is lower than zero or higher than the total number of available strings. Validation is often cited as one of the primary advantages of OOP. Objects can test information (new property settings, parameters passed to methods like this index number) coming into the object from the outside. Then, if the incoming request isn't valid, the object can display an error message and refuse to work. That's just what our object does:

```
        If ((index < 0) Or (index >= Count)) Then
            Throw New IndexOutOfRangeException()
        End If
```

(Of course, you can easily write functions that validate parameters passed from outside code.)

The `throw new` command means, "Create a new error 'object' of the `IndexOutOfRange-Exception` type." The message generated by this technique is for programmers, many of whom will understand what it means. If you want to provide a useful message for ordinary users of an object, substitute this:

```
If ((index < 0) Or (index >= Count)) Then
    msgbox ("You are asking for an index out of range")
    Exit Function
End If
```

In either case, your `StringArray` object's `GetString` method handles problems all by itself, without shifting that responsibility to the outside calling code. Typically, an object's properties also validate any incoming requests.

Finally, notice that the `Count` property is essentially public, but permits no outsider to change the count, only to read the count:

```
ReadOnly Property Count() As Long
    Get
        Count = StringArray.Length
    End Get
End Property
```

The `StringArray` (like all arrays in VB .NET) has a *length* property that provides the information you're after.

Now, how does outside code instantiate this `StringArray` object, and use its methods and properties?

Add a Button to your form, and then type this code into the button:

```
Private Sub Button1_Click(ByVal sender As System.Object, ByVal e As
System.EventArgs) Handles Button1.Click

    Dim s As String
    Dim n As Long

    Dim strc As New MySpecialLibrary.StringArray()

    n = strc.Count
    MsgBox(n)

    s = strc.GetString(2)
    MsgBox(s)

End Sub
```

If you were creating this example in a WebForm, you would have to replace those `MsgBox` lines with the following, because message boxes don't pop out of Web pages:

```
Response.Write(n)
Response.Write(s)
```

Note that you instantiate a new `StringArray` object by naming its namespace and then naming its actual name (`StringArray`):

```
Dim strc As New MySpecialLibrary.StringArray()
```

Technically, `strc` is called an *object variable* (or *object reference*) because it "holds" (or stands for) an object.

How can you avoid having to specifically name the namespace? Use the Imports command. That's the whole purpose of the Imports command — to permit you to avoid having to specify ("fully qualify") in your code the namespace for every class (object) within that namespace.

Once the `strc` variable contains the "object reference" after you've declared it as a new instance of your `StringArray` object, you can use `strc` to access the members (properties and methods) of that object.

First you get the ReadOnly Count property:

```
n = strc.Count
```

Then next we use the `GetString` method to get one of the strings:

```
s = strc.GetString(2)
```

So now you know how to create a class, add properties and methods to it, and then access those members from outside. But how do you permit the user to *change* a property? Make it `Public` and also add a Set structure. To see how this works, type this in just after the `End Property` line (just above the `End Class` line) in the previous example:

```
Private MoneyAmount As Long = 0 'Hold the value

Public Property Money() As Long

    Get 'outsider is querying
        Money = MoneyAmount
    End Get

    Set  'outsider is changing the value
        If Value < 1 Then
            Msgbox("Can't be less than $1")
        ElseIf Value > 1000000 Then
            Msgbox("Don't kid yourself. You don't have a
million!")
        Else
            MoneyAmount = Value
        End If
    End Set

    End Property
```

Note that you must declare a variable (`MoneyAmout` in this example) to actually hold the value should the outsider change that value. Also note that there is some validation code in the Set structure to test what the user is attempting to insert into this property. Also, there is a special Value command that contains what the user is attempting to store into this property.

To test this new property, change the code in the Button's Click event to this:

```
Private Sub Button1_Click(ByVal sender As System.Object, ByVal e As
System.EventArgs) Handles Button1.Click

        Dim strc As New MySpecialLibrary.StringArray()
        Dim n as long

        n = strc.Money
        msgbox(n)

        strc.Money = 12300

    n = strc.Money
        msgbox(n)


    End Sub
```

As you can see, the caller queries an object's property by assigning the *objectname.property* to a variable (n here). And the caller modifies an object's property by assigning a value (12300) to the *objectname.property*.

Another side benefit of OOP is that the other programmers (writing the "outside code" that uses your object) don't need to know the details of how the code in your object works. Indeed, they cannot know any details you don't make public. But when your code validates their input, they find out soon enough that they can, for example, send in any amount of money up to $1 million, but not more.

An outside programmer need not be concerned with precisely how an object's methods or properties work. The validation code should catch any errors — all the outsider need know is which properties are exposed, what they mean, and how to use the object's methods to get results. Needless to say, the outside programmer has no access to an object's programming code directly. No tampering is allowed.

This *encapsulation* concept can be compared to a receiver you might buy for your stereo system. It has publicly exposed properties (such as the loudness or tone knobs) and methods (such as a button to scan for the next FM station). However, it doesn't permit you to turn the volume knob below 0 or up to 1,400 — you are permitted a range of 1–10 for the loudness. (Though, as Spinal Tap famously revealed, some really expensive audio equipment goes up to 11.)

Additionally, the receiver doesn't let you see, or, worse, adjust, the internal programming that executes the Scan method. Put another way, it's a black box with some public properties and events you can mess around with — and lots of stuff inside that you cannot get to. That's just as well.

Note too that objects simplify code maintenance. Programmers often have to go back and make adjustments to a program perhaps a year after they wrote it. Maybe you want to add new features, or improve the user interface. In cases like that, unless you have a perfect memory you become the outsider to your own code. You'll then be glad that encapsulation relieves you of having to interpret the programming inside an object, and that validation helps you avoid feeding bad data to the object. You also avoid having to search throughout an entire application's source code to see if there are other places in the code where, for example, the StringArray members are located. They're always encapsulated within the class (object) they belong to.

One final point: Objects are more easily reused in future programs than ordinary source code. You write one object that accepts passwords, for instance, and you can reuse it in future projects as often as you wish. As you've seen, objects are, to a considerable extent, self-contained. Therefore, you can usually add them to other projects quite quickly, without worrying that a constant, variable, or codependency exists somewhere outside the object.

More about Classes

10 Min.
To Go

What's a class? Think of it as a blueprint, the code that describes how an object performs. There's code in the VB runtime library for the TextBox class. When you add a TextBox to a form, you've instantiated an object of the TextBox class. Recall that an important feature of objects is that you can instantiate (bring into existence) as many of them as you need. You can create two-dozen TextBox objects if that's what you want.

Suppose you start a real-estate business and need to write a program that keeps track of customers. You can design and code a customer class, and then instantiate a customer object for each customer. By changing the properties in an object during runtime — such as a CustomerName property — you can customize each object. The class, then, is a somewhat general container, and the objects instantiated out of that class can be customized during runtime.

Just as it's a good idea to plan the jobs that an application is supposed to accomplish before you start writing code, it's also a good idea to think through the properties and methods before you start coding a class. For example, using the real estate scenario again, the customer object should probably contain the following properties: name, address, phone number, annual salary, location preferences, house preferences, and perhaps others.

Inheritance

New in VB .NET is a cornerstone of OOP called *inheritance*. It's similar to copying and pasting — a new class can be built upon an already existing class. First you inherit the existing class, and then you modify it in your code.

Be warned: many people consider inheritance a dangerous technique, and rarely worth the trouble it can cause. I never use it. Others, however, swear by it (claiming that it improves productivity when you need to reuse some functionality, but occasionally want to modify it). I'm sure there's room enough in this world for people of both persuasions, just as some people swear by the Lexus and others wouldn't travel anywhere unless they can ride their Harley.

In VB .NET you can use the Inherits command to create a new class based on an existing class (known as the *base class*). Such secondary classes are called *derived* classes. They start off with an identical set of members as the base (parent) class, but an inherited class extends (modifies and adds to) the members. Sometimes it removes (ignores) inherited members.

The idea is that you need not invent the wheel if you have an existing class that does most or some of what you need done in a new class. Just inherit the older class, and then modify its members (and perhaps modify any self-contained data as well).

To see how to use inheritance, try this. Using the example class constructed earlier in this session, locate this line:

```
Public Function GetString(ByVal index As Integer) As String
```

Now add the term `Overridable` to the line, thereby giving a class that inherits the `StringArray` class permission to modify how this function works (by default, members are not overridable):

```
Public Overridable Function GetString(ByVal index As Integer) As String
```

Next, add your new class. Move down in the code window until you're located between the `End Class` and `End Namespace` lines, and type in the new ("derived") class:

```
Class InheritanceExample

        Inherits StringArray

        Overrides Function GetString(ByVal index As Integer) As String
             Return "This is the derived class and we don't have any
strings."

        End Function


End Class
```

Now, change the caller code to access the derived class:

```
Private Sub Button1_Click(ByVal sender As System.Object, ByVal e As
System.EventArgs) Handles Button1.Click

        Dim strc As New MySpecialLibrary.InheritanceExample()

        Dim s As String
        Dim n As Long

        n = 12

        s = strc.GetString(12)

        msgbox(s)


        End Sub
```

Notice that when you press F5 to run this example, the `GetString` method behaves quite differently in the derived class.

If you think you'd find inheritance useful, go ahead and explore it. Lexii or Harleys, it's good to have choices. (Forms are classes in VB .NET, so you can inherit forms, too.) There are several new VB .NET commands used with inheritance: `NotInheritable`, `MustInherit`, `NotOverridable`, `MustOverride`, `MyBase`, and `MyClass`. You can find more about them in VB .NET Help. My feeling is that you can just copy and paste code that you want to reuse, then modify it to suit your needs. To me, that's a less complicated process and is likely to prevent some kinds of bugs. Nevertheless, many intelligent people disagree with my view (including the technical editor of this book), so make up your own mind about the value of inheritance in programming It might suit you just fine.

Done!

REVIEW

You were exposed to an important programming philosophy in this session: OOP (Object-Oriented Programming), also known as OO. You learned that, in VB, a primary virtue of OOP is encapsulation — sealing off data and code from the outside world (including other programmers or even yourself a year later). In addition to preventing various kinds of bugs, reusing objects is simpler than attempting to read and understand ordinary source code. Objects also help prevent errors by validating changes made to their properties. Inheritance? Well, that feature of OO is debatable.

QUIZ YOURSELF

1. In which situations is object-oriented programming most useful? (See "Object-Oriented Programming.")
2. Why is validation a useful feature of encapsulation? (See "Encapsulation.")
3. Define the difference between a class and an object. (See "Classes Give Birth to Objects.")
4. Explain the concept of instantiation. (See "Classes Give Birth to Objects.")
5. What VB command do you use to assign an object to an object variable? Is it Get, Set, Let, or New? (See "Encapsulation.")

Sunday Afternoon
Part Review

1. How does an object differ from a variable?

2. What is the programming within an object usually called?

3. An object's properties, methods, and events are collectively known as what?

4. What does *OOP* mean?

5. What's a class?

6. When you reference a namespace in VB .NET code, you use the Imports command. How do you reference a namespace in ASP.NET?

7. How do you request a particular DataSet by using its name in?

8. Is it possible to bind an array to a control?

9. What property and method are used when binding a data source to a control?

10. Can you always use the Properties window to change the headers and data in a DataGrid?

11. What is a template when used with the Rich Data Controls?

12. Can you use a template with DataGrids or DataLists?

13. What is the purpose of ASP?

14. What language is ASP written in?

15. What is the successor to ASP?

16. Name some of the advantages of ASP.NET over ASP.

17. What does *deployment* mean when used with a VB project?

Answers to Part Reviews

Friday Evening Review Answers

1. Answers will vary based on how you do the exercise.

2. Answers will vary.

3. The Solution Explorer works in VB somewhat the way the Windows Explorer works in Windows. The Solution Explorer shows the overall organization of the project or projects you're currently working on — a tree view of the forms, and other elements in your projects such as modules, class modules, user controls, XML files, components, and so on.

4. TextBox1 and TextBox2. VB appends a number to the control's name to distinguish multiple components of the same type.

5. chk, lst, lbl, and mnu.

6. It's always possible — just choose File ➪ Add Project. One reason to work on two projects at once is that you can create your own components with VB .NET, and there must be a way to test them. To test components, one project needs to be a container application, and the second project needs to be the component you want to test, the one contained.

7. IDE means Integrated Design Environment — a fancy phrase for the VB editor. RAD means Rapid Application Development. The VB IDE was the first, and many still consider it the best, of the RAD environments.

8. F5 starts it running. There is no keypress that stops a running program in the VB IDE. You must click the X icon in the upper-right corner of the program's active window, press Ctrl+Break, choose Debug ➪ Stop Debugging, or click the square blue icon on the Debug Toolbar.

9. It specifies the order in which components on a window get focus as the user presses the Tab key.

10. In arithmetic, when you say $a = b$, you mean that both a and b are the same number. What you mean by TextBox1.Text = "Helloooo!" is: "When this line is executed, the contents of this TextBox will change to Helloooo!." An equals sign used this way in programming signifies assignment rather than equality. It means, if

this line of programming executes, the text "Helloooo!" will be placed (assigned) to this TextBox.

However, in other contexts, the equals sign in programming means the same thing as it does in arithmetic — that is, equality. In a line of programming that tests something, the equals sign really does mean equals. Here's an example: `If X = 12 Then DoSomething`. That means: "If X equals 12, then carry out the assigned job."

11. The design window is the form's user interface surface — where you add, position, and size components; and adjust their various properties. The code window is "underneath" the components and the form; you put your programming in the code window.

12. A sub is a little program within a program (sub is short for subroutine). The programming you put between the Sub and End Sub will sit there and wait to be activated by some outside event. Subs, or functions, are called procedures. A sub differs from a function in that a sub returns no data to the code that "calls" (triggers) it. Events are subs.

13. Press Ctrl+T, and then select one of the components in the Components dialog box.

14. They are used to display familiar, standard Windows dialog boxes to the user — File Open, Save, Font, Color, and so forth.

15. VB looks at lines of code as a single, cohesive statement of your wishes. If a logical line is quite long, you might want to break it into two physical lines so you can view the whole thing without having to scroll the editor horizontally. You can break a logical line of code into two physical lines by using a space character followed by an underscore character. Here's an example of a single logical line of code broken into two physical lines:

```
If OpenFileDialog1.FileName <> "" Then _
Text1.Text = OpenFileDialog1.FileName
```

16. `OpenFileDialog1.ShowDialog()`

17. This code puts the name of the file the user selected with the OpenFileDialog's dialog box into the TextBox named TextBox1. However, if the user clicked the Cancel button, the dialog's Filename property will be empty (""), and your code continues on without attempting to work with a no-name file.

18. An empty text variable.

19. End

20. It's something that happens to a class, component or form. I'd compare it to a summer's day. Seriously, folks, think of a toaster. Pressing its bar down (to start toasting) is one event. Pulling up on the bar to abort toasting is the other event. A typical toaster has two events — two things that an outside agent can do to it, and to which it should respond. Its own ability to pop up the toast when the toast is done is a method of the toaster, not an event. If the toaster itself does it, it's not "happening to" the toaster.

21. Double-click the Button in the Design window. You then see its `Click` event in which you can write some code if you wish. The event you see when you double-click a component is the event that VB thinks is the most often used of all of that component's events. So it's most likely the one you want to write programming for, too.

Saturday Morning Review Answers

1. Parameter information tells you what data you are expected to pass to a sub or function.

   Auto List Members provides you with a quick list of all of the properties and methods of an object. As soon as you type the period following openfiledialog1 in the code window, you see the Auto List Members feature pop into action. (When you type an object's name, such as openfiledialog1, followed by a period, you're telling VB that you are about to specify a property of that object next, or perhaps a method.)

   These features can be enabled or disabled in the Tools ⇨ Options ⇨ Text Editor ⇨ All Languages page.

2. It starts Windows Notepad running. The Shell command launches applications, just as if a user had double-clicked the application's filename in Windows Explorer.

3. Choose Project ⇨ Add Windows Form to add a new form to a project. Many applications include more than a single window. You might, for example, want to allow the user to customize some aspects of your application, and you could display a form with various option buttons or checkboxes where they can make such choices.

4. Grouped OptionButtons work together. When grouped, they become mutually exclusive. If the user clicks one of them, the rest become deselected. In other words, only one OptionButton in a group can be selected at a given time. This is useful for such choices as the BackColor of a form — it can be only one color at a time, so the user can click only one choice at a time.

5. CheckBoxes are never mutually exclusive. The user can select none, one, some, or all of any CheckBoxes displayed.

6. The Enabled property, if set to False, prevents users from typing anything into a TextBox (it is said to be disabled), or from clicking a Button, and so on. The control's text will appear light gray rather than black to indicate that the control is disabled. Components are disabled when it makes no sense for the user to try to use them. Many components — such as the OptionButton — can also be disabled and turn gray, refusing to respond to mouse clicks or keyboard actions.

7. A ToolTip (which used to be a property in previous versions of VB, but is now a control in VB .NET) displays a small help window that pops up to inform the user about the purpose of a component. It pops up when the user pauses the mouse pointer on top of a component. Unique among all controls, and indeed unique among the way that properties are handled, you must add a ToolTip control to your form, and *then* the other controls on the form have a ToolTip property in the Properties window.

8. When you select multiple components, the Properties window displays only those properties that all the selected components have in common. When you change the Font property with several components selected, for example, that property changes for each of the selected components.

9. Just what it sounds like: to describe to the user the purpose of some other component.

10. AutoSize causes a label to grow or shrink to fit whatever text is inside. This can be useful if you plan to dynamically add text (to add it during run time), and you do not know in advance how much text there will be. However, this kind of thing can cause unpredictable side effects, such as covering up other controls.

11. No.

12. To alphabetize, change the ListBox's Sorted property to True in the Properties window.

13. Use the Remove method: `lstIndex.Items.Remove`

14. Set the ListBox's MultiColumn property to True.

15. A ComboBox has a small TextBox at the very top. The user can select from the items in the list by typing only the first letter or first few letters, and then pressing enter. The typical ComboBox only displays one item — the user doesn't see the list unless the down-arrow button next to the TextBox is clicked.

16. A PictureBox displays graphics.

17. It loads a graphic named MyDog from the hard drive into the PictureBox named PictureBox1.

18. The MainMenu control.

19. `mnuNew.Enabled = False`

20. VB .NET includes many built-in constants. Constants are predefined values for such things as colors (`color.white`, for example), and other elements used in programming. Instead of using a complicated and, to humans, meaningless numeric value for powder blue, instead use: `color.powderblue` and let VB .NET translate that into the numeric value.

Saturday Afternoon Review Answers

1. An argument is data that is defined in a procedure declaration, data that is supposed to be passed to the procedure when that procedure executes. For example, the `MsgBox` function has a `prompt` argument, and you can pass "Display This Message" as the prompt when you use the function.

2. Sometimes. Some arguments are optional and can be omitted from an argument list. For example, the `Title` argument for the `MsgBox` function is optional. However, if you do leave out an optional argument, you must still insert a comma in the argument list to indicate that the argument is missing from the list.

3. A function returns information to the source code that calls it.

4. Open, Save, Color, Font, PrintPreview, PageSetup and Print

5. PageSetup and PrintPreview

6. Assign the data to the Return command: `Return VarValue`

7. Pressing F8 steps you line by line through your program — executing each line, and then stopping and waiting for you to press F8 again. This is an excellent debugging tool.

8. No. A function must be called from within an expression, such as `X = FunctionName ()`.

9. Text (or string) and numeric.

10. The value is the contents of the variable. In the code, X = "Moosie", Moosie is the value.

11. It must start with a letter, not a digit. It cannot be one of Visual Basic's own command words like For or Height. It cannot be larger than 255 characters. It cannot contain any punctuation marks or spaces.

12. Prior to VB .NET, when you needed to use a variable in a program, you could simply assign a value to a valid variable name, and the variable would come into existence. The following code implicitly creates the variable Z:

    ```
    Z = "Darby"
    ```

    In VB .NET, however, you are expected to explicitly declare every variable. You are, though, allowed to assign a value to a variable at the same time that you declare it, like this:

    ```
    Dim Z As String = "Darby"
    ```

13. Dim, ReDim, Public, Private, or Static

14. One. There are specialized kinds of variables, such as arrays, that hold multiple values. An ordinary variable can hold only a single value at any given time.

15. Yes, in essence, they are. However, they are predefined by the creator of each component. You can adjust their values, but you cannot define new properties for a component unless you are able to inherit the component as a class, and modify the members of that class.

16. The object.

17. It can contain only two values: True or False.

18. When you declare a variable inside a procedure, the variable only works within that procedure. While the program executes the procedure or event, the variable comes to life, does its thing, but then dies (disappears) as soon as the End Sub line is executed. Variables that live only within a single procedure are called local variables. Their scope is limited to the single procedure. Variables declared with the Dim or Private command in the General Declarations section of a form are accessible within that form. They have form-wide scope. Variables declared with the Public command have project-wide scope.

19. An expression is a compound entity that VB evaluates at runtime. An expression can be made up of literals, variables, or a combination of the two. In the following code, "Hello" & MyVariable is an expression, and it evaluates to "Hello Sandra":

    ```
    MyVariable = " Sandra"
    Response = MsgBox ("Hello" & MyVariable)
    ```

20. Operators are used in expressions to compare two elements (like two variables), to do math on them, or to perform a "logical" operation on them. The plus sign, for example, is an operator in this example: 2 + 4. The greater-than symbol (>) is an operator in this example, which says n is greater than z: n > z.

Saturday Night Review Answers

1. An array is a set of variable values that have been grouped together. Once inside an array structure, the values share the same variable name, but are individually identified by an index number.

2. Yes. Break the line by using a space character, followed by an underscore:

    ```
    N = N & "Hello" & _
    " Goodbye"
    ```

    However, you cannot use this technique within a string, like this:

    ```
    MsgBox "Toron _
    to"
    ```

3. By grouping many values under the same variable name, you can manipulate the values by individual index number. This means you can work with the values in a loop, using the loop's counter to reference each value by its index number. This technique permits you to accomplish certain jobs using fewer lines of code.

4. Step can be attached at the end of the For...Next structure to allow you to skip numbers — to step past them. When the Step command is used with For...Next, Step alters the way the loop counts. By default, without Step, For...Next increments by one.

5. It tests the truth of an expression, and then executes appropriate lines of code based on the answer to the question posed by the If. If...Then is a decision-making mechanism and is also sometimes referred to as branching because it can take one or more alternative paths in the code.

6. The lines of code that are carried out based on the results of the If expression are indented. Put another way, indent any line of code within an If...Then structure that does not begin with If, Else, ElseIf, or Then. This indenting helps clarify the structure and makes it easier to read and understand the code.

7. If...Then is great for simple, common testing and branching. But if you have more than two branches, If...Then becomes clumsy. Fortunately, there's an alternative decision-making structure in VB that specializes in multiple-branching — Select...Case, which should be used when there are several possible outcomes.

8. Case Else describes what the program should do if none of the other Case commands matches the Select Case expression.

9. Yes. Case Is < 200

10. Yes. Case "n" To "z"

11. The Timer component has several uses. It can make things happen at intervals (for instance, animation), remind people that it's time to do something, measure the passage of time, or cause a delay.

12. Most controls have more than a dozen properties; Timers have only three. Most controls have at least ten events they can respond to; Timers have only two. Most controls are visible and can be accessed and triggered by the user of the program; Timers work in the background, independent of the user. They are always invisible when a program runs. Most controls' events are triggered instantly; Timers don't carry out the instructions you've put into their events

until their Interval (a duration of time) passes. Most controls' events are only triggered once; Timers will repeatedly trigger their event until you either set their Interval property to 0 or their Enabled property to False.

13. They generally don't have any effect; the Timer keeps on ticking independent of whatever else is happening in Windows. In rare cases, an application might freeze the system, but for all practical purposes, you can consider Timers isolated from outside influence.

14. The millisecond.

15. In earlier versions of VB, yes. The default property was the most commonly used property. For a TextBox, it was the Text property. For compatibility with other .NET languages, the default property concept has been dropped in VB .NET.

16. Control Arrays have been dropped from the language in VB .NET.

17. Typos, because Visual Basic can generally alert you to them.

18. Very. A misplaced comma can crash a program.

19. `Try...End Try`

20. The feature is called *Run to cursor*. Click in the code where you want execution to stop, press Ctrl+F10, and the code between the original and new locations is executed fast.

Sunday Morning Review Answers

1. Some programmers prefer to first design the user interface, and then fill in the programming "underneath" the various controls (in their click event or other events). This is one meaning of the term *top-down*.

2. First use paper and pencil to create an outline of the various functions and features of their program, and then decide which user-interface controls are most appropriate.

3. If you were designing a database that would hold the information in your Rolodex, you would recognize that each card in the Rolodex is a single record, and that each of those records is divided into perhaps eight fields (zones): Name, Address, City, State, Zip, Voice Phone, Fax Phone, and E-mail Address. In other words, a record is a set of data (the actual name, address, and so on of an individual), and fields are the categories that define what data should go into the records.

4. In a complex database, there may be more than one group of records. If you have a huge Rolodex, you might divide the records into two categories: Personal and Business, for example. This kind of large-scale group of records is called a *table*. A database can have multiple tables — and they can be linked, searched, or otherwise interrelated in various ways.

5. When you specify that a field is to be indexed, it is maintained in alphabetical (or numeric) order by the database engine (the underlying, low-level support code that does jobs for a database). An index makes it easier to search for information in a database.

6. It's good to put sizing and positioning code into the Form_Load event. That way, it gets carried out before the form is made visible, and it happens only that one time when the form is first created.

7. Use the & symbol before the letter that you want to make the shortcut character. The Caption property is then displayed with that letter underlined as a cue to the user. Change a search button's Caption property to &Search, for example, and the user will see Search as the visible caption.

8. It determines the order in which components on a form get the focus as the user presses the Tab key to cycle through them.

9. It runs a VB .NET project in the IDE.

10. Stops program execution and shuts down the program.

11. Yes, but that approach can become confusing to the programmer. Also, you must keep track of the current status of the dual-purpose control so you know what programming to execute for each purpose.

12. It's the third dimension on a form (depth). The X coordinate describes a control's position horizontally; the Y coordinate describes verticality (see the Location property in the Properties window for a control). The Z coordinate defines which control is "on top" of another if they are overlapping each other.

13. A DataSet is a copy of some data (containing as many data tables as you wish) that is held in memory or stored as two XML files on a hard drive. A DataSet does not require any active connection to a database. A DataSet object is fairly self-sufficient — it contains a variety of commands (methods) and properties you can employ to manage its data.

14. Technically, no. A DataSet is a smaller, less complex structure than a traditional database. However, a DataSet has much in common with databases and could be considered a database, in the sense that a Little Leaguer could be considered a baseball player.

15. An .SLN file, for *solution*, is the file that describes all the various files that, together, make up a VB .NET program. In previous versions of VB, this file used to have a .VBP extension (for Visual Basic Project), but now, things have gotten a bit larger in scope, and a *solution* can contain more than a single *project*.

16. It tells you how many columns (fields) there are in the first table (in the tables collection) in a DataSet. (ds is an object variable that was previously declared to represent a particular DataSet.)

17. First the programmer uses the NewRow method to notify the DataSet that a new row of data is coming. Then you fill the new row's columns with the actual data you want to insert into the DataSet. Finally, you use the Add method to actually commit (store) the data to the DataSet.

18. There are actually *two* methods that sound as if they could delete a row in a DataSet: Delete and Remove. However, the Delete method doesn't actually get rid of a row; it simply "marks" the row for later deletion when (or if) the programmer employs the AcceptChanges method. Marking a row is useful for such jobs as later permitting an Undo option, restoring the row. The Remove method gets rid of a row completely.

19. ds.WriteXmlSchema(schemafilepath) saves the structure (its tables and their columns) of a DataSet. ds.WriteXml(datafilepath) saves the actual data into a separate file.

20. Making a change in one location in a fairly sophisticated application often causes a side-effect, a problem elsewhere in the project.

Sunday Afternoon Review Answers

1. An *object* is more powerful and sophisticated — it's like a self-contained mini-program. A variable contains a value, a single piece of data. An object, on the other hand, usually contains several pieces of data. In addition to its data, an object also includes programming — things it knows how to do with its data (or data it's given). Finally, objects can (but don't necessarily) have *events*.

2. An object's programming is known as its *methods*.

3. An object's properties, methods, and events are collectively known as the object's *members*.

4. OOP means Object-Oriented Programming.

5. A class is a blueprint or template, the code that describes how an object performs. Classes are also said to be like "factories" that stamp out objects.

6. When you want to reference a namespace in ASP.NET, you use this syntax:

```
<%@ Import Namespace="System.Data.ADO" %>
```

7. `DataGrid1.DataSource = ds.Tables("Them").defaultview`

Here you're not simply asking for the table and its structure (the schema). You're qualifying it by asking for a particular dataset by name ("Them"). You can also use an index number: `ds.Tables(0)`, for instance.

8. Yes. ADO.NET can accept data from a wide variety of sources, including arrays:

```
Dim MyArray as new ArrayList

    myArray.Add ("One")
    myArray.Add ("Two")
    myArray.Add ("Three")
    myArray.Add ("Four")
    myArray.Add ("Five")

    ListBox1.DataSource = MyArray
    ListBox1.DataBind()
```

9. Set the control's DataSource property to the name of the data source, and then invoke the control's DataBind method.

10. Not if the DataGrid isn't bound to a data store until runtime.

11. A template is a group of HTML elements (and any controls you place within each element) that specify the look of an area (a single cell for instance) of a container control. For instance, you can create a template that specifies how each row in a DataGrid looks.

12. You can use templates with DataGrids or DataLists, but only the Repeater *requires* a template for its visual output.

13. The core idea of ASP (Active Server Pages) is that somebody (or many people at once) is surfing around the Internet (or a local intranet) and arrives at a page in your Web site. When they arrive, their browser sends a request to your server to send the page. But instead of merely sending them a canned, previously written, static, page, you can dynamically generate the page on your server right then and there — as a response to their visit — and send the resulting *fresh* HTML page to the visitor. Your page can display the current time and date, the current status of an order they placed with you, your latest catalog, and so on.

14. ASP uses a script language (JavaScript or VBScript) to do its computing.

15. ASP.NET.

16. Faster, easier to maintain, segregated source files, written in full VB (not script), browser independence, better security, easier deployment, cross-language programming and debugging.

17. If you want to give your VB application to other people to use — sell it, pass it around to grateful coworkers, or make it available on the Internet — that's called *deployment*.

What's on the CD-ROM

This appendix provides you with information on the contents of the CD that accompanies this book. For the latest and greatest information, please refer to the ReadMe file located in the root directory of the CD. Here is what you will find:

- System Requirements
- Using the CD with Windows
- What's on the CD
- Troubleshooting

System Requirements

Make sure that your computer meets the minimum system requirements listed in this section. If your computer doesn't match up to most of these requirements, you may have a problem using the contents of the CD.

For Windows 9x, Windows 2000, Windows NT4 (with SP 4 or later), Windows Me, or Windows XP:

- PC with a Pentium processor running at 120 Mhz or faster
- At least 64 MB of total RAM installed on your computer; for best performance, we recommend at least 128 MB
- A CD-ROM drive

Using the CD with Windows

To install the items from the CD to your hard drive, follow these steps:

1. Insert the CD into your computer's CD-ROM drive.

2. A window will appear with the following options: Install, Explore, eBook, Links, and Exit.

   Install: Gives you the option to install the supplied software and/or the author-created samples on the CD-ROM.

   Explore: Allows you to view the contents of the CD-ROM in its directory structure.

   Exit: Closes the autorun window.

   If you do not have autorun enabled or if the autorun window does not appear, follow the steps below to access the CD.

1. Click Start ⇨ Run.

2. In the dialog box that appears, type ***d:\setup.exe***, where *d* is the letter of your CD-ROM drive. This will bring up the autorun window described above.

3. Choose the Install, Explore, or Exit option from the menu. (See Step 2 in the preceding list for a description of these options.)

What's on the CD

The following sections provide a summary of the software and other materials you'll find on the CD.

Author-created materials

All author-created material from the book, including code listings and samples, are on the CD in the folder named "Author".

This book's CD contains:

- All the source code from all the examples in this book.

- A very large Appendix C, which includes many important examples (such as how to print in VB .NET) and many brief tutorials.

- A file titled "Supplementary Notes," which includes several important topics that would not fit in the pages of this book.

- The VB .NET Weekend Crash Course Assessment Test.

- The complete Personal Database Manager (PDM) program.

Code Listings

The sample code developed for the book has been included on the CD-ROM. There is a folder for each of the 30 sessions in the book, named after the session number (1, 2, 3...and so on). In each folder you'll find a .TXT file containing all the source code from all the examples in that session, regardless of how few lines there were in the example. The source code examples are arranged in the .TXT file in the same order that they appear within the session. Each example is separated from the others by several blank lines.

The Personal Database Manager (PDM) application built in the Sunday sessions is also included in its entirety in the folder named, you guessed it, PDM.

Appendix C

If you want to know how to do something in VB .NET, you'll likely find it in Appendix C. Everything from file access to creating random numbers is covered. Take a look — it's a very useful reference.

Supplementary Notes

A few sessions in this book ran long — longer than the allotted 30 minutes. Nevertheless, rather than simply cutting important information, I've mentioned in the text that there is further discussion of a topic in the Supplementary Notes on this book's CD.

The VB .NET Weekend Crash Course *Assessment Test.*

This is a self-guided test that covers the majority of topics in this book.

The Complete Personal Database Manager (PDM) Program

This is the complete final version of the project that was built during sessions 21–25. To load it into VB.NET, right-click the PDM folder on the CD and then choose Copy from the context menu. Then right-click Drive C: in Windows Explorer, and choose Paste. This copies the entire PDM folder and its sub-folders to your C: drive. (You can put the PDM into a different drive than C: if you want to.)

Next, you must remove the read-only attribute from the entire PDM folder system. To do that, right-click the PDM folder in Windows Explorer, choose Properties, and deselect the Read-only checkbox. Click OK. In the next dialog box, click the *Apply changes to this folder, sub-folders, and files* option button. Click OK to close the dialog box.

Now open the PDM folder on Drive C: in Windows Explorer, and double-click the filename *PDM.sln* to load the PDM project into VB .NET. You can now double-click Form1.vb in the VB .NET Solution Explorer to work with and test the PDM program.

Troubleshooting

If you have difficulty installing or using any of the materials on the companion CD, try the following solutions:

- **Turn off any anti-virus software that you may have running.** Installers sometimes mimic virus activity and can make your computer incorrectly believe that it is being infected by a virus. (Be sure to turn the anti-virus software back on later.)

- **Close all running programs.** The more programs you're running, the less memory is available to other programs. Installers also typically update files and programs; if you keep other programs running, installation may not work properly.

- **Reference the ReadMe:** Please refer to the ReadMe file located at the root of the CD-ROM for the latest product information at the time of publication.

If you still have trouble with the CD, please call the Hungry Minds Customer Care phone number: (800) 762-2974. Outside the United States, call 1 (317) 572-3994. You can also contact Hungry Minds Customer Service by e-mail at techsupdum@hungryminds.com. Hungry Minds will provide technical support only for installation and other general quality control items; for technical support on the applications themselves, consult the program's vendor or author.

Index

Hungry Minds, Inc. End-User License Agreement

READ THIS. You should carefully read these terms and conditions before opening the software packet(s) included with this book ("Book"). This is a license agreement ("Agreement") between you and Hungry Minds, Inc. ("HMI"). By opening the accompanying software packet(s), you acknowledge that you have read and accept the following terms and conditions. If you do not agree and do not want to be bound by such terms and conditions, promptly return the Book and the unopened software packet(s) to the place you obtained them for a full refund.

1. **License Grant.** HMI grants to you (either an individual or entity) a nonexclusive license to use one copy of the enclosed software program(s) (collectively, the "Software") solely for your own personal or business purposes on a single computer (whether a standard computer or a workstation component of a multi-user network). The Software is in use on a computer when it is loaded into temporary memory (RAM) or installed into permanent memory (hard disk, CD-ROM, or other storage device). HMI reserves all rights not expressly granted herein.

2. **Ownership.** HMI is the owner of all right, title, and interest, including copyright, in and to the compilation of the Software recorded on the disk(s) or CD-ROM ("Software Media"). Copyright to the individual programs recorded on the Software Media is owned by the author or other authorized copyright owner of each program. Ownership of the Software and all proprietary rights relating thereto remain with HMI and its licensers.

3. **Restrictions On Use and Transfer.**

   (a) You may only (i) make one copy of the Software for backup or archival purposes, or (ii) transfer the Software to a single hard disk, provided that you keep the original for backup or archival purposes. You may not (i) rent or lease the Software, (ii) copy or reproduce the Software through a LAN or other network system or through any computer subscriber system or bulletin-board system, or (iii) modify, adapt, or create derivative works based on the Software.

   (b) You may not reverse engineer, decompile, or disassemble the Software. You may transfer the Software and user documentation on a permanent basis, provided that the transferee agrees to accept the terms and conditions of this Agreement and you retain no copies. If the Software is an update or has been updated, any transfer must include the most recent update and all prior versions.

4. **Restrictions on Use of Individual Programs.** You must follow the individual requirements and restrictions detailed for each individual program in Appendix B of this Book. These limitations are also contained in the individual license agreements recorded on the Software Media. These limitations may include a requirement that after using the program for a specified period of time, the user must pay a registration fee or discontinue use. By opening the Software packet(s), you will be agreeing to abide by the licenses and restrictions for these individual programs that are detailed in Appendix B and on the Software Media. None of the material on this Software Media or listed in this Book may ever be redistributed, in original or modified form, for commercial purposes.